Praise for *Healing the Wounds*

"A sequel rarely equals its predecessor, especially when the latter is on course for the rarified status of 'classic,' but David Noer achieves no less. Essential players in job loss dramas will applaud the expanded learning and implications sections, and the extensive treatment of leadership issues. Organizational career management is indeed indebted to David Noer's contribution."

> —Michael E. Hall, Ph.D., board-certified career management fellow

"Dr. Noer is absolutely right—there is no one big tool that will save you during a downsizing effort. It takes many little tools. This book will give you the tools and insights into how to save those who are left behind."

> —Kevin R. Planet, principle, Integrity Staffing

"Excellent guidance on how to deal with the most complex and difficult issues of anxiety, fear, and sorrow."

> —Ingar Skaug, president and CEO, Wilhelmsen Lines

"David Noer's book is a handy remedy for anyone caught up in today's corporate survivor illness. It contains a healthy dose of practical advice from an authentic management professional."

> —Walter F. Ulmer Jr., Lieutenant General, US Army (Retired), and former president and CEO, Center for Creative Leadership

"Much-needed insights on effectively managing downsizings while forging productive relationships with its surviving workers."

> —Joel Brockner, professor of management, Graduate School of Business, Columbia University

HEALING THE WOUNDS

OVERCOMING THE TRAUMA OF LAYOFFS AND REVITALIZING DOWNSIZED ORGANIZATIONS

REVISED AND UPDATED

David M. Noer

JOSSEY-BASS
A Wiley Imprint
www.josseybass.com

Published by Jossey-Bass
A Wiley Imprint
989 Market Street, San Francisco, CA 94103-1741—www.josseybass.com

Jossey-Bass books and products are available through most bookstores. To contact Jossey-Bass directly call our Customer Care Department within the U.S. at 800-956-7739, outside the U.S. at 317-572-3986, or fax 317-572-4002.

Jossey-Bass also publishes its books in a variety of electronic formats. Some content that appears in print may not be available in electronic books.

Library of Congress Cataloging-in-Publication Data

Noer, David M.
  Healing the wounds: overcoming the trauma of layoffs and revitalizing downsized organizations / David M. Noer.—Rev. and updated.
      p. cm.
  Includes bibliographical references and index.
  ISBN 978–0–470–50015–6 (cloth)
  1. Downsizing of organizations—Psychological aspects. 2. Organizational change—Psychological aspects. 3. Unemployment—Psychological aspects. 4. Layoff systems. 5. Employees—Dismissal of. I. Title.
  HD58.85.N64 2009
  658.4'06—dc22

                                                                              2009021546

Printed in the United States of America
FIRST EDITION
HB Printing   10 9 8 7 6 5 4 3 2 1

CONTENTS

PART TWO
THE SURVIVOR EXPERIENCE 31

PART THREE
INTERVENTIONS FOR HEALTHY SURVIVAL   75

PART FOUR
THE LEADERSHIP WAKE-UP CALL   179

PREFACE

It had been nearly a year since I'd visited my friend and client in Charlotte, North Carolina. At that time, Charlotte was buoyant and bustling, the banking capital of the South with glass-encased buildings filled with creative, optimistic people. This time it was different. From the profusely sweating employee who refused eye contact as he nervously scuttled out the front door carrying a cardboard box crammed with personal photographs, company trinkets, and carelessly packed papers, to the empty offices, eerie silences, and the thousand-yard stares that hovered above desks and conference tables. It was all too familiar. In the immortal words of Yogi Berra, it was "déjà vu all over again." I'd been here before.

My friend was a top executive in the financial services industry, and the economic meltdown had dealt his firm a staggering blow. It was entering its third round of layoffs: a hoped-for merger had fallen through, and federal bailout money, which my friend described as "fool's gold," wasn't helping. His employees were suffering the classic symptoms of layoff survivor sickness—a toxic combination of fear, anger, and anxiety—and he was struggling to hold his own anger and depression in check. At the very time that creativity and innovation were crucial to turn the organization around, employees at all levels were risk averse, hunkering down in the trenches, paralyzed by their survivor symptoms. This was not a team you would bet on to compete and thrive in the global economy.

As we near the second decade of the new millennium, that scene in Charlotte is being played out around the world. Organizations of all types—public, private, profit, nonprofit, government—are experiencing a pandemic of downsizings where people are viewed as expenses to be reduced as opposed to human resources to be grown and nurtured. Both employees and organizational leaders need to shed comfortable but outdated concepts of loyalty, motivation, and commitment and, in order to ensure their individual relevance and their organizations' survival, venture into the uncharted waters of the new reality.

As I left the building that afternoon, I saw an unmanned crane parked in front of a half-constructed high-rise building, initially intended to house still another bank, and was struck by the symbolism. Would it ever be finished? Was the glass half full or half empty, not just for the financial services industry, but for the global economy and the psychological employment contract between employee and organization? We've been there before, but the lessons didn't take. The layoffs of the late 1980s and early 1990s— what I call the first act—were an early wake-up call but one that was not adequately passed on and was overridden by the short-term noise of the recent boom. Today we have reached the tipping point, and we have no choice but to accept and accommodate the new reality. What is at stake is the survival of our organizations and individual relevance.

The new psychological employment contract has experienced a long and painful birth, but it is here, it is real, and it has a major impact on our ability to revitalize our organizations. My focus in *Healing the Wounds* is on those who remain in organizational systems after downsizing. For the employee, a primary danger is what I call *layoff survivor sickness*. I explain the nature of this disease and discuss ways to become immune to its toxic effects. For organizational leaders, I outline strategies, perspectives, and models congruent with the unique leadership challenges of the new reality. Too often organizations institute layoffs to cut costs and promote competitiveness, but afterward, they find themselves worse off than before. All they have to show for it is a depressed, anxious, and angry workforce that is confused, fearful, and unable to shake an unhealthy and unreciprocated organizational dependency.

Audience

Although anyone interested in the profound changes taking place in the relationship of person to organization will find *Healing the Wounds* useful, I direct my comments here toward three often overlapping audiences: organizational managers and leaders, layoff survivors, and layoff victims.

Organizational Managers and Leaders

If you are a manager or leader in an organization that has been, or is about to be, downsized, you have a tremendously important role and a difficult twofold task. First, you must come to grips with your own survivor status. You must deal with your own feelings while you work toward a relationship with your organization in which you are more empowered and less dependent. You cannot be of much help to other layoff survivors until you have helped yourself. Second, you must take on the most vital and complex managerial role since the industrial revolution. You must lead the other people in your organization through a painful and irrevocable shift in the terms of the psychological contract that exists between employee and organization.

This book can help you reach a personal understanding and acceptance of your own survivor feelings while also providing insight into the ways employees can develop a more autonomous and less dependent organizational relationship. Chapters Seven, Eight, and Nine offer examples of managerial actions that support the new psychological employment contract, which no longer guarantees job security. Chapter Ten sets out an important frame of reference for those striving to understand the basic shifts taking place in the new reality. Many organizational leaders feel a great deal of pain and guilt over what they perceive they have "done to" employees in the service of organizational downsizing. This chapter helps alleviate this guilt by pointing out that the organizational changes are systemic.

If you are a manager, you are caught up in a basic change in the relationship of individuals to organizations, and you are asked to play a vital leadership role during this painful transition. You must lead the change from within the change. Chapters Eleven, Twelve, and Thirteen provide valuable perspectives and models for leading in the new reality. This book will help you deal with your own survivor issues and frame the environmental changes underlying downsizing; it will help alleviate guilt you may feel for what you have "done to" employees; and it will offer practical ideas for exercising leadership in the midst of fundamental change.

Layoff Survivors

If you are among the increasing legions of people who remain in organizations that have been downsized, merged, or delayered, *Healing the Wounds* will help you understand that you are not alone. The anxiety, fear, and sometimes depression that you experience are normal survivor feelings. However, many who survive cutbacks work in organizational cultures that do not permit individuals to admit to natural survivor reactions. Even in organizations where emotions are considered valid data, it is difficult for most people to be truly open about their survivor feelings. After cutbacks, there is great, if often subtle, pressure to dig in, tighten your belt, grit your teeth, and work harder to move the organization forward. After layoffs in macho cultures, people feel it would be selfish or not teamlike to admit their true anguish and say how debilitating that anguish is.

If you are a layoff survivor, the most immediate benefit of this book may well be a clearer understanding of your normal and yet often unshared survivor feelings. The first three chapters show why those who survive layoffs universally feel such a deep sense of violation. In Chapters Four and Five, readers will discover both personal and organizational echoes in the actual voices of layoff survivors. Chapters Four and Five legitimize survivors' repressed feelings and begin a necessary catharsis, and Chapter Nine points the way for survivors and victims alike toward breaking an unhealthy organizational dependency and learning to create an empowered employment relationship, with reduced susceptibility to layoff survivor sickness.

If you are among those who remain after cutbacks, *Healing the Wounds* will help you toward a deeper understanding and acceptance of your survivor symptoms and give you strategies for an employment relationship in which you are more autonomous and less likely to feel like a victim.

Layoff Victims

Most layoff victims—those who have left involuntarily—eventually find themselves employed in another organization. A surprising number, particularly managers and professionals, rebound into organizations with worse epidemics of layoff survivor sickness than those the layoff victims came from. In this way, many employees simply transport their survivor symptoms from one place to another.

I have a friend, now in his third organization, who reports feeling less enthusiastic with each successive move. When it comes to life planning, his scarce and marketable skills, good network, and interviewing savvy ironically have made it easy for him to rebound. He has not taken the time to deal with his survivor feelings, take stock of what he really wants to do, or come to grips with the reality of the new employment contract, which calls for a more autonomous, less dependent employment relationship.

If you are a layoff victim, you must make your transition a learning experience. An understanding of the nature of this new employment contract (Chapter Ten), the personal perils of organizational dependency (Chapter Nine), the survivor symptoms that probably exist in many of the organizations to which you are applying (Chapter Four), and the empowering possibilities of your choices (Chapter Fourteen) will be of great help in your personal transition.

Overview of the Contents

Layoff survivor sickness debilitates both organizations and individuals. Organizations should develop systems to accommodate the new linkages that are called for between individuals and organizations, and individuals should develop more entrepreneurial and less dependent connections to organizations. What is at stake is nothing less than the survival of our organizations and of our self-esteem and autonomy as employees. That survival is also the subject of this book.

Because denial is a primary symptom of layoff survivor sickness, its effects are nearly always underestimated. Moreover, the higher a person is in an organizational system, the more she or he denies the symptoms. For these reasons, I devote the first six chapters to an explanation of the pathology of layoff survivor sickness. In the remainder of the book, I show what to do about the sickness using a four-level intervention model (Chapters Seven to Ten), and then I outline leadership strategies and perspectives that fit the new reality (Chapters Eleven to Fourteen).

I have divided the book into four parts. Part One outlines the profound changes in the relationship of person to job that leads to the mistrust and sense of violation that survivors of organizational layoffs feel. Chapter One examines the dynamics of layoff survivor sickness through a case study and a metaphor. Chapter Two outlines the fundamental paradigm shift that has occurred in the relationship of person to organization.

The universality of the survivor experience and the similarities between the feelings of layoff survivors and the feelings of survivors of other traumatic situations are the subjects of Part Two. Chapter Three explores the universal traits of survivorship, demonstrating the emotional links between layoff survivors and others who have survived trauma and tragedy. Archetypal survivor themes emerge that are also apparent in the statements of layoff survivors.

Most research on layoff survivors is conducted in a laboratory or is a summary of questionnaire results. Chapter Four presents raw data on actual layoff survivors, bringing home to readers the depth and complexity of these survivors' symptoms. It will be a rare person who is not reminded of his of her own organizational situation. The host organization for the research sample in Chapter Four was revisited five years later, and the results of a second sample are presented in Chapter Five. It is apparent that, unlike wine, layoff survivors do not automatically improve with age.

Part Three is centered around a four-level intervention model that serves as a road map to reestablishing healthy and productive relationships between employees and organizations in the midst of continual downsizing and trauma after layoffs. Chapter Six sums up the research and introduces this model. Chapter Seven explores level 1, or process, interventions. These are basic first-aid interventions at the point when layoffs take place. Level 1 interventions will not cure layoff survivor sickness but will provide damage control until more permanent solutions are found.

Layoff survivors carry heavy emotional baggage, and unless they are given the opportunity to drop it, they are unable to progress beyond their debilitating funk. Level 2 interventions allow survivors to grieve. Chapter Eight outlines processes for breaking blockages and stimulating catharsis.

Chapter Nine applies the concept of codependency to organizations. Level 3 interventions deal with the painful but liberating process of breaking away from organizational codependency. Employees are codependent with an organization to the extent that they index their self-worth by their success in that organization and attempt to control and manipulate the organizational system. Organizationally codependent people are always susceptible to layoff survivor sickness. Those who break the bonds of organizational codependency are immune.

Chapter Ten reviews the series of shifts that have made a new employment contract necessary. It explores processes for making organizational systems relevant to the new contract, which demands profound and evolutionary changes in our organizational systems and in us as individuals. On the personal level, they often require us to behave in accordance with a reality that opposes the values conditioned into us through organizational cultures that were formed just after World War II.

Level 4 interventions alter organizational systems to accommodate the reality of the new employment contract. In discussing levels 1 and 2 (Chapters Seven and Eight), I have been as prescriptive as possible and include case studies and specific advice to both the employee and the manager. My advice is more general for levels 3 and 4 (Chapters Nine and Ten). Implementing the new employment contract demands complex individual and organizational changes. Therefore, I help readers explore the changes in their own organizations and personal careers.

Part Four deals with the critical leadership challenges within this new environment of change, ambiguity, and violated employee expectations of long-term job security. Today's leadership requires new skills and a great deal of courage. Chapter Eleven examines leadership competencies relevant in the new reality that are not often found in business schools or corporate training programs. Chapter Twelve reviews the critical leadership task of reconceptualizing perspectives of loyalty, commitment, and motivation from the old paradigm. Chapter Thirteen outlines the core skills and relevant models necessary to lead organizational systems in a new paradigm.

The death of the old patterns of organizational thought and behavior, painful though it may be, opens up the possibility that we as individuals will acquire greater personal empowerment and autonomy and that more organizations will survive these competitive times.

Chapter Fourteen discusses the ultimate existential choices that individuals and organizations now confront.

Healing the Wounds is the culmination of multiple ways of perceiving and responding to the global epidemic of downsizing and the need to put the pieces together—both individual and organizational—and move on. It combines research, case studies, and methodologies from my own consulting practice and specific advice based on my experience. The case studies have been disguised to ensure client anonymity. Although this book is based on research, it is for practitioners and can be used at several levels: to help line managers intervene in their organizational systems, consultants and consulting managers develop intervention techniques, and individual survivors understand what is happening to them and see that they are not alone.

Healing the Wounds views layoff survivor sickness as the symptom of a condition even more toxic to the human spirit: unhealthy dependence. For organizational leaders and employees who respond courageously to the call to combat this symptom, there is the exciting promise of reclamation of lost autonomy, the ability to index self-worth by good work, and the exciting potential of a quantum increase in organizational productivity and customer service.

June 2009   David M. Noer
Greensboro, North Carolina

HEALING
THE
WOUNDS

PART ONE

THE SHATTERED COVENANT

CHAPTER 1

Employees who perform and fit into the culture can count on a job until they retire or choose to leave.

Forgotten Survivors

What Happens to Those Who Are Left Behind

"No one is happy anymore. I think a lot of people are under stress, and it tends to balloon out, and everybody is absorbed by it. You don't have anybody coming in in the morning, going, 'God, it's a great day!'"

Layoff survivor sickness begins with a deep sense of violation. It often ends with angry, sad, and depressed employees, consumed with their attempt to hold on to jobs that have become devoid of joy, spontaneity, and personal relevancy, and with the organization attempting to survive in a competitive global environment with a risk-averse, depressed workforce. This is no way to lead a life, no way to run an organization, and no way to perpetuate an economy.

The root cause is a historically based, but no longer valid, dependency relationship between employee and employer—a type of cultural lag from the post–World War II days when employees were considered long-term assets to be retained, nurtured, and developed over a career as opposed to short-term costs to be managed and, if possible, reduced. The first act of the harsh reality of this new psychological employment contract became painfully evident in the late 1980s and early 1990s. Then there was an intermission when both employees and employers were seduced back into complacency by the liquidity and economic boom of the early years of the new millennium. The curtain abruptly rose for act two with the financial meltdown of 2008, and we are now facing the jolting reality of a worldwide wake-up call. The second act is much more somber and represents the final shattering of the old psychological employment contract. We are caught up in an unprecedented global epidemic of layoffs, and the toxic effects of layoff survivor sickness on both individuals and organizations are approaching a pandemic tipping point.

The battle to ward off and eventually develop immunity to these survivor symptoms must be waged simultaneously by individuals and organizations. This battle is among the most important struggles that we and our organizations will ever face. Individuals must break the chains of their unhealthy, outdated organizational codependency and recapture their self-esteem; organizations must reconceptualize their paradigms of loyalty, motivation, and commitment in order to compete in the new global economy.

The old psychological employment contract began to unravel about twenty years ago, and some people are still feeling the effects. Although we are well into act two, the dynamics haven't changed, and we can learn much from the past. For the organization, managing according to outdated values will no longer work. For individuals, struggling to hold on to a meaningless, deflated job can be a Faustian bargain that is hazardous to their mental health, as the following examples illustrate.

Lessons from Act One: Juanita and Charles—Victim and Survivor

When the layoffs hit, Juanita and Charles were both department directors, the lower end of the upper-management spectrum in the high-technology firm where they worked. Juanita was in her late forties, Charles in his early fifties. Although they had traversed very different paths to their management jobs, they were equally devastated when their organization started "taking out" managers to reduce costs. They experienced similar feelings of personal violation when the implicit psychological contract between each of them and their organization went up in smoke. Although this contract was only implied, Juanita and Charles had assumed that the organization shared their belief in the importance of this contract.

It wasn't long before both were experiencing survivor symptoms of fear, anxiety, and mistrust.

Juanita had achieved her management role. She had returned to school in midcareer, earned an M.B.A, and—through talent, determination, and the efforts of a good mentor—moved quickly through Anglo-male management ranks that were lonely and uncharted for a woman. When Juanita lost her job, the official explanation was that her department was "eliminated" and no other "suitable" positions were available. In reality, she was done in by the existing old-boy network, which at least in the early stages of the layoffs looked after its own. (In a form of layoff poetic justice, the network fell apart as the "rightsizing" continued.) Juanita was a "layoff victim."

Charles evolved into his management role. He was a classic organization man, joining the company right out of college and following the traditional career path of working his way up the system by punching the right tickets, knowing the right people, wearing the right clothes, and generally walking the walk and talking the talk. This career path was a hallmark of the large hierarchical public and private organizations that dominated the post–World War II era in North America, Western Europe, and Japan. The psychological contract that Charles and Juanita trusted was a legacy of this organizationally endorsed career path. Charles believed he had made a covenant that unless he violated the norms and standards of his company, he could count on his job until he retired or decided to leave.

Although Charles lost his influence, watched his support network disintegrate, ended up taking a substantial salary cut, and lived in a constant state of anxiety, guilt, and fear, he managed to hang on long enough to qualify for early retirement. He carried anger and depression with him when he left. Although technically a survivor, he is a victim of layoff survivor sickness. He would have been better off psychologically if he had left, and his company certainly would have been much wiser to invest in helping him make an external transition than living with his anger, guilt, and anxiety for fifteen years.

When Juanita was laid off, the company helped her take stock of her life and career. It spent some time and a fair amount of money on her psychological counseling and outplacement services. Juanita took over two years to grope her way through a time of exploration, regeneration, and ambiguity that William Bridges (1980) has called the "neutral zone." She emerged as a principal in a small but vibrant and thriving consulting firm. She has cut back her hours somewhat in the past few years, but is still excited about life and stimulated by her work, and she has merged her career and personal life into a balance she found impossible in her previous job. She become a much more integrated and congruent person as a layoff victim.

Charles is still living an anxiety-ridden life. His guilt, fear, and anger have spilled outside the job. He is now divorced and emotionally isolated, and he continues to struggle with alcoholism. His company, which after twenty years and two mergers, is still mostly intact, is going through another round of layoffs. Once again, in act two, it is spending some of its very scarce recourses to help those who are leaving but doing nothing to re-recruit those who have survived. As a result, the legacy of Charles lives on in a whole building filled with angry, unproductive, risk-averse employees. This is the team the company is fielding to compete in a global marketplace where innovation and creativity are the only true competitive advantage.

The Basic Bind: Lean and Mean Leads to Sad and Angry

Layoffs are intended to reduce costs and promote an efficient lean-and-mean organization. However, what tends to result is a sad and angry organization, populated by depressed survivors. The basic bind is that the process of reducing staff to achieve increased efficiency and productivity often creates conditions that lead to the opposite result: an organization that is risk averse and less productive than it was in the past.

The key variable is the survivors' sense of personal violation. The greater their perception of violation, the greater their susceptibility is to survivor sickness. The perception of violation appears directly related to the degree of trust employees have had that the organization will take care of them. Since nearly all organizations in the past had strategies of taking care of their employees, this basic bind is alive and well (Figure 1.1).

One symptom of layoff survivor sickness is a hierarchical denial pattern: the higher a person resides in an organization, the more

Figure 1.1. The Basic Bind

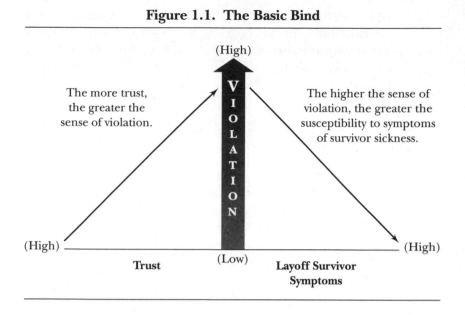

The more trust, the greater the sense of violation.

The higher the sense of violation, the greater the susceptibility to symptoms of survivor sickness.

(High)

V I O L A T I O N

(High)

(High)

Trust

(Low)

Layoff Survivor Symptoms

he or she will be invested in denying the symptoms of the sickness. This is one of the reasons that managers are often reluctant to implement intervention strategies, despite the increasing evidence of an epidemic of survivor symptoms, despite entire organizations filled with people like Charles. Understanding and dealing with survivor symptoms requires personal vulnerability and an emotional and spiritual knowledge of the symptoms. Most top managers are excellent at playing the role they and their employees have colluded to give them. Their egos require that they present an image of cool control and that they appear skilled and comfortable with rational and analytical knowing rather than emotional knowing. The management job in a downsized organization is extremely complex and demanding.

Metaphor of the Surviving Children

Managers and organizational leaders play a vital role in bringing about the emotional release necessary to begin the survivors' healing process after layoff. Their denial must be dealt with before there can be any release. In my experience, confronting denial head-on serves only to reinforce it. Methods that help people reach out to and legitimize their emotions and spiritual feelings are more useful in helping these people to understand the dynamics of their layoff survivor sickness. For example, I find that the metaphor of the surviving children is a compelling way to demonstrate the emotional context of survivor sickness to managers and help them move past denial:

> Imagine a family: a father, a mother, and four children. The family has been together for a long time, living in a loving, nurturing, trusting environment. The parents take care of the children, who reciprocate by being good.
>
> Every morning the family sits down to breakfast together, a ritual that functions as a bonding experience, somewhat akin to an organizational staff meeting. One morning, the children sense that something is wrong. The parents exchange furtive glances, appear nervous, and after a painful silence, the mother speaks. "Father and I have reviewed the family budget," she says, looking down at her plate, avoiding eye contact, "and we just don't have enough money to make ends meet!" She forces herself to look around the table and continues, "As much as we would like to, we just can't afford to feed and clothe all four of you. After another silence, she points a finger: "You two must go!"
>
> "It's nothing personal," explains the father as he passes out a sheet of paper to each of the children. "As you can see by the numbers in front of you, it's simply an economic decision. We really have no choice." He continues, forcing a smile, "We have arranged for your aunt and uncle to help you get settled, to aid in your transition."
>
> The next morning, the two remaining children are greeted by a table on which only four places have been set. Two chairs have been removed. All physical evidence of the other two children has vanished. The emotional evidence is suppressed and ignored. No one talks about the two who are no longer there. The parents emphasize to the two remaining children, the survivors, that they should be grateful, "since, after all, you've been allowed to remain in the family." To show their gratitude, the remaining children will be expected to work harder on the family chores. The father explains that "the workload remains the same even though there are two fewer of you." The mother reassures them that "this will make us a closer family!"
>
> "Eat your breakfast, children," entreats the father. "After all, food costs money!"

After telling this story, I ask surviving managers to reflect individually on the following five questions. Then I ask them to form small groups to discuss and amplify their answers:

1. *What were the children who left feeling?* Most managers say, "anger," "hurt," "fear," "guilt," and "sadness."
2. *What were the children who remained feeling?* Most managers soon conclude that the children who remain have the same feelings as those who left. The managers also often report that the remaining children experience these feelings with more intensity than those who left.
3. *What were the parents feeling?* Although the managers sometimes struggle with this question, most of them discover that the parents feel the same emotions as the surviving children.
4. *How different are these feelings from those of survivors in your organization?* After honest reflection, many managers admit that there are striking and alarming similarities.
5. *How productive is a workforce with these survivor feelings?* Most managers conclude that such feelings are indeed a barrier to productivity. Some groups move into discussions about effects of survivor feelings on the quality of work life and share personal reflections.

What most managers take away from the metaphor of the children is a powerful and often personally felt understanding of the radical change the managers are experiencing in their own organizations. The vast majority of managers were hired into organizations that encouraged employees to feel part of a family in which the managers performed the benevolent parent role. The reward for such performance was that all organizational employees, from executives to production people, would be taken care of.

The harsh reality of the new psychological contract is that many "family" members are no longer cared for and are treated as dispensable commodities. It is not my intent to label this situation as good or bad. It is a sad situation for many, and the existing situation for everyone. The fact is that the old "family" contract is ending and the new competitive realities are creating a fundamental shift in the relationship of individual and organization. Managers and nonmanagers alike are part of this fundamental change in the system. It is how to respond to this change, how to make it good rather than bad, that I am concerned with here.

Acts One and Two: A Family Legacy

George was a casualty of an act one layoff. He was manager of production control coordination for the manufacturing division of a computer company. What that title actually meant was that he was highly skilled at managing an administrative system that was of value to only one company at one point in time. When he lost his job, he found himself with large mortgage payments, loans on two cars, quarterly payments for a country club membership, the prospect of twelve years of private school tuition payments for his first-grade daughter, Betsy, and no transferable skills. Like the metaphorical children who left the family, he too was a victim; he had trusted that if he did his job well, the organization would take care of him. When that didn't happen, he went into an emotional tailspin that took him nearly five years to pull out of. He eventually went back to school and leveraged his increasingly irrelevant degree in industrial engineering for a teaching certificate in math. He moved to a smaller town, bought a smaller house, downsized to one smaller car, sent Betsy to a public school, and played golf at a public course. He is about to retire from his job as a high school math teacher.

Betsy developed into a smart, independent, and ambitious woman. With the aid of scholarships and student loans, she went to an expensive private college, majored in business administration, and went directly to graduate school, where still more loans helped her get an M.B.A. with a concentration in finance. She took a job in New York with a financial service firm and used her signing bonus and lucrative new compensation agreement to finance a flat in Manhattan's notoriously expensive real estate market.

Enter act two: soon after the 2008 meltdown, Betsy lost her job. She was enmeshed in debt, far from home, with no realistic prospects of a job that would pay even a quarter of her brief, but liberal, previous compensation. Demographically, she was representative of generation Y values. She had great comfort with technology, a need for instant gratification, and, most relevant to the layoff symptoms of her generation, had never before experienced failure. Unlike her father, whose symptoms when he was laid off were depression and anxiety, Betsy emerged angry and cynical. Unlike her father, she did not expect the mutual commitment and lifetime contract of the old paradigm, but she had not expected to lose her job. If she had left, she figured it would be her own choice.

The story of George and Betsy illustrates that although the causes and symptoms often vary by generation, the dynamics of layoff survivor sickness for victims and those who remain are alive and well. Although the old covenant is irrevocably broken, its power lies deep within our collective psyche. If our economic system is to survive, individuals and organizations need to find ways to move on.

Issues to Be Explored

Metaphors or analogies tease out underlying issues and move them past our defense mechanisms. The metaphor of the surviving children allows survivors to bypass their denial. They begin to understand the dynamics of layoff survivor sickness by looking at the symptoms through the experience of others. This metaphor, along with the stories of Juanita, Charles, George, and Betsy, illustrate the following layoff survivor issues, which we will explore in this book.

Common Symptoms

Those who remain in hierarchical organizations after layoffs share feelings of anger, fear, anxiety, and distrust. These feelings are particularly strong when the organizations have been nurturing and have captured the spirit of their employees. Employees have these feelings regardless of employment level. In the metaphor, the children and the parents shared the same feelings. In real organizations, those in the executive suite and on the assembly line share similar survivor feelings.

Norm of Denial

Employees follow a norm of denying and blocking layoff survivor symptoms. This psychic numbing is also commonly found in survivors of other forms of trauma. The chain of denial among layoff survivors is difficult to break systematically because it is hierarchical:

the higher the employee's rank, the stronger the denial. Denial also seems to be stronger in those who must plan and implement the layoffs. Human resource people, for example, often seem to exhibit a "Judas complex" and engage in extensive rationalization and explanation to justify workforce reductions. If there were a character equivalent to a human resource person in the surviving children metaphor, that character would be a caring aunt, uncle, or cousin who planned the separation, helped decide who would go, and either scripted or delivered the layoff notifications. That character would present rational arguments as to the economic need for the downsizing.

Shared Symptoms Among Survivors and Victims

The feelings of those who stay and those who leave are mirror images of each other. In fact, some evidence shows that the terms could reasonably be reversed: those who leave become survivors, and those who stay become victims.

Helping Resources Restricted to Those Who Leave

As the example of Juanita and Charles illustrated, the laid-off employee, Juanita, was helped by life and career counseling, outplacement assistance, and a variety of transitional support services, all paid for by the organization. But the survivor, Charles, was expected to report to work the next morning as though nothing happened, be grateful, and work harder. A strong norm of denial within the organization made him suppress his anger. The suppression resulted in survivor guilt, depression, and, in Charles's case, alcohol abuse. The organization devoted no resources to help Charles deal with his layoff survivor sickness.

Long-Term Symptoms

The literature about survivors clearly shows that survivor feelings exist for the long term. Although more research is needed, current evidence indicates that layoff survivors are no different from survivors of other forms of tragedy in that their symptoms do not go away unaided.

Needed Intervention Strategies

The family in the metaphor was a system in need of an intervention. Given the persistence of survivor symptoms, the norm of denial, and the general atmosphere of risk avoidance, the people in an organizational family tend to lock into a pattern of codependency with their survivorship. The codependency is also change resistant and persists. Multilevel intervention strategies at both the individual and systems levels are needed to break the unhealthy and counterproductive pattern.

Definitions

Layoff survivor sickness and the organizational realities that accompany this sickness are a relatively new topic in management writings, and some of the terminology is also new. These are the definitions of the terms I use to help people understand layoff survivor sickness and the need for new leadership strategies:

- *Layoff.* The term *layoff* is used generically to refer to all involuntary employee reductions for causes other than performance. Layoff in this sense does not imply that the employee may be recalled when business improves. Other common terms that convey the same meaning are *reduction-in-force* and *termination.* I do not use *firing* because it implies poor performance.
- *Layoff survivor sickness. Layoff survivor sickness* is a generic term that describes a set of attitudes, feelings, and perceptions that occur in employees who remain in organizational systems following involuntary employee reductions. Words commonly used to describe the symptoms of layoff survivor sickness are *anger, depression, fear, distrust,* and *guilt.* People with survivor sickness have often been described as having a reduced desire to take risks, a lowered commitment to the job, and a lack of spontaneity.
- *Victim.* The term *layoff victim* is used in this book, and increasingly in both academic and popular literature, to refer to the person who involuntarily leaves the organization, who is laid off. I hope to show how organizations can be "lean and mean" without creating people who feel victimized.
- *Survivor. Layoff survivors* are the people who remain in organizational systems after involuntary employee reductions. The

boundary between victims and survivors is blurred, however, because survivors often behave as victims.

- *Old employment contract.* This is the psychological contract that implies that employees who perform and fit into the culture can count on a job until they retire or choose to leave. I use this term interchangeably with *the old reality.*

- *New employment contract.* This psychological contract, which I sometimes describe as *the new reality,* says that even the best performer or the most culturally adaptive person cannot count on long-term employment. It replaces loyalty to an organization with loyalty to one's work.

- *Act one.* This is a generic term for the first significant round of layoffs (approximately between the late 1980s and early 1990s) that began the unraveling of the post–World War II covenant and violated the old employment contract.

- *Act two.* This is a term for the global pandemic of layoffs that followed the financial meltdown of 2008 and irrevocably shattered what was left of the post–World War II convenient.

- *Organizational codependency.* The concept of codependency originated in the treatment of alcoholism and has since been expanded to other addictive relationships. It is used here to describe the employee's relationship with an organization under the old employment contract.

- *Old paradigm.* This is the broad context, or setting, within which the old employment contract was played out. It describes the boundaries or limits once used to understand organizations, employees, and their relationship.

- *New paradigm.* This is the broad context within which the new employment contract is manifested. *New paradigm* describes the boundaries of a new way of understanding employees, organizations, and their relationship.

- *Good work.* This term describes task-specific behavior from which individuals derive worth, self-esteem, and value. *Good work* is part of the new employment contract.

- *Survivor guilt. Survivor guilt* describes a fundamental condition that leads to, and is often expressed in terms of, other survivor symptoms, such as depression, fear, or anger. In the context of layoff survivor sickness, *guilt* may be generally defined as "a feeling of responsibility or remorse for some offense; an emotional reaction that one has violated social mores" (Gottesfeld, 1979, p. 525).

Learnings and Implications

The stories of Juanita, Charles, George, and Betsy and the meta-phor of the surviving children illustrate the dynamics and multi-generational aspects of layoff survivor sickness. These stories introduced themes I explore in future chapters: the denial chain, shared symptoms among survivors and victims, the propensity of organizations to help those who leave and take for granted those who remain, the persistence of survivor symptoms, the necessity for intervention strategies, and new dimensions of leadership.

Before individuals or organizations can formulate healing strategies, they need a deep literal and symbolic understanding of the pathology of layoff survivor sickness. To help managers avoid the trap of instant diagnosis, or the ready, fire, aim strategy to which many organizations often succumb, it is necessary to explore the depth and breadth of this sickness. Chapter Two begins this process with a review of the fundamental change in the relation-ship of people to organizations, the change that is causing such agony today.

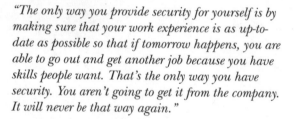

CHAPTER 2

Changing Organizations and the End of Job Security

> *"The only way you provide security for yourself is by making sure that your work experience is as up-to-date as possible so that if tomorrow happens, you are able to go out and get another job because you have skills people want. That's the only way you have security. You aren't going to get it from the company. It will never be that way again."*

I had a colleague whose second least favorite word was *empowerment*. At the top of his list was *paradigm*. Although both words are often overused and misused, I nevertheless use them a great deal in this book because they convey powerful and unique meanings. The profound and basic change in the typical relationship between employee and organization, and between organization and society, is nothing less than the fundamental change in worldview originally envisioned by Thomas Kuhn (1970) when he rescued the word *paradigm* from obscurity. We *are* in the midst of a fundamental paradigm shift. This chapter examines that shift in detail, because both individuals attempting to shake the symptoms of layoff survivor sickness and regain meaning and relevance in their work and organizations struggling to compete in the new global

economy need to understand the significance of this basic shift. Although it is difficult to see change when we are in the middle of it, we have four organizational yardsticks to measure it. These yardsticks have an old worldview at one end and a new worldview at the other (see Figure 2.1). The changes they measure occur in the assumptions organizations make about the purpose of employees, the language patterns organizations use to talk about employees, the long-term versus short-term time orientation of organizations, and the optimum operational size of organizations.

Figure 2.1. Paradigm Shifts

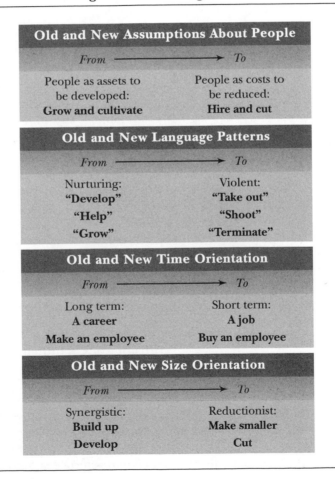

Old and New Assumptions About People	
From ⟶	*To*
People as assets to be developed: **Grow and cultivate**	People as costs to be reduced: **Hire and cut**

Old and New Language Patterns	
From ⟶	*To*
Nurturing: **"Develop"** **"Help"** **"Grow"**	Violent: **"Take out"** **"Shoot"** **"Terminate"**

Old and New Time Orientation	
From ⟶	*To*
Long term: **A career** **Make an employee**	Short term: **A job** **Buy an employee**

Old and New Size Orientation	
From ⟶	*To*
Synergistic: **Build up** **Develop**	Reductionist: **Make smaller** **Cut**

From Assets to Costs:
The New View of Employees

Perhaps the clearest evidence of the paradigm shift is that organizations that used to perceive people as long-term assets to be nurtured and developed now see people as short-term costs to be reduced. This basic change has a radical impact on the staffing and development cycle of hiring, training, career planning, and succession planning. Even more important, it represents a fundamental shift in the psychological covenant between the organization and the individual. Under the values of the old contract, employees in most large business, military, government, and religious hierarchies were perceived as assets to be nurtured and grown over the long term, often through organizational training and developmental programs. Even Frederick Taylor's "scientific management," mechanistic though it was, never envisioned a throwaway employee. For adherents of Taylor's principles, employees, like machines, were intended to be properly fit into the system, tuned, lubricated, and maintained over the long haul. As mechanistic and dehumanizing as scientific management was, many organizations are one-upping Taylor by not just viewing employees as "things" that are but one variable in the production equation, but as "things" that can be discarded when the bottom line does not come out as desired. However, as became apparent in act one and is again evidenced as act two unfolds, unlike machines, people who are discarded have a significant effect on those who remain within the system and in the system's ability to rebound.

"They Believed 'til the Door Hit Them in the Ass on the Way Out!"

A common employee response to the shift in organizational viewpoint is captured in these bitter words of Tony, a human resource manager who helped plan layoffs until he was laid off himself:

> Now that I'm out, I can see how things really changed—and not for the better! It sounded like God and motherhood, but we really meant it. In the early days, we said people were the most important things. Without good people, there wouldn't be an organization. The thing is we really believed that BS and acted on it. We paid

well, sent a lot of people to school—we had a super tuition refund process, lots of internal training and management development. We were in the human resource development business. It was part of everything we did. In the last few years, all we did was cut, cut, cut. They didn't give a damn about development. It was cut your head count, look for ways to get people out—the old meat grinder. The thing is, some of the lifers, the old-timers, still believed in all that crap—believed it 'til the door hit them in the ass on the way out! Talk about walking your talk: when we were cutting the hell out of the place—taking out whole layers, functions—we still said that people were most important. What a crock!

Better Planning and Management for "Inhuman" Resources

Another clue to the paradigm shift in the way organizations view employees surfaces in an exercise I sometimes use with clients. I first used it as part of a planning session after a postmerger layoff. I asked managers to write a paper contrasting their organizational considerations and decision-making processes for purchasing or leasing a facility with those for hiring a new M.B.A. The results were striking. The facility decision would be made carefully: the organization would use a number of analytical screens, look at the long-term perspective, and amortize the cost over a number of years. The final decision would be made at a high level and only after a number of functions had weighed in on it. The hiring decision, in contrast, would be made at the discretion of the supervisor, with no corporate overview. The time frame would be the present—what the M.B.A. could contribute on day one—and there would be no consideration of any long-term amortization of cost, which would be considerable given the pay, benefits, and office and support costs of a thirty-year-old M.B.A. until age sixty-five. I often also use a follow-on exercise in which managers decide whether to sell a building or lay off employees. After the two exercises, most managers experience varying degrees of the following insights and conclusions:

- Surprise at the true long-term cost of just one employee.
- Concern that there is such a striking difference between the rational decisions made about nonhuman resources and the random decisions made about human resources.

- Agreement that although the idea of looking at people as long-term investments makes a lot of sense, it does not work in the current organizational environment. (All groups agree on this.)
- A great deal of variance over the option of selling or subleasing a building and letting the employees work at home, where they could still be productive, or laying them off and keeping the building. Interestingly, most top management groups favor getting out of the building, whereas most middle managers say this option would not work because top management would not support it.

The discussion of the ways decisions are made about people and facilities often focuses on the possibility of organizations' treating people in the same manner as other assets, or human resource accounting. Human resource accounting never really made it into organizational systems in the old paradigm or in response to the early wake-up call of the first act. However, the concept of treating people like other capital assets, conceptualizing their training and development as "human capital" (Becker, 1993) and amortizing their costs over time, is an excellent way to think in the new paradigm. One of the criticisms of human resource accounting was that it dehumanized people, and it was difficult to translate human potential to the balance sheet. There have, however, been a number of improvements to the techniques in human resource accounting (Flamholtz, 1999), and clarity about the true costs and commercial nature of the employment relationship can actually produce a more open and honest relationship.

The Message from the Media

One way futurists gain insight into trends and directional shifts is by studying and distilling themes from newspapers, magazines, books, and journals. From the mid-1980s on, the popular press presented overwhelming evidence that we were in the midst of a major paradigm shift. Throughout the first act, the data continued to scream out at us undiminished from the daily newspapers, both underscoring the velocity of that change and providing a paradigmatic frame of reference for the even more significant change we are experiencing in the second act.

As early as 1987, journalist Jerry Flint captured the trend and provided an eerie harbinger of the situation twenty years in the future when he wrote that "hardly a day goes by without a headline on some major bloodletting: AT&T to cut its payroll by 27,000; IBM letting go 10,000; GM chopping 29,000; United Technologies cutting 11,000; a merged Burroughs/Sperry (UNISYS) 10,000; Eastern Airlines another 1,500; Illinois Central another 1,500; Wang, Tenneco, RCA, Exxon, ALCOA, why go on? The list seemingly never stops" (p. 38).

The first act gave us a preview of the now-apparent shift from people as long-term assets to be nurtured and developed to short-term costs to be managed and reduced. During the first act, even such staunchly nonlayoff organizations as IBM reversed decades of strong cultural norms and joined the frenzy. The numbers are still being tallied in today's second act and are certain to greatly eclipse those of the past. Nonetheless, it is useful to look back. Here are some other benchmarks of the first act:

- Two million jobs were eliminated in the 1980s, 1 million of them in middle management. Half of the 1980 Fortune 500 are missing from the 1990 list (Marks, 1991a).
- "More than eighty-five percent of the Fortune 1000 firms . . . downsized their white collar work force between 1987 and 1991. Almost a million American managers with salaries exceeding $40,000 lost their jobs [in 1990]. Between one and two million pink slips have been handed out each year [from 1988 to 1990]" (Cameron, Freeman, and Mishra, 1991, p. 58).

As the paradigm shift continued, the press also provided glimpses of a related value shift among organizational leaders. Steven Prokesch (1987), in a chronicle of what he calls the new creed of "ruthless management that puts corporate survival above all else," wrote, "The new order eschews loyalty to workers, products, corporate structure, businesses, communities, even the nation. All such allegiances are viewed as expendable under the new rules. With survival at stake, only market leadership, strong profits, and a high stock price can be allowed to matter" (p. 1). Prokesch also reported the comments of business leaders such as Gulf and Western's Martin Davis, who said, "You can't be emotionally bound to any particular asset," and Eaton's Stephen Hardis, who saw business as combat and said, "We're more like wartime leaders, in that all we can promise [employees] is blood, sweat and tears" (Prokesch, 1987, p. 8).

Leaders heading those organizations once credited with demonstrating "transformational leadership" (those of Chrysler, GM, Burroughs, and Honeywell) all had a strategy of helping the transformation by major layoffs. At Chrysler, for example, twenty thousand white-collar positions and more than forty thousand blue-collar jobs were eliminated in the initial "transformation." At the top of the organization, chairman Lee Iacocca reduced his staff by thirty-five vice presidents (Tichy and Devanna, 1986). Flint's description of Chrysler (1987) shows a battle-weary army of survivors rather than a transformed organization. He quotes Iacocca: "When we finally held the victory parade, a lot of our soldiers were missing. A lot of people—blue collar, white collar, and dealers— who had been with us in 1979 were no longer around to enjoy the fruits of victory" (p. 38).

Flint also showed the potential for layoff survivor sickness when he wrote of the dark side of efficiency: "The blood bath of firing goes on. That's the dark side of the current improvement in corporate efficiency. . . . After all, those workers from the production line now laid off, and those middle managers now adrift didn't hire themselves. They didn't create bureaucratic bloat. They didn't make the foolish acquisitions, or product choices. . . . In all of this, business is building up a good deal of resentment that will one day come to haunt it" (p. 38).

If the layoffs of the first act represented a paradigmatic shift, those we are experiencing in the second act are an earthquake. It is like comparing an arithmetic to a geometric progression or a swollen stream to a raging river. Here are some differences:

- Layoffs are deeper (affecting more levels), broader (affecting a greater variety of organizations: for profit, nonprofit, and government), and occurring at an accelerating pace (with shorter lead time from announcement to implementation and more organizations).
- Layoffs are much more global in scope, and in some locations, they began earlier than in the United States. Friedman (2007)

articulated it well: the world is flat, we are interconnected by technology, and what happens in one part of the world quickly and directly affects all other parts. The layoffs of the first act primarily affected North America, the United Kingdom, parts of Western Europe, and, to some degree Australia and New Zealand. The shock wave of second act layoffs is being felt throughout the world in places like China (Wudunn, 1993), India (Poornima, 2009), Mexico, and even Saudi Arabia, where there is an accelerated government-mandated involuntary exodus of expatriate guest workers in an attempt to preserve Saudi jobs (Looney, 2004).

- We were lulled into compliancy. The economic boomlet caused by excess liquidity and irresponsible credit practices caused us to forget the harsh reality of the first wave. The current crop of new college graduates missed the lessons entirely, and with their generation Y sense of entitlement, lack of experience with failure, and need for instant gratification, they are experiencing shock and anger at the second-wave realities.

From Nurturing to Violence: The Symbolism of Layoff Language

The symbolism of layoff language patterns provides powerful evidence of a paradigm shift. I began an ongoing research process by partnering with a manager investigating the language patterns within her own layoff environment.

Semantic Sensing

Sally, a human resource manager, was convinced that "no one [was] talking about development" anymore in her organization after layoffs were planned. She and I decided to test that feeling. For two weeks, Sally kept track of both "nurturing" and "violent" phrases. She jotted them down during group meetings and after one-on-one meetings. She captured hallway talk during a half-day top management planning meeting. The outcome? Violent terminology won hands down. While this was not surprising (the organization was intensely engaged in layoff planning), what was interesting was the size of the victory of violent terms over those that described nurturing relationships. For all the human resource group meetings, there were only four "nurturing" entries as opposed to over twenty "violent" entries, yet this was an organization with a long tradition of training and development and a strong and professional human resource staff. Violent words such as *take out, kill, shoot,* and *terminate* outscored helping words such as *develop, grow,* and *train* by about three to one. Although we used a simple sensing process rather than a sophisticated scientific study, the results were nonetheless illuminating. When they were fed back to a human resource committee, the consensus was that violent words had markedly increased over the past few years and that ten years ago, the group would have had "an opposite outcome."

I have since asked small groups of managers planning postlayoff revitalization efforts to come up with words and phrases that described the way they wanted to relate to their employees. Although the small group results were not as spectacular as the two-week study, the managers were surprised at the language patterns that had emerged within their organizations, particularly when these patterns were contrasted with the managers' intentions. During one session, a vice president turned to a comptroller and said, "The last time I came for an increase in my R&D budget, you asked me 'How many have you shot?' As if I had to pay for my new product development with the blood of employees!"

The Language of Layoffs as the Language of Assassination

Clinical behavioral practitioners have always carefully examined and given credence to the symbolism of communication patterns. Leaders struggling to revitalize organizations should do the same. Robert Marshak and Judith Katz (1992, p. 2) provide a good guideline for leaders when they say, "Explore literal messages symbolically, and symbolic messages literally," because "when symbolic communications are looked at, or listened to, for their literal as well as symbolic meaning a wider range of diagnostic speculation and/or inquiry is revealed." If leaders follow this guideline and understand the language of violence literally, they can see that managers who are "taking out" or "terminating" their fellow employees see themselves at some level as doing severe harm to others. Consequently these managers experience anger and survivor guilt. It is neither a coincidence nor a matter to be lightly dismissed that the language of layoffs is the language of assassination.

Language as a Safe Abstraction

Individuals also use symbolism to distance or somehow abstract themselves from the pain or embarrassment of reality. We have spawned a number of euphemisms for the act of separating people involuntarily from their jobs. It is easier for top executives to talk to the public about "restructuring" than to production workers about "termination." "Downsizing" feels better than "reduction in force," and "rightsizing" has an almost moral ring to it. Organizational leaders' invention of "safe" words is a clue to their repressed feelings and a window on their own survivor sickness.

From Long Term to Short Term: The Shrinking Planning Horizon

Another harbinger of the new paradigm is the shrinking time frame that organizations apply to almost everything. Organizations are reducing cycle time, planning time, budgeting time, travel time, development time, and, significantly, employee tenure time.

The Just-in-Time Employee

Stimulated by the current frenzy, driven primarily by security analysts, to make short-term (sometimes less than quarterly) incremental profit gains, many organizations find that their strategic horizon has been drastically shortened. In one organization, the so-called long-range strategic plan is now an eighteen-month document, and even that time period seems contrived and artificial to those who are leading and managing the organization. Employees too are affected by the short-term frenzy. Their long-term careers have become short-term jobs. In the new reality, people are becoming task-specific disposable components of a system that is already short term, and getting shorter. We are living in the era of the *just-in-time employee*. The increasing number of temporary help agencies offering both clerical and professional employees, a growing contract employee industry, and a marked increase in employee classifications such as part-time, temporary, permanent part-time, and on-call testify to the changed paradigm.

Bait-and-Switch Time Victims

Employees who accepted jobs under the old employment contract but are now ruled by the new may feel that they are victims of a type of bait-and-switch operation because the ground rules have changed in the middle of the game. When they joined, they expected a long-term relationship. Their tenure was often rewarded by periodic celebrations and organizational trinkets such as tie bars, earrings, key chains, and wall plaques. Now, under the new contract, leaving is more often the desired outcome. Even employees who joined organizations after the first act with no intention of remaining throughout their careers are surprised at the degree to which they are seduced into putting their social and emotional eggs in the organizational basket and the sense of anxiety they feel when facing the probability that the basket will be dropped.

From Synergistic to Reductionistic: Taking Apart Is Better Than Putting Together

Synergy is an old-paradigm word. Once, organizations added components, built themselves up, developed people for the long term, and a form of magic happened: two and two came out to more than four. No longer. The new paradigm is reductionistic. The shift in preference is from large to small. In human resource terms, the shift is from long-term employee development to short-term employee fit.

When Big Was Better

In the era after World War II, big was in. The United States had won the war by mobilizing large hierarchical organizations. What was good for General Motors truly was perceived as good for everyone. Books such as Sloan Wilson's *The Man in the Gray Flannel Suit* (1955) and William Whyte's *The Organization Man* (1956) provide a window on the work ethic and organizational culture of the time. Large, hierarchical, bureaucratic, male-dominated (*man* was appropriate in the book titles) organizations were the norm. Many organizations indexed the importance of managerial jobs by the number of people supervised. Job evaluation systems were developed that gave great weight to this span-of-control factor.

Many of these organization systems are in use within organizations that now value downsizing. Organizations that valued size also tended to value development. The party line was, "My primary job is developing people." The refrain toward the top of the organization was, "I can't go anywhere until I develop a replacement." The assumption was growth, the payoff was promotion, and the currency of the realm was size. Contrast that paradigm with today's reality: the assumption is quarter-to-quarter bottom-line survival, the payoff is that you get to keep your job and do it again next quarter, and the currency of the realm is getting the job done with a smaller, more flexible organization.

An Executive's New Reality

Robert once headed a large division of an organization attempting to rebound from layoffs triggered by a merger. After he too was laid off, he said, "I used to get kudos for hiring and developing people—used to give them myself to my people. That was the payoff: growing people, running big organizations. Now [the board of directors] gives [the CEO] big raises, stock, every other damn thing for cutting back, for taking people out. The headhunters that call don't care about who I mentored—the money I spent on training. They want to know how I did more with less."

Layoff Survivor Sickness: The Legacy

The reality of the paradigm shift is becoming increasingly clear, and we can live in only one paradigm. We can't go back. What we can do, what we must do if we are to revitalize our organizations, is deal with layoff survivor sickness, the legacy of the demise of the old paradigm and the old employment contract.

In a classic internal AT&T memo, written for the first act but even more applicable for today's environment, Joel Moses (1987) provided a clear articulation of this bitter legacy:

> We have very "disturbed" managers. Managers who are forced to make work force reduction decisions without any guidance, training, or support are becoming cynical. Or those who really care are being torn apart when making decisions that they are unprepared to make.

Open hostility is surfacing as never before and its focus is toward the company rather than toward the competition or the marketplace where such energies can be productively channeled.

The amount of suppressed, covert hostility lurking just below the surface in many people is truly frightening. Unfortunately, much of the frustration, anger, and depression is taking its toll on the non-work lives of our people.

Frequently, its manifestations are deteriorating physical and psychological health. The impact on managers' health in the future can't be ignored and may be approaching crisis proportions.

At the same time, we have noted a marked increase in symptoms of depression among managers we have studied. Today's survivors are often disillusioned, frustrated, bitter, and, most of all, lacking in hope.

One can't help wondering what kinds of managers they will be like in the future as they populate senior levels at AT&T [pp. 35–36].

Another first act writer, Jeffrey Hallett (1987), offered a prophetic prescription for dealing with second act survivor sickness when he called for "self-reliance," a theme that will be discussed in later chapters. He writes that organizations should "never, never say to an employee that the job is steady, guaranteed long-term, permanent or safe." Instead, Hallett suggests that self-reliance can become "a powerful statement about or expectation regarding work and society. The concept connotes a complete reversal of the fundamental notion that we 'work' for someone else. Instead, it says we work only for ourselves, that we take the responsibility for our own performance and progress, that we take responsibility for our own futures, and that we have the knowledge and the capabilities necessary for success" (p. 62).

Learnings and Implications

We are experiencing four dimensions of a basic shift in the relationship between people and organizations. Insights into this paradigm shift are found in organizational assumptions about the purpose of people (from assets to be grown and nurtured to costs to be cut), the symbolism of organizational language (from nurturing to violent), organizational time horizons (from long-term career development to short-term job fit and short-term profit orientation), and organizational preferences (from building up to taking apart).

The legacy of these profound changes is often an embittered work-force and reduced productivity at a time when organizations most need an optimistic workforce and high productivity.

This is a no-fault, long-term change. There are no "good" people and "bad" people. Managers did not make the paradigm shift happen or set out to trade off people for cost reduction. All levels of employees—top executives, middle managers, first-level supervisors, exempt and nonexempt employees—are in the same boat, part of the same uncomfortable, often painful cultural voyage. Nevertheless, people tend to blame others—usually the next person up on the organizational chart—for what is a basic systemic change that is beyond anyone's control. This survivor blaming phenomenon, described in more detail in Chapter Four, is not a productive way to deal with the fundamental change facing individuals and organizations.

Those occupying leadership roles are key to the survival of organizations and the rekindling of the spirit and creativity of the workforce. The new challenge to leaders is much more complex and stressful than operating within the predictability of the old paradigm. Both organizational leaders struggling to compete in a global marketplace and individuals seeking relevance in a time of change must learn to let go of the comfort of the predictable past. This is not a simple intellectual or rational decision. It involves struggling with the same inner demons that have confronted survivors of other forms of trauma.

PART TWO

THE
SURVIVOR
EXPERIENCE

CHAPTER 3

Learning from the Past

The Survivor Syndrome Across Time

"I didn't realize that I was probably suffering from some form of depression, but it was going on, and on, and on. I mean day after day, feeling the same way."

A general manager once asked for help with what he saw as the "short-term motivation problems" of the layoff survivors in his organization. He wanted to get on with business and thought a one-shot external intervention would do the job. Unfortunately, his diagnosis of the depth and staying power of layoff survivor symptoms was wrong. You do not fix survivors as you do a leaky faucet by calling in a specialist for a mechanical repair. As I show later in this book, a true fix requires a deep culture-breaking change for individuals and their organizations.

In the confusion of the postlayoff environment, it is easy for managers to underestimate the severity of survivor symptoms in both those they manage and themselves. However, layoff survivors suffer long-lasting symptoms that are in many ways similar to the symptoms of other survivors. An awareness of these similarities not only defines the seriousness of layoff survivor sickness but also stimulates the emotional release and grieving that must take place before organizations and survivors can move forward. The example of the Gunslinger shows how a deeper understanding of universal survivor symptoms can unblock organizational denial.

The Saga of "No Toes," the Gunslinger

The CEO of a regional financial services organization retained a headhunter and hired a new chief operating officer who had a reputation as a "tough, take-no-prisoners" turnaround expert. At the bank, his initial nickname was "Gunslinger," but later in his reign, because he made quick decisions without consulting others or adequate data, he was more frequently called "No Toes." Figuratively speaking, he would approach problems in a "ready–fire–aim" sequence, pulling the trigger before drawing his gun from its holster, thus blowing off his toes.

The bank was in bad shape when he arrived. It was internally focused, overbureaucratized, and overstaffed, and it had made too many bad credit decisions. If ever an organization needed downsizing, this one did, and the Gunslinger was only too happy to oblige. He initiated a series of rapid and substantial layoffs, at times eliminating entire functions and an entire level of middle management. He followed up with a requirement that each remaining department "totem-pole" its employees and terminate the bottom 10 percent.

There is nothing wrong with reducing the staff of a fat and marginally productive organization, and reducing the number of middle managers can eliminate bureaucratic bottlenecks and facilitate communication. The process of totem poling, although arbitrary with a one-solution-fits-all-departments bias, can also lead to the establishment of objective performance standards. The reason these results did not materialize in the Gunslinger's bank was that the changes were accomplished through a terrible process. There was no management participation, layoff decisions seemed random and arbitrary, and survivor feelings were repressed and denied. A bad process was then compounded by the organizational culture. For thirty years, the bank had valued tenure and emphasized loyalty. Its culture was accurately described by one long-term employee as "low pay, low stress, high security." When this old paradigm organization tried to become a new paradigm organization through an ineffective process, the basic bind came into operation, and the organization was paralyzed with survivor sickness.

A courageous vice president of computer operations, who worked for the Gunslinger, formed a cross-functional task force, despite the lack of any real support from his boss, in an attempt to get things moving again. The group, made up of eight upper-middle managers from across the organization, asked me to help them, but after a few meetings, it was apparent that they were going in circles. They would discuss in weighty intellectual terms the way that the past layoffs and future uncertainty had paralyzed the organization, nod their heads, and turn to me for suggestions. When I asked them to talk about their own feelings, they either talked about their pain with calm, nonpainful affect or talked about others' feelings.

A behavior common to layoff survivors was taking place: they were denying the personal emotional impact of the reductions and consequently blocking the necessary catharsis and grieving. Before this task force could do much for their organization, they had to recognize and deal with their own survivor issues. However, talking about feelings and emotions was never a part of the bank's culture, and with No Toes still the top decision maker in the organization, in charge of their fates, and wondering what they were up to, this task force was particularly resistant to experimental behavior.

In order to try to break the circular process, I set up a meeting outside the office and for a longer period than the normal two hours. We met at a conference center, starting after lunch and continuing well into the evening. What then occurred was one of those special times in group dynamics that can neither be predicted nor artificially recreated. I offer it here to illustrate the importance of overcoming denial, not to suggest that this particular intervention be routinely applied. The process we went through had four steps:

1. After some general relaxing and centering exercises, which helped everyone feel more at ease and in touch with their individual boundaries, each group member was asked to think of a major survival situation that he or she, or someone he or she knew, had experienced. With the exception of layoffs, all survival situations were fair game. What came out were events such as car crashes, divorces, and unexpected deaths. After individually fixing a chosen event in their minds and reexperiencing the feelings, the task force members wrote down the feelings.

2.　The participants were invited, still working alone, to think of a major survivor event to which they could relate but had not experienced. Examples of what they came up with were surviving a plane crash, a prisoner-of-war experience, and a potentially fatal illness. Again, they were asked to put themselves in the survivor's position and write out their feelings.

3.　The participants shared the events and their feelings. It soon became clear that their feelings for both the real and the fantasized events were similar. They had experienced fear, anger, depression, and anxiety, all grounded in a core sense of violation.

4.　The task force members fantasized further survivor situations and collectively used them as metaphors for layoff situations. What they came up with was exceptionally vivid and powerful: they were travelers over the Donner Pass, staying alive through the winter by cannibalizing their fellow travelers; they were in charge of life rafts and had to decide who could stay and who had to be thrown overboard; they were soldiers parachuted into hostile territory and abandoned while their generals took early retirement and forgot about them. Metaphors like these flowed uninterrupted for almost an hour and served to break through the norm of denial and calm rationality and help them personally come to grips with the depth of survivor symptoms.

It was an emotional session that served to break patterns of denial by dramatizing the shared sense of violation the task force members felt. These insights helped them own up to their own issues and paved the way for a much better layoff process for future layoffs and programs to facilitate the necessary grieving and emotional release for those who remained.

This intervention example is not meant to be a recipe but only to provide one example of the rich variety of exercises that can be used to get survivors in touch with and clarify their emotions. I have found the metaphor of the surviving children discussed in Chapter One to be a consistently reliable tool in this regard. Also, the intervention's positive results would not have resulted in any action if the Gunslinger had remained at the bank. Shortly after the breakthrough session, he was terminated. The story in the hallways was that, like his Old West counterparts, he wore out his welcome. The CEO, like the town mayor in the Old West, had hired the Gunslinger to rid the town of bandits—the fat, overbureau-cratized organization. The Gunslinger did clean out the bandits, but then he stayed on and became a bigger problem than the bandits themselves. He had fixed one problem but had to leave before the wounds he had created in the process could heal.

Lessons from the Gunslinger's Task Force

- It is easy to underestimate the depth and tenacity of layoff survivor feelings.
- In the heat of battle, as change, confusion, and uncertainty swirl throughout the organization, it is easy, and often seems safer, to block and deny survivor feelings.
- Understanding, in both your head and your heart, that the feelings of layoff survivors and those who have survived other forms of trauma are connected is a necessary means of getting past blockage and denial.
- Those attempting to help others deal with survivor issues must first work on their own feelings.
- A take-no-prisoners, macho, "suck it up" and uninformed cut-and-slash top management approach may initially seem appealing to outside stakeholders, but it always does more harm than good to recovery and productivity.

Universal Survivor Linkages

All those involved in layoffs should broaden their cognitive and emotional (head and heart) understanding of the linkages among survivors of trauma. This broad understanding is necessary if managers in particular are to heal themselves and then help others. I will use powerful well-known historical examples of survivorship to define survivor linkages. In comparing layoff survivors to survivors of much more life-threatening events, I do not intend to trivialize or dilute the pain and horror that these other survivors endured. Nor am I equating the violation experienced by a layoff survivor with, for example, that experienced by September 11 survivors. The difference in magnitude is immeasurable. That is not to say, however, that layoff survivors do not experience violation.

The forty-six-year-old middle manager who joined an organization as a new college graduate and has been conditioned into relying on the organization to meet his social, financial, and self-esteem needs is exceptionally vulnerable. When he wakes up one morning in midcareer to find that the organization can no longer honor its end of the psychological employment contract, he does indeed experience violation. His sense of personal relevance and value has been taken away. When a single survivor understands that all survivors share the same emotions, though in greatly varying degrees, he or she gains head and, more important, heart insight into both the seriousness and the normalcy of these emotions.

There are three primary linkages: similar symptoms, a common sense of violation and a preoccupation with death imagery, and blurred distinctions between those who do and those who do not survive and a shared sense of victimization among victims and victimizers.

Similarity of Symptoms

After the space shuttle *Challenger* disaster, the thousands of people who had worked in the shuttle program felt like disaster survivors. Descriptions of the symptoms experienced by these survivors and by layoff survivors at Occidental Petroleum provide an example of survivor symptom similarity. Shortly after the disaster, observers said that the shuttle survivors experienced "guilt, anxiety, and fear," with the full intensity of these feelings yet to be dealt with because of "denial" (Schwadel, Moffett, Harris, and Lowenstein, 1986, p. 27). Very similar words were used by human resource consultant Marshall Stelifox when he described the symptoms of "anxiety, distrust, fear, and insecurity" among survivors at Occidental Petroleum (Fowler, 1986, p. 23). Stelifox may also have been the first to use the term *survivors' syndrome.*

Preoccupation with Violation

In a classic study, psychiatrist Robert Lifton (1967) analyzed the survivors of the Hiroshima atomic bomb and found they had a fixation with "death imagery." He also found that a preoccupation with images of death and destruction is common among survivors of other traumatic situations. Tragically, we do not suffer for more recent examples: the September 11, 2001, attacks; the April, 20, 1999, Columbine shootings; the April 16, 2007, Georgia Tech killings;

the November 26, 2008, Mumbai attack. Layoff survivors too have recurring images of destruction, although these are obviously significantly more diminutive in tragic consequences. A review of the direct quotations of layoff survivors in the next two chapters reveals both symbolic and literal descriptions of violation and destruction.

I have also found gallows humor common among layoff survivors. At one level, this is a form of comic relief. At a symbolic level, it is also a variant on survivors' unconscious use of the imagery of destruction. An example of the ease with which violent imagery is integrated into day-to-day layoff discussions is the human resource manager who attended a meeting on the administrative aspects of implementing an impending layoff and afterward said in an off-hand way that she felt she had just attended a Nazi staff meeting in which the number of Jews who could fit in a boxcar was "rationally" decided. These extreme images of destruction are common among those who process layoff victims out the door. The ease with which this manager conjured up this horrible image is evidence that a survivor connection was percolating in her unconscious while she sat through that meeting.

Feelings of Victimization by Victims and Perpetrators

The metaphor of the surviving children often leads managers to the conclusion that those who make layoff decisions, other layoff survivors, and the layoff victims are all in the same boat. Survivors of layoffs share similar feelings of guilt, anxiety, and depression. Jerry Harvey, author of the well-known *Abilene Paradox* (1988), a parable that describes how people collude collectively to do things they do not want to do individually, perceives what I call survivor sickness as a dulling of our "moral sensibilities," which "decreases the probability of our individual and collective survival" (1985, p. 41). He also describes it as marasmus. Derived from the Greek, *marasmus* means "'to waste away.' It generally refers to the progressive emaciation which occurs in infants when they are denied the loving care of an adult. It is caused by 'anaclitic depression,' which, in turn, means depression which is induced by being separated from someone you love or care for or need" (1981, p. 1).

Wasting away—mental and emotional withdrawal and loss of affect—due to depression is a symptom that both survivors and victims experience. Most managers who work in organizations hit hard by layoffs have had experience with organizational units where marasmus seems to be the operant condition. The survivors do seem to be wasting away. In Harvey's model, the irrevocable outcome of unchecked marasmus is death for the organization and, at the least, what Richard Leider (1992) calls "inner-kill" for the individual. The behavior of declining organizations that Uri Merry and George Brown describe in *The Neurotic Behavior of Organizations* (1987) also is found in organizations suffering from marasmus. The characteristics are:

- Negative self-image; failure script of organization [a negative self-fulfilling prophecy].
- Energy down; organization pervaded by low motivation, frustration, unhappiness, boredom, and hopelessness.
- Disagreement on goals and values throughout organization; norm disruptment with extreme deviations; organized life loses meaning.
- High magnitude of dysfunctioning, lack of reserve resources, failure of self-image, and fear of letting go make change extremely difficult; rational organizational development methods give no results [pp. 44–45].

Lifton's Model of Hiroshima Atomic Bomb Survivors

An illuminating way of viewing the universality of survivorship is through the symbolic lenses of psychiatry. Robert Lifton's analysis of Hiroshima atomic bomb survivors created a model that can be applied to all survivor situations. The left-hand column of the list shows the themes Lifton found in the survivors of Hiroshima as these themes are manifested in both Hiroshima and death camp survivors. The right-hand column shows my interpretation of these themes in layoff survivors:

Hiroshima and Death Camp Survivors	*Layoff Survivors*
Death imprint	**Death imprint**
The bombing	The layoffs

Symbolic reactivation

News reports of atomic deaths

Annual August 6 ceremony

World destruction imagery

Visions of "ultimate death, ultimate separation"

Psychic mutation

Altered perception of reality— "coping mechanisms" necessary to survive death camps

Death guilt

Resentment toward those who died

Feeling that those who left escaped the consequences of survivorship

Psychic numbing

Perception of oneself as an object—"These dreadful, degrading things are not happening to me"

Miscarried repair

Vitality perceived as immoral

Victim bonding and suspicion

Resentment by Hiroshima survivors toward Bikini atoll survivors

Delayed paranoia

Formulation

"Establish new internal and external relationships"

Symbolic reactivation

News reports of mergers, layoffs, and acquisitions

Empty offices, vacant parking slots

World destruction imagery

Projections of failure of capitalistic system

Psychic mutation

Joy in work, spontaneity, and creative energy no longer part of reality

Death guilt

Guilt feelings associated with luck—being in the right place at the right time

Psychic numbing

Process of denial—"That's the way it is in business organizations"

Miscarried repair

Lack of risk taking: going through the motions

Victim bonding and suspicion

Resentment by line personnel toward staff personnel

Survivor status hidden at outside social gatherings

Formulation

Break organizational codependence

Death Imprint

In Lifton's terminology, a *death imprint* is the initial violation. In Hiroshima the triggering event was the bombing; in organizations it is the layoffs. This event starts the chain of emotional response. Death imprinting causes mourning for the way things were, "for beliefs that have been shattered" (Lifton, 1967, p. 484).

Although there is an immense difference between the horror and fear faced by Hiroshima survivors and the disruption and uncertainty faced by those who remain in organizations after reductions, layoff survivors are indeed imprinted by the layoffs. They do mourn the way things were—the old paradigm days that have been destroyed. When survivors wish former bosses were still in charge (because, they say, those bosses wouldn't let this happen) or when they lament the loss of an organization's founder (because, they say, he would run the company better), the survivors are looking back, searching for beliefs that have been shattered.

A death imprint has three subprocesses: symbolic reactivation, world destruction imagery, and psychic mutation. Lifton found that symbolic reactivation occurred for Hiroshima survivors when they saw media reports of atomic deaths or were reminded of their survivorship through events like an annual commemorative ceremony. Organizational parallels occur when each succeeding wave of layoffs reminds survivors of their status. Reactivation triggers symptoms of guilt, fear, and anxiety. It also makes layoff survivors feel paranoid, inauthentic, and disinclined to take risks. Although they do not envision their "ultimate death," newspaper and television reports of bad economic conditions, layoffs, divestitures, and mergers encourage a form of world destruction imagery among those survivors. In some old paradigm organizations with a history of paternalism, layoffs trigger such a deep erosion of trust that survivors question whether any for-profit organization can survive with, as they see it, the permanent loss of motivation and commitment.

Psychic mutation describes the altered perception of reality that individuals succumb to in order to get through terrible events. It is a process of numbing one's feelings and blocking our previous ideas of the way things ought to be. Death camp prisoners developed a type of apathy, make-it-through-one-day-at-a-time resignation, and a type of acceptance that the horror of their environment was "normal." Long-term layoff survivors also undergo a form of psychic mutation. They often accept fear and anxiety and just try to make it through the day. Creative energy, spontaneity, and joy in work are no longer part of their reality.

Death Guilt

A number of mental health professionals believe that all deaths cause guilt in those who survive. Deep and often unexpressed or not understood feelings of resentment at being abandoned lead to this survivor guilt. Hiroshima survivors suffered from survivor guilt directly attributable to the deaths caused by the atomic bomb. The early work of Brockner and others (1985, 1986) gave evidence that a form of survivor guilt exists in layoff situations even though no literal deaths are involved. Survivor guilt is alive and well in the second act. Leadership IQ (Business Wire, 2008) reports that in a study of 4,172 layoff survivors, 74 percent reported reduced productivity, and the most common words from an open-ended question asking for a description of feelings were *guilt, anxiety,* and *anger.* Layoff survivors who feel "depressed" or "saddened" by empty offices, or, in the case of one person, by all the extra parking slots in the executive parking garage, are manifesting survivor guilt, triggered by a form of symbolic reactivation.

Psychic Numbing

In Lifton's study, psychic numbing not only occurred immediately following the survivor experience, it dominated the survivors' entire lifestyle. Numbing begins with denial: "The survivor's major defense is the cessation of feeling" (Lifton, 1967, p. 500).

As an example of psychic numbing, Lifton quotes the following description of the psychic numbing of prisoners from Primo Levi's *Survival in Auschwitz.* It is similar to the condition Harvey calls marasmus: "An anonymous mass, continually renewed and always identical, of non-men who march and labor in silence, the spark dead within them, already too empty to really suffer, one hesitates to call them living: one hesitates to call their death death, in the face of which they have no fear, as they are too tired to understand" (p. 502).

Miscarried Repair

The ultimate effect of psychic numbing is *miscarried repair,* which is analogous to an overreaction of the body's immune system. The defenses against infection become a noxious force. In Hiroshima survivors, miscarried repair took the form of fatigue and other bodily complaints. Lifton (1967) observes that these survivors' "numbing is such that vitality is perceived as immoral" (p. 503).

Layoff survivors are seen as flat, tired, and risk averse. Being "up" and positive often seems countercultural. Hunkering in the trenches, not taking risks, and keeping a tight rein on emotions that need airing are defensive reactions that are neither healthy for the individual nor productive for the organization. This defensiveness, or miscarried repair, causes layoff survivors too to perceive vitality as immoral.

Victim Bonding and Suspicion

Survivors often have difficulty establishing authentic relationships with others for two reasons. First, they are invested in a victim identity: they are survivor-victims. Second, they are suspicious of others. This suspicion can turn into a form of "delayed paranoia." Hiroshima survivors have "a group tie built around common victimization. . . . The survivor feels drawn into permanent union with the force that killed so many others around him. His guilt is intensified as is his sense that his own life is counterfeit" (Lifton, 1967, p. 511). Identity as a survivor can lead to rivalry with other survivors. The Hiroshima survivors, for example, resented the attention given to the survivors of the 1954 Bikini atoll hydrogen bomb fallout. Layoff survivors continually index the severity and ruthlessness of the layoffs in their organization against that of other organizations. Another prevalent index of severity is the line-staff, headquarters-field, or top-bottom balance. Line units will lament that they "took harder hits" than staff units, saying, "After all, we bring in the revenue." Field units resent layoff leniency in headquarters units, and lower levels resent top management for not taking its fair share. And so it goes: all units are invested in their I'm-a-bigger-victim-than-you syndrome.

Survivors are suspicious of others. One form this suspicion takes in layoffs is the survivor-blaming phenomenon: everyone blames everyone else. The Hiroshima survivors turned inward and clung to their victim identity. As both types of survivors struggle over time with repressed rage, their isolation and suspicion are reinforced by what Lifton (1967) describes as others' contagion anxiety: "The essence of contagion anxiety is, if I touch him, or come too close, I will experience his death and his annihilation. Hence the universal tendency to honor martyrs and reject survivors" (p. 518). Survivors in organizations known to be going through severe layoffs often worry about how their outside contacts are affected by this knowledge. Some layoff survivors say that they do not own up to their place of employment when they attend outside social events. Others report limiting their social life and spending more leisure time at home. Contagion anxiety flourishes in many organizations during the awkward time between layoff victims' getting the word and leaving the organization. Survivors are reluctant to engage with these victims. Conversation is stilted or nonexistent, and empathy and concern are often suppressed.

Formulation

Lifton's cure for survivor sickness involves a process of structuring a new relationship with the world and coming to terms with the permanence of loss. He describes how "the dropping of the atomic bomb in Hiroshima annihilated a general sense of life's coherence" among the survivors, and he points out that Freud "described the survivor's need to come to gradual recognition of the new reality, of the world which no longer contains that which has been lost" (1967, p. 525). Similarly, the cure for layoff survivor sickness requires that survivors accept the new reality and let go of the old paradigm. As I discuss later, the cure demands that survivors muster up the courage to break organizational codependency and live organizational life as adventurers, not victims.

Learnings and Implications

Those of us who must revitalize ourselves or our organizations must understand the true depth and staying power of survivor symptoms. We can increase both our head and heart understanding by examining the archetypical linkages between layoff survivors and survivors of more severe traumas. I have used the ideas of Jerry Harvey, the psychodynamic theories of Robert Lifton, and a story of survivors confronting their symptoms in order to illustrate the universality of survivor symptoms. Unfortunately, there are countless contemporary examples. Another historical look at survivor symptoms is found in the work of Aleksandr Solzhenitsyn, who wrote with a passion fueled by his own survivor sickness. One need only journey with him through the Gulag Archipelago (1974) or spend a day with him examining the marasmus of Ivan Denisovich (1963), to visualize the specter of a gulag of organizations, populated by demoralized employees with spirits atrophied by a plague of survivor sickness.

My primary purpose in this chapter was to broaden managers' understanding of survivorship and set the stage to analyze layoff survivor sickness through the literal and symbolic descriptions of survivors' feelings in the survivors' own words. As I listen to the layoff survivors in the next two chapters, it often seems to me that the voices of many earlier survivors have reached across time and mingled with those of the layoff survivors to reflect the universality of survivor feelings.

CHAPTER 4

Speaking for Themselves

Layoff Survivor Stories

"There is a sense that you have done something wrong if you get laid off. I don't think anyone escapes that. Even if, in their rational minds, they say, 'I was good, it just happened to be the job I was in,' there's something down deep that says, 'You weren't good enough, there's something wrong, you pissed somebody off, you didn't play the game.'"

With a few exceptions, most of the research on the effects of layoffs on survivors is limited by its laboratory orientation. Although valuable, it has not captured the gut-wrenching trauma or plumbed the true emotional depth of layoff survivor sickness. To allow readers to experience the turmoil and anger of survivors, this chapter and the next report on an ongoing field study of real survivors in an existing organization. These chapters consist mainly of direct quotations from the survivors to provide readers with a personal, undiluted sense of the true emotions and thoughts of layoff survivors. The universal survivor feelings explored in Chapter Three and the pain of living through the transition to the new paradigm described in Chapter Two can be heard in the voices of these survivors. The intervention strategies I describe later also build on the foundation of personal understanding developed in this and the next chapter. I encourage you to allow yourself to be flooded by the layoff survivors' feelings and perceptions as you read. For those preferring a different journey, the quotations are organized by theme and therefore may be read selectively.

Organizational Characteristics

The initial study took place in a large multinational firm head-quartered on the East Coast of the United States. The organization was experiencing severe financial problems and implementing a downsizing that called for significant across-the-board layoffs. A prototypical old employment contract organization, it had a number of programs to integrate employees into the organization over a long period of time. In the spirit of "modern" employee relations, the organization had support services that promoted employee dependency, and the psychological bond supporting this relationship was seen to be violated when the organization instituted layoffs. Although there was no formal nonlayoff policy, the shared expectation was that an employee with acceptable performance could count on her or his job no matter what the economic conditions. Although the initial study began during act one, the survivor symptoms and personal stories are directly applicable to organizations today, and it is the rare manager who won't discover the sentiments of employees in her organization in the voices of these survivors.

Research Methodology

The initial study consisted of two samples: structured interviews of small groups of layoff survivors and individual interviews with human resource professionals involved in layoff administration. A second, more limited follow-up study (discussed in Chapter Five) was conducted five years later. In the initial group interviews were ten randomly selected groups of eight to fifteen survivors from recent layoffs. These groups represented a variety of businesses and job levels. The interview sessions were taped and the transcripts analyzed. The quotations that follow, excerpted from the interview transcripts, provide an appreciation of the depth and seriousness of layoff survivor sickness.

Survivors' feelings and concerns are separated into fifteen categories: job insecurity; unfairness; depression, stress, and fatigue; reduced risk taking and motivation; distrust and betrayal; optimism; continuing commitment; lack of reciprocal commitment; wanting it to be over; dissatisfaction with planning and communication; anger over the layoff process; lack of strategic direction; lack of management credibility; short-term profit orientation; and sense of permanent change.

Job Insecurity

Job insecurity was an interview theme that cuts across all levels and was discussed in all groups:

- "I go home and I wonder at night, am I going to be here tomorrow, the next day, or three days from now?" (manager)
- "I find it frightening. At my age, I would really hate to go out and walk the sidewalks. I wouldn't even know which sidewalk to start on. I think it's very frightening." (clerical employee)
- "I've come up through the ranks. I started in assembly. I don't have a college degree, and now I'm doing work [for which] other companies hire those people with master's degrees. If I was tapped on the shoulder tomorrow, and they said, 'Well, find a job,' I don't know where I would find one. If I went outside, I probably wouldn't know what to do. I would be lost. That scares me." (professional/technical employee)

Unfairness

Like job security, unfairness as a theme came up in all groups. The discussions had two dimensions: a sense that top executives and people from other parts of the organization were not doing their share and perceptions that the choice of who stayed and who left was unfair:

- "I think there are too many instances where they took the wrong people. The ones that have kept their jobs are short termers and haven't contributed in the short time they've been here. Then they've taken senior people because they're paid more. They've made a conscious decision to cut these out and keep people whom I don't consider contribute at all." (field employee)

- "They're padding their pockets. In the good times, the bonuses and everything go to the top executives, and during the bad times the workers get cut out. The company hasn't shown me that they care as much about me." (professional/technical employee)
- "I personally feel like I've seen a lot of good people lose their jobs because somebody screwed up down at headquarters." (professional/technical employee)
- "I asked my manager how they decide, because I was curious after the layoffs were happening. He said, basically, they go by your performance overall. That's what he told me. To me it is just like favoritism. . . . If they like you, they'll keep you; if they don't, they won't." (clerical employee)
- "Sometimes we hear in the news or in the business reports [about] executive levels and the gold parachutes. It's something that can cause resentment because you feel that these guys have enough connections or networking that if the plug is pulled on them, they're going to land on their feet elsewhere." (administrative employee)
- "The criteria are very political. . . . They just laid a guy off who did a super job, and he had been there about eighteen years. He was very, very upset because he had no idea; he worked so hard. And the reason he was upset was because there was another guy at the same level that he felt was doing such a terrible job, and they don't do anything about it." (administrative employee)

Depression, Stress, and Fatigue

The themes of depression, stress, and fatigue occurred in all discussion groups, and as the first two quotations show, those in leadership roles shared these feelings:

- "But I did walk through, talked with a lot of people. . . . My biggest personal reaction to a lot of what went on was the feeling of depression as I would talk to people." (executive)
- "You see a lot of good people being let go, and that's very demoralizing, to know that an excellent person is being let go. It affects your credibility with your company, and it also affects your productivity." (manager)
- "I walk around with a knot in my stomach. Honestly, two weeks ago I told my boss I'd either take a week off or I'd quit. I had

to get away from the job, away from the paper, away from the dispatchers, away from the problems, the customers." (field employee)

Reduced Risk Taking and Motivation

Employees at all levels saw a direct relationship between the layoffs and reduced risk taking among the survivors:

- "Some of the folks I have talked to in the last couple of months have specifically said it's the ones most outspoken that get hit. [We] had sales representatives who had exceeded quota for several years in a row, and then suddenly they're workforce reduced. They were the pushy ones saying, 'I need more product, I need this, I need that,' and the perception was that we've lost the risk takers. We lost the people who are willing to speak up." (executive)
- "The most dangerous [result] is refusing to take any risks at all. Keeping your head down. You see that from the executive level all the way down to that programmer whom you're asking to reassign to something. They're looking to see if [the reassignment is] at all dead-ended. If it is, they don't want it. The same thing is true of executives." (executive)
- "Why should I take a new position within this corporation [with] the risks of that project failing or not being funded next year so that I'm exposed? Why should I take that risk?" (professional/technical employee)
- "I don't go that extra step anymore, whereas I [used to take on more, on] my own initiative. Because when I would go that extra, I felt I owed the company that. [Now] I don't necessarily feel like I owe the company that." (field employee)
- "I feel there are some people in our department who are afraid to speak up on their feelings about the way things are being run or the way their job is being handled—in the sense that [they think], 'If I see something that goes against the grain, or if I say something about my dissatisfaction here, perhaps the next time our department is looked at as to who should be let go, it will be me, because I am the one who has expressed some dissatisfaction in the way that things are being handled.' I think there's a real fear of that." (administrative employee)
- "I think we feel kind of intimidated about speaking up to our management. When it comes time to lay off, they'll think, 'Well,

that loudmouth—we don't need her around here.' So I find myself holding back, not saying things I should be able to say and stating my opinion." (clerical employee)

Distrust and Betrayal

Feelings of distrust and betrayal emerged as themes in the field, headquarters, and professional/technical groups:

- "My attitude is affected by what's gone on in the company, and I'm not so positive when I go out there and work. [I think,] 'That's not my problem,' where before my attitude was a lot different. I don't care whether the company, and I say *the company,* can support that customer in the middle of the night. It shouldn't be my problem; it's their problem. Let them find somebody else. I'm not going to go out there. That's the attitude I had to take a couple times because I don't care anymore." (field employee)
- "I've lost trust in the company. I've been with them for eleven years, and I have no idea whether or not to trust them anymore because of what you hear positive [from them] about the company. The next day you come in to work and it's 180 people out. You can't believe what they say. My key word is that I've lost trust." (field employee)

Optimism

Some managers and executives expressed a sense of optimism. It was their opinion that necessary tough actions had been taken and that the organization was on a painful but clear road toward recovery. These feelings of optimism were unique to executives and managers:

- "I think I feel that, more than ever, I know where the company is going—especially in the decentralized mode that we're in in our division. We know where we are, and we know what we've got to do in order to survive. It's been pretty well laid out to me and to the people who work for me. I feel good about it. I think that the company is doing things now that it had to do ten years ago, and it's got another five years to go before it's going to get there, and it's going to be bloody. But I feel good about it because the alternative is to get the hell out. If [we] don't do those things, . . . we ain't going to be around." (executive)

- "When you look at the beginning of it, we were all in a total survival mode. We had to make changes in the company and downscale the way we were doing things in order to survive. And that's good—the overall change of downscaling the entire staff has been good for the company. There's no question about that." (manager)
- "I hear a lot of good vibes about the cooperation of those survivors, or pseudo-survivors, that a meaner, leaner corporation we're going to be, and I'm proud to work for it." (manager)

Continuing Commitment

Despite the uncertainty and with layoffs going on around them, some employees expressed a continuing sense of commitment to the organization:

- "It's difficult when people are being laid off all around you, but I still feel committed to the company. I get concerned about overmanaging the company on a quarterly basis, but I recognize the need for profitability. I still feel committed to the company." (manager)
- "In the last six months, I've turned down two good offers. People say, 'Why? Are you crazy?' And maybe I am, but I still have a commitment to this company. I want to see them succeed. I don't want to bail out and say, 'No, we couldn't get the job done.' That's the way I am. I believe that I should follow a job through, but I still feel insecure in my job, and tomorrow I may not have one, no matter of the fact that I did make that commitment to this company." (field employee)
- "I just like doing my job, I look at the organization, and I see a company with a hell of a lot of potential. I mean the products, the services, and the like. I don't want to get laid off, and I don't really want to quit. I don't want to go to some other company because it's not going to be much better anyplace else." (field employee)

Lack of Reciprocal Commitment

Although some employees expressed a continuing commitment to the organization, no one felt the organization had a reciprocal ongoing commitment to him or her. Some were angry and bitter about the abrupt change:

• "There seems to be an absolute fundamental change in the company as far as its attitude toward people. People are viewed as commodities. The first reaction to problems is to reduce head count. That fundamental attitude seems to have changed the company. [The change] seems to be permanent." (executive)

• "I've talked to people, . . . senior executives [who have] been around twenty, twenty-five years, who have been given two minutes total to see their HR rep. So what's come out of all that is people just wonder where they stand. The biggest problem, I think, that we have as a company in going forward is, in fact, being able to demonstrate by the behavior of executives and each manager in dealing with their people, that they really give a damn about people as individuals, and [give] some dignity and respect to the people." (executive)

• "I think that it is a cultural change that's going on in the industry. I think a lot of people have the feeling that if they went to work for a company, enjoyed the company, and gave the company a day's work for a day's pay, they could stay there until the day they retire. There's not that guarantee anymore. It's been a real wake-up to the American public." (manager)

• "They owe me a little bit more than just saying . . . , 'You ought to be grateful that you have a job.' They ought to be grateful that I put eleven years into this company and I've done what I consider to be a good job. I never had a poor performance review." (field employee)

Wanting It to Be Over

There was a widespread desire to get on with the downsizing, to get it over. Employees felt fatigued and drained by the continuing reductions. Some felt misled by what they perceived as unfilled promises that the layoffs would end:

• "When you get wave after wave and the statement, 'Just around the corner, just around the corner, we're almost there, things are looking up, things are looking up,' wave after wave after wave, it just emotionally drains you." (executive)

• "This thing is dragging out too long, and that's what the problem is. We're hearing it from this one, we're hearing it from that one, we're hearing it over there. If everything was done all at one time, at least within a three- or four-month period, but here we're dragging it out six, eight, ten, twelve, fourteen months!" (manager)

- "We are essentially over, . . . and all that time there has been low productivity from everybody. I feel that even trying to motivate your people and keep up to speed and do additional work is a very difficult task." (manager)

- "I guess it seems like it's never ending. If there had been a large workforce reduction in the beginning of the year, or at a particular time, and you say, 'That's it, that's what we're going to do. Now we can go off and do our business,' I think that would be easier for the employees to accept. Our group has been hit two or three times since October. It feels like they came back and said, 'Oops, we need some more money. Let's take some more,' and then, 'Oops, let's take more.' I don't know when they are going to stop. I don't see the end. There's no light at the end of the tunnel that you can say, 'If I can just make it until here, then I'll be okay.'" (professional/technical employee)

Dissatisfaction with Planning and Communication

The planning, administration, and communication of layoffs was a topic of widespread discussion. Of particular concern among many was the need for longer notice and a more open flow of information:

- "We could have given them a little bit more warning, been up front with them and told them, 'Hey, the end of the year, you're going to have to go,' in time for them to go out and find a job. We didn't do that. That made it even a little more strenuous on me. There's a lot of mistrust right now. That's going to be tough to overcome." (manager)

- "All of a sudden somebody hands you a slip of paper, they have you into HR, in with your boss, and say, 'We don't need you anymore.' That's rough." (manager)

- "Everybody knew there was going to be a layoff, and a janitor comes in on Friday night, brings up thirty boxes, sets them by the elevator. Now, those people went home and they knew . . . they counted the boxes . . . they knew thirty people were going to go. And nobody knew until Monday morning who the thirty of them were. . . . That's bad news! Nobody slept out of the whole group over the weekend because everybody thought it was going to be [him or her]. Just a little bit of coordination could have prevented something like that." (professional/technical employee)

• "If cutbacks are needed, planning how you are going to do a total cutback would be better than doing it in little steps and see where you are and then do a little more." (technical/professional employee)

• "If they don't know how to plan for the types of cuts that they put in last year, we've got some real bad problems at the top." (field employee)

• "Who is making that decision? Where is it really coming from? How did they decide on this person?" (field employee)

• "I think a lot of that came through communication problems. If they would at least let us know in advance what was going on, but they keep saying, 'We're doing fine, we're doing fine,' and then all of a sudden people are gone." (field employee)

• "So why aren't they letting us know ahead of time that this is what we're planning and be honest? As everybody's saying, be honest with us and let us deal with it." (field employee)

• "Invariably, when you ask them, 'Are there going to be more layoffs?' you're told, 'We don't foresee any. There probably will be some. We don't know.' So it's a real secretive type thing." (production employee)

Anger over the Layoff Process

The groups had widespread anger and concern over how layoff victims were treated. The concern was for both the feelings and dignity of those who left and what the process said about the organization's values:

• "You can say all the right things in that private meeting between you, HR, and the employee, and handle the situation. Then you are forced to walk them out to their desk, gather up their personal effects in full public view. Employee after employee, going through a whole bunch of them. It's demoralizing for the employee, for the management, for personnel, for the people that are sitting out there on the line. It's just archaic, terrible." (executive)

• "Some of the people are ushered out of here coldly, like it's all over and you can't even say good-bye to your friends. They come in here and clean off their desks at night. All of a sudden, the desk is clear; it's gone. They've disappeared. They've vanished into the woodwork." (professional/technical employee)

• "They walk them out the door, which I think is a bad thing. It's a humiliating thing. You shouldn't have to do that. That's one thing they've got to quit. Don't humiliate your employees when you lay them off. It's your fault you hired too many. Don't do that. That's the number one thing they've got to do is quit that damn thing." (professional/technical employee)

• "My boss tells me, 'You will do the process. Make the cut. Don't tell me that you can't cut expenses, Goddamn it, go do it.' But how do I translate that back to the guy who's about to get cut?" (executive)

• "It goes to the long-term image that we had of being people centered. I see a lot of people being eliminated where the files don't support the action. And then the organization looks and says, 'Holy cow! We thought this guy was a good guy!' and he doesn't have a job—what's it say about us?" (executive).

Lack of Strategic Direction

The following quotations illustrate deeply felt concerns, expressed primarily by executives and managers, over the perceived lack of strategic direction and the gap between the strategy planners and the implementers:

• "We focus really well on what we're going to do tomorrow, and we're going to try and make it through this year, and we're going to have a profitable year, and the bankers are going to be happy, and Wall Street is going to be happy. But where are we going? What is the direction? I understand the total quality processes and all of that. What I don't understand is what the future is. I don't understand how many more business segments are going to be pulled off because we had this problem. What does that leave us, and what do we have left of the company? So, I think it's more openness, honesty, and real communication on those issues that would make me personally feel better about where we're going." (executive)

• "We've got short-term cash problems, sure, but we have a strategy, and by God, if the people down there would just implement it, we would be okay. That worries the hell out of me more than anything else." (executive)

Lack of Management Credibility

All groups blamed others, usually a generic "management," and felt that what these others said had limited credibility:

• "Thursday and Friday, knowing it was coming to this, I went out and visited all my people, especially at remote sites, and had a chat with them in groups about this, and just tried to get a feel for what their morale was—where they felt the company was right now—and the standard flavor I got out of everybody was, 'I don't believe what I hear from the corporation.'" (manager)

• "I think we could say that we do not have confidence in our upper management." (professional/technical employee)

• "They keep saying we're going back to the core business, but I don't see it. . . . I see absolutely no evidence that indicates that's taking place." (field employee)

• "[There are] numerous morale builders. . . . They say we're going to do this and do this, and then two months later, somehow, miraculously it's dropped. Nobody's heard of it. . . . They never follow through with anything as far as you can see." (field employee)

Short-Term Profit Orientation

"They," the generic management, were perceived by some as fixated on short-term profits and willing to pay for them with workforce reductions:

• "You've got to understand the only indicator of this whole damn thing is the second-quarter profits. They don't know what the business is going to do; the only thing they can do is try to keep a status quo until they look at the second and third quarter profits." (manager)

- "I know all they want to do right now is turn a profit, and they'll get as many people as they need to do that. That's short term. They're not looking long term anymore." (field employee)
- "I say if we don't make a profit at the end of the first quarter, there's going to be more people that are going to be cut, and they'll just keep cutting and cutting until they make a profit." (field employee)

Sense of Permanent Change

There was a widespread sense of permanent and sudden change, and this sense resulted in stress, resignation, and fear:

- "I've gone through a pretty significant change over the last ten months. Last March, I stood before my group and told them that we were sitting with twenty-six people, and that by the end of the year, we would be at no more than fifteen. That was probably the toughest thing I've had to do since I've been with the company. I've been here over twenty-one years. There is a lot of distrust now. It's like all the work I've done and all the work they did in the past is for nothing." (manager)
- "The whole organization is 50 percent of what it was. One of the more stressful things is the fact that a lot of full-time employees who have put an awful lot of life into the company have been going by the boards. That's a lot different than the environment in the past." (manager)
- "For the first time, I'm scared, really scared. In my case, it's my whole livelihood. I'm the sole supporter in the family, and it's scary to think about what happens to my kids if I lose my job. I didn't worry about that before, but I sure as hell do now." (production worker)
- "I feel generally upset with the whole situation. When I come to work I feel tired, even though I don't have much to do. I've never felt that way before, and it isn't fear. I don't give a damn if I get laid off. I'm just tired. That's real news for me." (administrative employee)
- "I don't feel good anymore about my decision to come to work here. I made that decision twenty-five years ago, and up until last year, I felt good about it. Not anymore. I don't tell my kids to come and work for this company." (professional/technical employee)

Unexpected Findings

Most of the study findings were consistent with previous research on layoff survivors. Fear, anger, insecurity, depression, and guilt seem to be the core survivor feelings. The perceptions of the layoff survivors in this study were consistent with many of these core feelings. There were, however, some unexpected results.

Few Expressions of Survivor Guilt

Guilt was not identified as a major theme, and it was only a minor theme within three of the ten groups. Since other researchers believe that feelings of guilt are central to survivorship (Chapter Three), the absence of these feelings in this study is notable. One explanation could be that guilt is a difficult human emotion for an individual to own and disclose in a group situation. The general concern over management competence, lack of information, and feelings of betrayal may be an external projection of internal guilt feelings. Likewise, the extensive reports of fear, depression, and stress could be an acting out of deeper survivor guilt. Such diagnoses, however, are speculative, and their proof would require individual analysis. Even with such analysis, clear boundaries would be difficult to establish since guilt is an abstract emotion and difficult to distinguish through only symptoms.

Expressions of Optimism

Although they also had feelings of uncertainty, stress, and reduced motivation, some managers and executives expressed feelings of optimism—perceptions that a tough but needed job had been done and that the organization was back on track toward profitability. These perceptions occurred exclusively in the three groups made up of managers and executives.

Since managers and executives were often involved in layoff decisions and administration, they had more control or advance knowledge than other survivors. Their optimism may therefore have been related to participation in the process. By focusing on projected organizational outcomes, managers and executives may also have escaped dealing with their personal feelings.

The feelings and perceptions reported by managers and executives are complex and often contradictory. The same executives who expressed feelings of optimism also expressed strong feelings of depression and reduced risk taking.

Emergence of a Layoff Survivor Blaming Phenomenon

All groups blamed others. In some cases, they blamed a generic "management," or they blamed the next level up. Top executives blamed other executives or the company president. These feelings were intense across all groups. Dissatisfaction with company direction, management credibility, and long-term strategy were particularly strong among executives, professionals, and managers. This was all the more interesting because these people were responsible for these very functions.

The survivor blaming phenomenon may be a form of projection that serves as a defense mechanism, so that the individual can avoid confronting his or her individual survivor guilt. Certainly such survivor guilt is discussed throughout the survivor literature, and projection of one's own undesirable traits onto others is a widely recognized ego-defense mechanism.

Thirst for Information

Better, clearer, and more consistent information during layoffs were consistent recommendations. Partially this seemed a reaction to their widespread fear and uncertainty. In addition, executives, managers, and technical professionals said they needed a clearer understanding of the organization's strategy and plans. In a number of cases, survivors perceived a lack of adequate plans, and their recommendations for improved communication may translate into recommendations for better and more effective planning and goal setting. In a sense, the expressed need for better communication was a form of survivor distrust. Many of the layoff survivors seemed not to trust that management actually had a plan for the survival of the business. The lack of trust that someone in the organization had a plan to pull the organization out of its problems may have helped to produce such survivor feelings as fear, uncertainty, anger, or depression, or the lack of trust may have arisen from those feelings.

Either pattern illustrates the interaction and interdependence of survivor feelings and perceptions.

Sense of Change

Survivors in all groups indicated that the layoffs had triggered changes in their relationship to the organization. Whether they were discussing job security, feelings of betrayal, commitment, or coping strategies, the layoff survivors felt a strong sense of change, and these changes were perceived as permanent and wide ranging.

Learnings and Implications

In this chapter, I intended readers to feel the anger, fear, and anxiety of layoff survivors, to be flooded with the depth and intensity of survivor feelings. The organization I studied was not unusual. These survivors are mirrors of other layoff survivors, and most readers will find some themes that are all too familiar for themselves and their organizations. A large number of organizations seem to be populated by people who share these symptoms. The organization studied here was, in fact, in better shape than many others since its management recognized the seriousness of the problem. There are methodological issues (sample bias, group dynamics, and content analysis error) that affect the results of this type of study, and care must be taken in generalizing. Nonetheless, learning the true extent of layoff survivors' hurt is important for anyone attempting self- or organizational transformation and empowerment.

Time marched on. The economy continued to decline. The organization struggled for survival. Thanks to cooperative management, I revisited it five years later. What had happened? The story continues in Chapter Five.

CHAPTER 5

Time Does Not Heal All Wounds

The Effects of Long-Term Survivor Sickness

"Our group has been hit two or three times since October. It feels like they came back and said, 'Oops, we need some more money. Let's take some more,' and then, 'Oops, let's take more.' I don't know when they are going to stop, I don't see the end. There's no light at the end of the tunnel that you can say, 'If I can just take it until here, then I'll be happy.'"

Time, it would appear, does not heal all wounds. In order to assess the impact of time on layoff survivor symptoms, a second study took place at the same organization five years after the initial effort. The methodology was similar to that of the initial study: group interviews, using the same standard set of questions, were recorded, transcribed, and analyzed for the major themes. The second study's scope was more limited (three as opposed to ten groups) and the content analysis was less rigorous (interviewers and coders were not separate people). Nonetheless, this is one of the few attempts to assess the continuity of layoff survivor symptoms over time, and the results are of interest to any individual or organization attempting to escape the debilitating effects of layoff survivor sickness.

There were a group of twelve production workers (skilled non-exempt and exempt production engineers) from a manufacturing operation, a group of fourteen engineers and professional/technical employees from a design and development operation, and a group of ten administrative staff from corporate headquarters. For logistical and administrative reasons, managers and executives were not included in this study. Also, unlike the first groups, these groups included only long-term employees (the groups were voluntary, but no one was accepted with fewer than six years of experience). In reality, the groups attracted very long-term employees; the median length of service was sixteen years. Two of the three groups were in parts of the organization represented in the original sample; owing to organizational changes, the third group, professional/technical employees, represented a blend of three organizational areas, two of which were in the original sample. To protect confidentiality in the first study, no names had been recorded. However, the participants in the second study were asked if any of them had participated in the earlier study, and no one indicated she or he had. Therefore, I assumed that none of the participants in the second study had been in the first study. In the intervening years, the organization had gone through a series of major downsizings, and layoffs continued unabated.

What is especially important about the groups in the second study is that the employees grew up under the full flowering of the old employment contract; survived a continuing series of organizational consolidations, spin-offs, and layoffs; and were now attempting to cope with the reality of the new employment contract. They had one foot in the old, another in the new, their heart was on the border between the old and the new, and their spirit was infected with layoff survivor sickness. The reader will come closer to feeling the concerns of these survivors by once again reviewing the raw data rather than abstracts of results.

Stress, Fatigue, Extra Workload, Decreased Motivation, Sadness, and Depression

The symptoms of stress, fatigue, decreased motivation, sadness, and depression, combined with an extra workload, persisted over the five-year time frame. The sense of resignation, fatigue, and depression seemed heavier and more pronounced than in the past:

• "I didn't realize that I was probably suffering from some form of depression, but it was going on, and on, and on. I mean day after day, feeling the same way." (administrative employee)

• "Everything is negative, and when you do good things, it's not recognized; whether it's the media, whether it's your manager, everything is always, in my opinion, on the down. So when you come to work, you are on the down." (professional/technical employee)

• "It's much worse just by accumulation. It's gone on for so long." (professional/technical employee)

• "I kind of look back to when the layoffs first started, and I felt very devastated. I felt very sad for these people, and, personally, as it started to continue on, I felt like the people who were left kind of got callous. Now it's gotten so commonplace that I think sometimes we hardly say good-bye." (administrative employee)

Insecurity, Anxiety, and Fear

The symptoms of insecurity, anxiety, and fear also continued. There was an attempt to understand and accommodate a state of permanent job insecurity, but it was not always successful:

• "One thing none of us have come up with is a model of how to behave in a situation like this. We grew up with [the] model that our parents worked hard and they didn't have as much as we do, but it seemed, in the eyes of a child, [to have] more safety in it. Now we're adults; we're fifty years old, and we don't have an example in our life to follow as to what to do when you're fifty and the rug is totally pulled out from under you. It's a little more difficult at a mature stage to go back and act like a teenager and say, 'Oh boy, the whole world is great!' I think it is hard for us to do that because people are watching us: our spouses, our children, our parents, our sisters, our brothers. There is a sense that you have done something wrong if you get laid off. I don't think anyone escapes that. Even if, in their rational minds, they say, 'I was good, it just happened to be the job I was in.'"

• "The only way you provide security for yourself is by making sure that your work experience is as up-to-date as possible so that if tomorrow happens, you are able to go out and get another job, because you have the skills people want. That's the only way you have security. You aren't going to get it from the company. It will never be that way again." (professional/technical employee)

• "Five years ago, you felt more secure. You had a future with the company. At the present time, you don't know whether you are going to be sold out, you are going to be downsized. That's a big difference." (professional/technical employee)

• "Decisions on . . . should I buy a car, should I put a new roof on the house, these are things that have been on hold. I don't see an end in sight. My boss says, 'I don't know what the plan is, and I'm not going to ask.'" (administrative employee)

Loyalty to Job (Not Company), Nonreciprocal Loyalty, and Self-Reliance

There seemed to be a much stronger feeling among the second round of layoff survivors that the organization was not in the business of looking out for its employees and that their loyalty was to themselves and to their unit, not to the overall organization:

• "I am committed to my customers. I am committed to the people who use my services, and it doesn't matter where I work, it's the people that I work with that I really enjoy, and I really want to do a good job for them." (administrative employee)

• "At one time, we kind of felt the company was responsible for your job security and that they would look after you, but I think we all know today that has shifted." (professional/technical employee)

• "I think it's changed dramatically. For myself it has. And I think we see that from the company's side too. Many meetings that we've had, we've been told, 'You're responsible for your future.' It's not like it used to be." (administrative employee)

• "The distinction for me that it isn't necessarily a commitment to the company, it's a commitment to the kind of work that I do. So it's a commitment to my own self, and it's a commitment to my department too. But not necessarily a commitment to the company." (administrative employee)

Sense of Unfairness and Anger over Top Management Pay and Severance

These survivors had much more anger than the earlier survivors over the perceived unfairness of top management severance and bonus payments:

- "There was such a wave of anger that people felt about that [severance payments to top management]. It was shameful to be part of the organization, that they would do that!" (administrative employee)
- "We took away from employees, we took away from retirees, we took away from everybody. Where did it go? Right to those people that walked out the door with the million-dollar parachutes. It was so shameful! Even now, after all these years, I realize everybody has the same anger about it." (administrative employee)
- "My message to top management is that you should spend as much time as you use trying to figure out how your gold parachute can do good for you, take that same energy and start making the company work. It's absolutely unacceptable for people to walk away with that kind of money in a downsized environment. Absolutely unacceptable! You have no credibility at all." (professional/technical employee)
- "I never felt so angry in my life. When I had gone out and stood up to all kinds of people who said, 'Oh yes, you work for that great company. Nobody can be that good,' I defended them, and then the company still wants the same kind of commitment out of me! My time, my hours, my life! No, I'm too old for that." (administrative employee)

Resignation and Numbness

There appeared to be an increase in the sense of resignation and numbness, and one survivor seemed embarrassed to tell outsiders where she worked:

- "I think that when it first started I felt confident that things would get better. I don't feel that way anymore. I don't think my feelings about the losses have changed. I feel, I think, just as horrible as the day when one person loses their job as I did when ten thousand did, but what made me feel better then was I felt we were going to turn a corner. Things were going to get better. I don't think that I'm a pessimist at all, but I don't see any evidence that we're turning any corner." (administrative employee)

• "Twenty-five years ago, there was a real sense of group and a sense of two-way loyalty that was very strong. I see none of that anymore. There's no sense of continuity. I see a lot of people that seem to spend as much emotional energy in preparing for possibly losing their job [and positioning] themselves to get another job, should that actually happen, as they do in actually doing their job." (professional/technical employee)

• "On the floor there are a lot of guys who would just as soon get it over with, get it done. They are just tired of going through it every three months. They feel unemployed. Something's got to give; it's just not right." (production employee)

• "Sometimes I almost feel like an idiot just for staying here this long. When people ask me where I work, I feel like an idiot when I tell them." (production employee)

• "It's always downsizing. We hear that so much, you almost become numb. All of us think, 'Well, who's next?' It's always something. It never seems to just settle down and let us work for a little while. It's constant pressure. It's not a happy environment to be in for me." (professional/technical employee)

Lack of Management Communication

Although five years had passed, the thirst for information and the survivor blaming phenomenon continued to be important:

• "People are interested in having a company make money because that's how we get paid, but a lot of management's concept of communication is to put out a financial report. There's a lot more to it than that." (professional/technical employee)

• "We call them sunshine meetings because it comes across like everything is wonderful, and two weeks later there's another layoff." (production employee)

- "I think [lack of communication is] a true dynamic with all downsizing. [But] some management withholds information for purposes of power, security. It's threatening for them to let go of too much information." (administrative employee)
- "The truth gets lost. I go to communication meetings with the higher-level managers, and the numbers they're putting up on the charts are absolutely impossible when you are out on the floor and you know what's going on." (production employee)

Helpful and Communicative Managers

Not all survivors blamed all managers. Some saw certain managers as accessible and as facilitators of communication:

- "My immediate manager, I can talk to him about what's going on real comfortably, and he's more worried about his job than I am with mine. He's gone through six location changes, so he knows what it's all about. He's pretty open, pretty honest. He's even told me to polish up my résumé, that it wouldn't hurt to send it around because things aren't looking good." (production employee)
- "To the defense of management, they're trying to find their spot too. They don't know where they belong either. They don't know what's going on with them the next time either." (administrative employee)
- "In our department, I see that top management is trying very hard and is trying to squeeze out the management that isn't going to make this company go forward by meeting with employee groups and empowering them, by bypassing all these other layers. But I think that we might be looking for some of what we had in the past, and we're not going to have that, and I do believe that top management is communicating, but I think they need to just come out a little bit stronger." (administrative employee)
- "I will say in defense of these men that they are working their fannies off right now." (administrative employee)
- "I would like to say about top management that I think they have the right spirit. They talk about empowering the people, letting the people have more authority to make changes and stuff like

that, but unless they get middle management motivated to get involved in some of the changes that the employees are trying to make, it's not going to happen." (production employee)

Honest Communication

All groups were very clear on their need for direct, open communication, a concern that was not as pronounced in the initial study:

- "Treat us like adults. Treat us like we can handle the real information." (administrative employee)
- "I think it is time to show us that we are really going to do something besides liquidate." (administrative employee)
- "You should never suppress any information because it can come back to haunt you. Be very honest, and I think most people will accept things if you are honest with them. I think you can get in trouble when you skirt around the issues and act like nothing's going on." (professional/technical employee)
- "[They should] be stronger in their decisions . . . instead of riding the fence. Say yes or no." (professional/technical employee)
- "All of us have to make decisions every day, but just be honest. I think that's the answer." (professional/technical employee)
- "I guess I would say, 'If nothing else, just please be honest with us.'" (production employee)
- "Tell us something that sounds like it's coming from someone's heart and not from their ledger." (administrative employee)

Short-Term Plans and Strategy

Survivors in the professional/technical group, who had experienced the most mergers and organizational change, expressed dissatisfaction with short-term planning. However, the concern was more limited and focused than in the initial study:

- "It's quarter-by-quarter management, and that really hurts. If you are in a declining environment and you manage strictly quarter by quarter, you will never grow." (professional/technical employee)

- "The number one objective for the last several years has been quarterly profit. . . . In order to make that quarterly profit, we've had indirect people have to take time off without pay, whatever it takes to make that quarterly profit. And if that's all you're looking at, one quarter ahead—I mean, we have these long-range strategic plans, but they seem kind of pie-in-the-sky because we are always focusing quarter by quarter. There's no real long-range philosophy. You don't see that practiced." (professional/technical employee)
- "Last July when they came through, so-and-so sat down and looked at the numbers, management came in with some numbers, and we were so many million short, and they said, 'Go back and come up with some new numbers.' We [had] just cut down thirty-one people. 'Try fifteen or twenty more in September—do it!' And that gets out to us folks, and we say, 'Why are they doing that?' It just doesn't make sense." (professional/technical employee)
- "They really think that manpower planning and skills can be turned on and off like a faucet as opposed to a smooth-flowing, blending arrangement." (professional/technical employee)

Layoff Process Problems

Survivors in the second study told the same kinds of horror stories concerning the way layoffs were handled as the earlier survivors had. However, they seemed clear on the difference between "good" and "bad" process:

- "I think that [layoffs] are handled very poorly. I worked with a guy for twenty-two years. We knew there was going to be a layoff in our department, but nobody was told ahead of time who it was going to be. When the day arrived, it was minutes before quitting time, and the boss came down and told him, 'You're it.' He had to pack his tools, clean out. It was a big shock. I don't think it was a very fair way of treating someone who had worked for a company for twenty-two years." (production employee)
- "I see that a lot. The people who actually have the person-to-person contact with the person who is being laid off aren't the ones who made the decision. They often didn't have any input into which of their people would go. There is something wrong with that process." (professional/technical employee)

- "I think it's a shotgun approach to how you maintain numbers and how to get rid of people legally without getting taken to court." (professional/technical employee)
- "I don't think any of us can get hold of any data that say, 'This is the process of how to treat a person humanely when you lay them off.' There are terrible managers, and there are good ones. I think [among] individual managers, some do a good job and some do a bad job." (professional/technical employee)
- "I'm often in a position to be talking to people very shortly after they have been given notice, and I can get very angry seeing the difference between when it's done well and when people have been left with so many unanswered questions." (administrative employee)
- "You really see a difference in the process if they are treated well than if they are not." (administrative employee)

Resentment over Being Made to Feel Guilty

The headquarters administrative group expressed two themes that did not come out in the earlier study: resentment over being told to be thankful they had a job and a perception that being positive was countercultural:

- "I get angry when I get out on the line and I hear management and [human resources] saying to their employees, 'You're just damned lucky you have a job. Go away and quit complaining.'" (headquarters administrative employee)
- "[They say], 'Don't complain. You're lucky you have a job.'" (administrative employee)
- "It gets difficult to just come in and say, or for managers to say, 'You're lucky you have a job.' It's more difficult for me to even feel that I am one of the lucky ones. I'm still staying here, and I'm going through all of these changes. The other people at least know where they are and, hopefully, know where they are going to go, or at least they are in the process of going somewhere." (administrative employee)
- "It's not that . . . I'm feeling cheated because I'm not let go, but I do feel it's very difficult to come in and continue to be positive about being a survivor when there are some people out there saying, 'You're damned lucky you've got a job.'" (administrative employee)

- "Are you really lucky, or are they the lucky ones because they've left?" (administrative employee)
- "You have to justify it, that you're still here. Even when you walk out of here, you meet somebody and you say where you work, and they say, 'How did you survive?' It just kind of feels that even to the outside world, you have to justify yourself, that you're still there—'How do you rate that you still have a job?' Why do I have to justify myself? It wasn't me who stood there and said, 'I want this job.' They kept me for one reason or another. I don't know why, but they probably have their reasons." (administrative employee)
- "My positiveness has oftentimes been almost a negative because everybody's so down. They feel I am insensitive, that I'm naive, that I don't know what's going on around me, which is not the case." (administrative employee)
- "I think it can make people feel uncomfortable if you seem to be having a good time in this environment." (administrative employee)

A Look Back from the Second Act

The first act (the initial wave of layoffs from the late 1980s to the early 1990s) was followed by an intermission stimulated by an economy of easy credit, liquidity, and technology-based globalization. For better or worse—in the short term probably the worse—the second act, triggered by a global meltdown of our financial infrastructure, act is upon us. During the intermission and in the early stages of the second act, I have remained in contact with the client organization as an executive coach and consultant. I have also worked with many other similar organizations. Here are three observations:

- The survivor feelings outlined in this and the previous chapter are just as relevant to the organizations of the second decade of the new millennium as they were during the first act.
- The lessons of the first act have not been passed on to the managers or the employees of the second act, and the pyramid four-level intervention model, introduced in the next chapter, is even more relevant for individual satisfaction and organizational survival.

- We are truly participants in a global economy, and the long-term effects of the reality of the new psychological contract on high-context cultures such as those in Asia (Hofstede, 1997), where relationships and social status are inseparably ingrained in organizational identity, remain to be determined. Consider the impact of the reported 20 million laid-off migrant Chinese workers returning to their rural villages (Anderlini and Dyer, 2009) in a country with a traditional history of rebellion.

Learnings and Implications

Layoff survivor symptoms persevered and evolved over time within the client organization. Survivors seemed more tired and depressed. They appeared to have been ground down by five years of job insecurity and flux. Although they had reduced their reliance on the organization to take care of them and seemed resigned to non-reciprocated loyalty, they were still struggling to understand and accommodate permanent job insecurity. They were an angry group, with much of their ire focused on top executive compensation, bonus payments during a time of financial loss, and excessive severance payments. In this regard, there is a direct correlation with the feelings of second act survivors. They had little tolerance for false optimism and fuzzy answers. They wanted straight talk and honest communication. Some employees resented being made to feel guilty over simply surviving and having a job. Others expressed resentment over being made to feel they did not understand the environment because their behavior was positive.

Layoff survivor sickness is complicated, and the cure does not lend itself to a one-dimensional prescription. The next chapter introduces the four-level model of intervention for curing this complex disease.

PART THREE

INTERVENTIONS FOR HEALTHY SURVIVAL

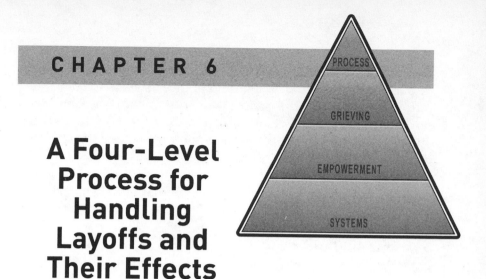

CHAPTER 6

A Four-Level Process for Handling Layoffs and Their Effects

*"I feel generally upset with the whole situation.
When I come to work I feel tired, even though I don't
have much to do. I've never felt that way before and
it isn't fear. I don't give a damn if I get laid off. I'm
just tired. That's real news for me."*

I recently had lunch with a caring but emotionally devastated and harassed executive from a rapidly melting down financial services company. He didn't eat much and, with a desperate look in his eyes, brought me back to his painful reality by interrupting my what I realized in retrospect was an overly logical academic explanation of survivor sickness, and blurting out, "Okay, let's just cut to the quick! What is it? Why is it important? And what in the hell can I do about it?" This chapter summarizes the answers to the first two questions and introduces a four-level process to help organizations not only deal with the symptoms, but develop a long-term strategy that will immunize them to the toxic effects of layoff survivor sickness.

Beneath the sterile and analytical charts, graphs, and purportedly objective reports of organizational downsizings, mergers, and restructurings lurks something that is decidedly not as antiseptic as these sanitized presentations would lead you to believe. Turn over the layoff rock in most organizations, and you will find some ugly and toxic creatures. Beginning in the first act and continuing into today's environment, other observers in both the academic and popular press and I have both turned the rock over and written about our observations. We have all seen the same creatures, but like the blind people exploring the elephant, each of us has had a different view of these phenomena and labeled our observations accordingly. It is the "dirty dozen": a combination of scapegoating, decreasing morale, increased conflict, and other "dysfunctional effects" (Cameron, Kim, and Whetten, 1987). It is the acting out of survivor guilt (Brockner and others, 1986). It is a combination of guilt, depression, loss of control, increased substance abuse, sleeplessness, and tension (Marks, 1991b). It is "discarded" and "demoralized" employees (Hoffman, 2006). It is a form of depression that leads to wasting away (Harvey, 1981). Despite the varying labels, what is becoming increasingly clear to everyone is the magnitude of damage done by these phenomena.

Many layoffs are planned by isolated and desperate executives and their number crunchers who erroneously conclude that a layoff on a Friday afternoon will lead to a productivity gain on a Monday morning. Unfortunately, it is not a simple linear exercise in mathematical extrapolation. The only predictable Monday morning outcome is that surviving employees will hunker down in the trenches, and at the very moment you need them to be creative, innovative, and take the risks necessary to ensure a turnaround, they will keep their heads down.

Although the results are clouded by intervening variables such as further layoffs, mergers, closings, and accounting practices, evidence is increasing that without exceptional attention to the survivors, layoffs not only may not result in any long term gains but may actually increase the losses. In a pioneering best-practices survey of automotive industry downsizing, Kim Cameron, Sarah Freeman, and April Mishra (1991) found that the way most of the downsizings were implemented had caused quality and productivity to deteriorate rather than increase. Consulting companies, long in the front lines of the downsizing movement, have made similar reports. An early study of over one thousand downsized organizations by the Wyatt Company (1991) indicated that most of these organizations did not meet their initial goals. Dorfman (1991) reports on a study conducted by Mitchell and Company that followed sixteen large restructurings from 1982 to 1988. At the end of this period, the organizations' stock performance trailed that of their competition by an average of 26 percent. In a survey of 909 managers, Right Associates (1992) found that 70 percent reported that survivors felt insecure about their future and had reduced confidence in their ability to manage their own careers. Seventy-two percent of the managers indicated that the survivors felt the restructured organization was not a better place to work. A study by Cascio (2002) using return on assets as an index found no evidence that downsizing worked and that profitability actually decreased in organizations with more than a 5 percent decrease in people and less than a 5 percent decrease in plant and equipment.

Layoff Survivor Feeling Clusters and Coping Strategies

Whether layoff survivor sickness is perceived as the result of ineffective downsizing strategies (Cameron, Freeman, and Mishra, 1991), a moral issue caused by collusion and a lack of courage (Harvey, 1988), or a result of survivor guilt (Kiviat, 2009), the outcome is the same: layoffs drain the work spirit, creativity, and productivity from many organizations. The archetypal stories of survivors of more traumatic events, my own experience with downsized organizations, and layoff survivor research all show that layoff survivors experience the following feelings.

Clusters of Feelings

Although general clusters of feelings are apparent among layoff survivors, the research has not shown any universal hierarchy of causality for these feelings. Of course, every individual's definition of a particular emotion is slightly different from others' definitions, so these clusters are broad rather than narrow. For example, some survivors saw depression and fatigue as outgrowths of stress, while others described stress as a result of fatigue and depression. Also, the stories of other survivors suggest that a strong theme of guilt might have been expected to emerge in the study presented in Chapters Four and Five.

One reason this did not appear may be that guilt is difficult to disclose. However, some researchers see the survivor blaming phenomenon as a projection of guilt feelings. Layoff survivors' extensively reported fear, depression, and stress may similarly be emotions reflecting a deeper survival guilt.

Nevertheless, the clusters of feelings that follow may be considered a working definition of layoff survivor sickness:

- *Fear, insecurity, and uncertainty.* These feelings cluster together, are among the easier ones to identify, and are found in every layoff survivor situation.
- *Frustration, resentment, and anger.* Layoff survivors are often unable to openly express these emotions within their organization. Suppressing these emotions, however, creates further problems.
- *Sadness, depression, and guilt.* Layoff survivors often mask depression and sadness in order to fit in with false group bravado or calls to "suck it up" in the period after the layoff. However, these feelings are usually easier to spot than guilt, which is often suppressed and manifested in other behavior.
- *Unfairness, betrayal, and distrust.* These feelings are often acted out through coping mechanisms, such as blaming others, and a seemingly insatiable need for information.

Coping Methods

Layoff survivors cope with their feelings in ways that are neither personally healthy nor organizationally productive:

- *Reduced risk taking.* Layoff survivors tend to hunker down in the trenches. They report risk-averse behavior, reluctance to take on new products, and fear of finishing existing ones. They are seen as becoming more rigid and conservative.
- *Lowered productivity.* Layoff survivors are initially consumed with seeking information and understanding their new environment rather than producing, but the relationship between survivor stress and productivity is complex. Some evidence exists that moderate job insecurity increases productivity (Brockner, 1992). But as time progresses and layoff symptoms solidify, it appears that survivors lose their work spirit and creativity.

- *Unquenchable thirst for information.* Layoff survivors soak up and demand information. Questing for information not only from formal channels and newspapers but also from rumors and nonverbal messages from management is a core survivor coping mechanism.
- *Survivor blaming.* Layoff survivors cope by blaming others, usually those above them—a generic management. Top managers tend to blame the chief executive officer (CEO), each other, or those below them. CEOs I have worked with tend to blame the economy, competition, other executives, the work ethic, or, in one case, the labor union.
- *Justification and explanation.* This is a coping method for those "in the know," that is, those involved in layoff administration. I have observed it most in staff managers and executives: lawyers, public relations executives, accountants, and human resource managers. In my research I often found it among human resource professionals who spent a great deal of time and energy on explaining and justifying the need for layoffs.
- *Denial.* Many organizations exhibit a hierarchical pattern of denial. The higher a person is in the organization, the greater his or her denial. This denial chain must be broken before any meaningful intervention strategy can be implemented.
- *Self and other abuse.* Organizations with employee assistance programs that track intake records report that layoffs cause a significant increase in cases of alcohol and drug abuse. They also find increased incidences of family issues such as spousal abuse. With few organizationally sanctioned outlets, survivors act out in destructive and abusive ways toward themselves and others. Although there are no immediate data, I predict that our communities and our social system will pay a heavy toll in response to second act layoffs.

Persistence of Symptoms over Time

Those who survive other forms of psychological or physical trauma require helping interventions because their survivor symptoms do not automatically disappear on their own. It is the same with layoff survivors' symptoms. Not only do they persist over time, but certain of them seem to intensify:

- *Increase in resignation, fatigue, and depression.* In organizations undergoing continuing reductions and change, survivors seem to lose their spark, be flat and tired, and simply go through the motions without hope.
- *Deepening sense of loss of control.* Long-term layoff survivors tend to give the organization control of their work life and, often, their self-esteem. Instead of taking control of their own destiny, they hang on and wait for external events to direct them.
- *Heightened and more focused anger.* Long-term layoff survivors are very angry. Compared to the anger of others, their anger seems sharpened and more personally focused. In the large organization study, this anger was directed at top executives' compensation and severance payments. In other organizations, the anger is focused more on individuals and is a clear extension of the survivor blaming phenomenon.

The Four-Level Intervention Model

Layoff survivor sickness is complex and does not lend itself to a simple solution. It contains conflicts of values centered on organizational codependency and self-empowerment. To be cured of it, people must let go of the familiar old and venture into the untested new. Healing layoff survivor sickness is, in the final analysis, an individual effort, requiring great personal courage. Creating organizational systems that will prevent the reoccurrence of this sickness ought to be one of the most fundamental priorities of organizational leaders.

Only compelling interventions can deal with the pathology of layoff survivor sickness. These interventions will be powerful acts, attention-grabbing and stimulating forces that compel survivors to choose personal and organizational change.

Four levels of intervention are needed to deal with layoff survivor sickness (Figure 6.1):

1. *Process interventions.* Level 1 interventions deal with the process—the way layoffs take place from the survivors' perspective. These interventions do not provide a cure for survivor sickness, but they do keep survivors from sinking further into survivor symptoms.

Figure 6.1. Four-Level Intervention Model

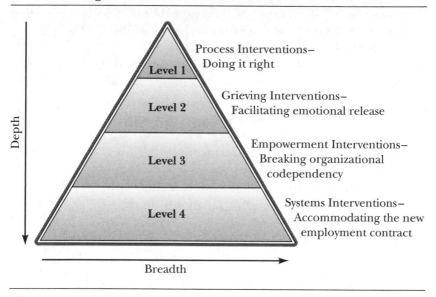

2. *Grieving interventions.* Level 2 interventions help survivors grieve. These interventions deal with repressed feelings and emotions and provide the opportunity for a catharsis that releases the energy invested in emotional repression.
3. *Interventions that break the chain of organizational codependency.* Level 3 interventions help survivors recapture from the organization their sense of control and self-esteem.
4. *Systems interventions.* Level 4 interventions create the structural systems and processes that immunize people against survivor sickness.

   Although the four-level pyramid is a stage model (level 1 interventions proceed to level 2, and so on) and is intended to convey the increasing depth and breadth of each successive intervention, the real world is much more dynamic than any model. Level 1 process interventions sometimes lead directly to level 4 system changes without going through levels 2 or 3. Breaking the shackles of organizational codependency (level 3) often stimulates level 2 grieving and vice versa. The four-level model is a general conceptual one, not an exact road map. However, the model generally holds true: process interventions are less complex and deep than those that facilitate grieving; interventions to break organizational codependency are yet deeper and broader than the first two; and interventions that change organizational systems from those that reinforce the old paradigm to those that encourage the new are the most difficult of all.

Learnings and Implications

Mergers, downsizings, and the resultant layoffs are not as neat, tidy, and sterile as accountants and security analysts make them out to be. Those looking under layoff rocks have found sad and toxic thoughts and feelings. They are not always labeled in the same manner by all rock turners, but under any name, they are hazardous to individual and organizational health. In my findings, layoff survivor sickness is not cured by a simple prescription. In the next four chapters, I describe the four-level intervention model that can reduce layoff survivor sickness.

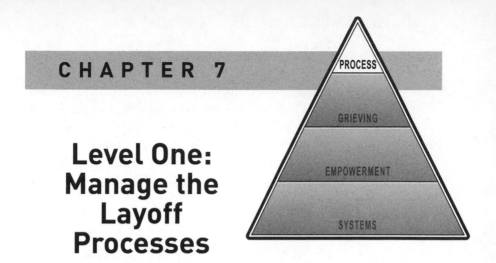

CHAPTER 7

Level One: Manage the Layoff Processes

"Compassion makes a huge difference. In some cases, you can tell there wasn't any in existence."

Level 1 interventions involve the way people are handled when they are laid off, and since they deal with the process of doing layoffs, I call them *process interventions.* Although they are just the tip of the intervention iceberg, they are important because the perception of the way layoffs are handled by survivors is a significant tactical factor in their ability to recover. As with actual icebergs, only the tip is visible, and although much more is going on beneath the surface, level 1 interventions keep survivors from sinking too deeply into the quagmire of depression and guilt and keep them afloat until deeper interventions can be applied.

Survivors are often forgotten in the frenzy of layoff planning. Planners, under unnecessary veils of secrecy, work out the processes of severance pay, communication sequencing, benefits, outplacement services, and often (sadly) how desks get cleaned out and surprised victims are escorted to the door, with little or no consideration of the impact on those who stay. Line managers and staff groups commonly exist in a cloak-and-dagger prelayoff environment, obsessing over the most intricate details of notification and implementation, with no concern over the transparency of the process.

Most—and perhaps too much, given that it is the tip of the layoff iceberg—research focuses on process issues. Nonetheless, the data are clear: the way layoffs take place has a significant impact on the productivity and prospects for recovery of those who stay. Survivors' involvement in the decision-making process, their level of attachment to the victims, and their perception as to the fairness and equity of layoffs have all been documented as important process factors that planners should consider.

"Clean Kills" and the Survivor Hygiene Factor

Frederick Herzberg (1964) developed a motivational theory that divides motivational factors into those that do motivate (such as satisfaction with the work itself) and those that simply keep employees from becoming *de*motivated (such as pay and working conditions). Herzberg calls the latter "hygiene factors." Level 1 interventions are the layoff equivalent of Herzberg's hygiene factors: they do not cure survivor sickness, but they blunt its symptoms and permit a more rapid recovery. When I explained this concept to a battle-weary manager who was planning yet another round of layoffs, he summed up my elegant theory by saying, "You mean a clean kill is better than a messy one!" Despite the violent language, a survivor symptom in itself, his response contains a hard truth, and it conjured up a vivid image from my youth in Minnesota. I remember a grizzled professional hunter standing on a snow-covered knoll, rifle in hand, thinning out a herd of deer who did not have enough food to survive a tough winter. Doing it right, making a "clean," direct kill, was better than making a mess of it, leaving a wounded animal lurching through the herd. The clean process did not ensure the survival of all the remaining deer, but it did prevent a collective panic.

Redundant Communication Is Essential

Communication is a level 1 process. Layoff survivors have an unquenchable thirst for information, before, during, and after reductions. Their need leaps from the pages of data in Chapters Four and Five. It is impossible for managers to overcommunicate during layoffs. Survivors suck up data like desert sand absorbs water. They are information junkies. If they do not get needed information, they go through withdrawal and then guess at what's going on and develop theories, often erroneous, based on fragments of information. If you are a layoff planner, it is extremely important for you to respond to this need. Flood the system with information—oral, written, formal, informal, verbal, and nonverbal; up, down, and laterally—over and over again. You cannot communicate enough. Even when you know you are saying the same thing to the same audience in the same way, still redouble the effort. I have yet to find an organization that has satisfied layoff survivors' information hunger.

What to Communicate

Layoff planners should *communicate everything that is going on*. During layoffs, employees are concerned not only with the obvious questions of who is going, when they are going, and how they were identified. Employees are desperately seeking assurance and striving for control over a frightening environment. They want to know that the cafeteria will be operational, the paychecks will not bounce, the softball league will continue, the dental plan will stay in effect, the Monday morning staff meeting will still happen. You name it, they want to know about it.

Written communication is important, but writing memos, sending e-mails, and producing newsletters are not enough. A surprising number of younger employees just don't like to read, and some either prefer oral communication or the jargon-laden shorthand of texting or twittering. Regardless of technique, employees want to see their leaders face-to-face in troubled times. Nonverbal messages are stronger than words. Bosses must be visible. They do not need to exhibit false bravado; they do need to be authentic and use the currency of authenticity: eye contact; touching, if it fits the culture, or handshakes; and empathic body language. Managers should think of how they would behave when they are the authority figure at a funeral or during a time of crisis, confusion, or emotional tension in a small group or family. The bottom has just dropped out from the survivors' world, and they are in dire need of consistency and continuity. Managers and top executives have similar needs: when they become involved in communicating to employees, they will also reassure themselves.

Control Traps That Block Communication

Despite the overwhelming evidence of a data feeding frenzy at all levels, it is often difficult for managers to stimulate and maintain the free flow of information. Instead, during layoffs managers often set for themselves what I call *control traps:* barriers that block needed self-insight and authentic communication.

Free-flowing communication, emotional honesty, and personal authenticity are the basic ingredients of level 1 interventions. It is therefore important to confront and spring the jaws of the control traps that block communication, honesty, and authenticity.

Control Trap 1: Managing Communication

Managers set up this control trap when they artificially manage and monitor the natural, authentic communication flow. In nearly every organization, someone has a vested interest in managing information. In normal times, this activity falls to the staff function that handles external public relations and internal employee communication. Usually the strategy is to control the way things are said—or, often, not said—so that the organization, and especially top management, looks good, or at least does not look bad. In times of crisis, the natural reaction is to tighten up these controls. Top managers' announcements are carefully crafted and scripted. Their "spontaneous" comments to employees while "walking around" are often rehearsed. At the very time when organizational leaders need to be most human and accessible to their fellow employees, they become artificial and controlled.

Earlier I suggested that managers think of how they would behave at a funeral. What effect would it have on surviving family members if the authority figure communicated from clear, conservative scripts, written in advance by lawyers? In organizations facing layoffs, contrived leadership communication does not fool anyone; employees see right through it.

At the very time when authentic and empathetic communication is needed, what is delivered is often controlled and cold. This does not mean that top managers and the staffers who write their scripts are bad people. In fact, they too are survivors, and at one level, their attempts to control interpersonal relationships are a means of escaping from the authentic sharing of emotions that would help purge their survivor symptoms and force them to give up their denial of these symptoms. Therefore, the attempt to control communication is a particularly toxic form of denial: it separates top management from the rest of the organization and leads to the bunker mentality found in many executive suites during layoffs.

Employees at the opposite end of the organizational hierarchy are not immune to their own version of this control trap. They displace their fear and anxiety through anger at management. They control their own communication by developing ritualistic blaming behavior that speaks of "we" and "they." Much of their communication can be seen as a projection of their anger. This control trap allows them to escape the painful but necessary task of exploring their survivor guilt and depression. The end result of overmanaged communication at the top and ritualized blaming at lower levels is a politicized organization in which all real communication has been shut down at the time when the organization most needs authenticity.

All levels need the courage to go against the grain. For top managers, this is the courage to interact authentically and naturally with their fellow survivors. It often means ignoring, or at least tempering, the advice of lawyers and communication experts. While managers should not say and do things that will result in lawsuits or will hurt people, my experience is that a wide gap, often a chasm, exists between the kind of communication that will be harmful to the organization or its people and the kind that normally takes place during a crisis situation such as a layoff.

It is genuinely lonely at the top, and top executives become isolated even more during downsizings and layoffs. They need someone to talk to. Some hire a consultant or an executive coach not so much for management advice as for someone to listen to their sadness over having to terminate their fellow employees and their frustration over being the one that fate designated to make the hard decisions. Some of the executives I have worked with have not shared their natural human feelings with anyone inside or outside the organization. Yet they have a deep and suppressed need to share these feelings with their fellow survivors because this sharing would also be a way of asking for absolution for executive actions. Employees have a reciprocal need to hear that the top manager is human and authentic and shares their pain. It is a tragic irony when neither need is met because top executives believe that they are expected to manage not only the organization but also the authenticity of their emotions.

Control Trap 2: Managing Emotions

In most executive suites, even at the best of times, talking about feelings and emotions is unacceptable. The air at the top is dry, analytical, and rational. When people ascend to the top of an organization, they do not leave their feelings and emotions behind, but they do enter a culture in which issues are seen as cool and orderly, not warm and messy. Shareholders, corporate boards, security analysts, lenders, and years of tradition mold corporate executives' behavior, while administrative assistants, senior staffers, walled-off offices, corporate jets, and executive garages and lunchrooms serve to protect and seal off the top from the middle.

Does that mean there is no stress at the top? No. Leading a complex hierarchical organization is a difficult, unpredictable, and enormously stressful job. Moreover, because there is no culturally acceptable external outlet for this stress, it is internalized. Top executives are like ice cubes that have not quite frozen. They are cool and firm on the outside, but tepid and viscous on the inside. Most executive suites are not healthy places to dwell over time. When the guilt and anger generated by a financial crisis and survivor sickness are added to this normal stress, executives' initial, and often only, response is to redouble the effort to manage their emotions.

Organizational leaders are often "helped" in this response by their staffers. Human resource people buffer and filter the executive impact of a fearful and anxious workforce. Communication officers write speeches and sanitize official communiqués. Lawyers find words that hedge and equivocate. As a result of this institutionalized management of emotions, any honest attempt to make a human contact with survivors is stifled.

Employees at the lower end of the organization also manage their emotions. At times they are victims of cultural trickle-down, as they emulate the mushy ice cube culture at the top. Much of the time, their own past socialization also encourages a controlled response. It is not easy or culturally acceptable, particularly for males, to talk about their real feelings. It is more acceptable to joke or engage in the kind of projection that leads to blaming others.

The control trap of managing emotions leads to isolation at the top, projection and repression at the bottom, and a mixture of both in the middle. Managers can break out of this trap through level 2 interventions, the topic of Chapter Eight. Briefly, these interventions involve facilitating dialogues about feelings. The focus of the first dialogue is intrapersonal, as the facilitator helps survivors get in touch with their true underlying feelings. The next dialogue is interpersonal, as the facilitator helps survivors to talk to each other.

Control Trap 3: Managing an Unproductive Image

Image management is an artifact of the old employment contract. Wear the right clothes, say the right things, live in the right suburb, join the right club, and you will, if you keep doing these things correctly, rise up in the organization. Individuals often act out unproductive or irrelevant images. The new M.B.A. from a prestigious quantitatively oriented school, who feels able to master any situation through decision matrices and objective, analytical thought, suffers a severe dose of reality when he or she encounters the unpredictable, time-constrained, confusing, and ambiguous realities of organizational life. The prevailing image of management as a controlling, evaluating, analytical function is not productive when the management skills needed for results are empathy, sharing, and authenticity. Leaders who rose up by perpetuating the image of control are armed with the wrong tools to be useful in organizations suffering from layoff survivor sickness. These leaders need a new self-perception—one that emphasizes helping others and honest communication.

I once attended a regularly scheduled staff meeting in an organization with a strong norm of image management. Cool, unemotional rationality was the currency of the realm. At 8:00 A.M. a well-liked junior executive received unexpected notice that he was losing his job. Still, he was required to attend the staff meeting at

10:30. Everyone else in that meeting—his friends and peers—knew he had received the bad news. This was an up-or-out organization, where professionals had a limited time to make partner. If they failed, they either had to leave or accept the fact that they were plateaued. The norm was macho and tough. It was not safe to get too close to one's peers because they were also competitors. Not one person in that meeting said a thing about what had happened, even though it was obvious that the laid-off executive was devastated and everyone else also felt badly. They ended up enduring a painful, contrived, unproductive, ritualistic meeting rather than engaging in authentic communication. After the meeting, I met individually with several attendees who told me that any public statement of sympathy would not be good for their image.

Breaking Control Traps

Individuals break control traps through insight, coaching, support, and a great deal of personal courage. Top executives are bright people and cognitively recognize the harm of control traps. But it takes coaching, support, and feedback for them to turn their cognition into behavior. It takes courage for them to go against the cultural grain and share personal vulnerability. However, once taken, the risk almost always pays off; authenticity begets authenticity, and a control trap, once sprung, loses its power for a long time.

Balancing Feeling and Thinking

Despite the desire for a rational and objective system by some researchers and management "scientists," organizations are social systems, and employees don't leave their feelings and emotions on the doorstep when they come to work. In times of organizational stress and trauma, helping employees deal with anger, fear, and anxiety is the managerial currency of the realm. Because organizational cultures suppress the authentic expression of emotions, most managers are more comfortable dealing with matters of the head (thoughts, concepts, and analysis) than matters of the heart (emotions, feelings, and subjective perceptions). In order to facilitate authentic communication, managers must become equally adept at dealing with the heart and the head.

The Hazards of Head-Heart Communication Conflicts

What often happens in turbulent organizational environments such as those in times of downsizing is a head-heart communication mismatch between leaders and employees. One familiar way to illustrate the dynamics of this dysfunctional pattern is in the all-too-familiar example of a conflict between significant others. In this example, I use the man as the employee and the woman as the person at home. The reverse or a same-gender couple could illustrate this pattern of escalation equally well.

The man arrives home late after a long, stressful day. He feels beaten down, tired, and drained of all empathy and desire for human interaction. All he wants is dinner, a drink, and an escape into the comfort of television.

The woman is also tired, but her fatigue is a result of the tedium of her new day-to-day role as a home-bound mother. She loves her husband and baby but feels conflicted, neglected, and emotionally isolated. She says, "I'm lonesome. We need to talk about our relationship" (heart statement).

He responds, "You shouldn't feel that way!" (judgmental head statement). "When the baby came, we decided that you should stay home because I made more money. It was the logical thing to do" (follow-on head statement).

"But, I feel so isolated, and we never seem to communicate" (heart statement).

"Let me give you some data," he responds, raising his voice. "It's a jungle down there. We're missing our numbers by a mile; there's a third round of layoffs coming up, and I'm in a combat zone all day. It just makes sense for me to drop out when I come home; it's the rational thing to do" (head statement).

"But," she responds, the tears beginning to come, "I'm not happy!" (heart statement).

"You shouldn't feel that way! If you understood the facts of what I'm going through, you would be happy to stay home!" (judgmental head statement).

And so goes the inevitable escalation of a heart-head conflict. The more she sends out heart (feeling) messages, the more he replies with head (logic and data) responses. The more she perceives that her feelings are diminished, judged, and not acknowledged, the deeper her emotional distress and the more she sends out feelings. And so it goes.

Unless resolved, heart-head conflicts among significant others can have tragic unintended consequences: divorces, isolation, and meaningless shared lives bonded only by inauthenticity. Heart-head communication conflicts are not restricted to interpersonal relationships; they are ubiquitous in organizations going through downsizing. Breaking the escalation cycle is essential to authentic communication both inside and outside organizational environments. Here are some ideas:

- People in pain or caught in the grip of emotions are not interested in facts and figures. They need their feelings and emotions acknowledged before they can move on. This does not mean that you have to agree with their issues, but you must acknowledge the validity of their feelings.
- You can't tell people they "shouldn't" feel they way they do. They feel the way they feel, and to judge and attempt to discount their feelings will only generate deeper, more intense feelings (Figure 7.1). Layoff survivors are angry and fearful. To tell them they "shouldn't" feel that way and to compound the problem by attempting to "sell" them a feeling (as in, "You should feel lucky to have a job") will just magnify their anger and anxiety.
- The way to break the heart-head mismatch is to go to the lowest common denominator, feelings, and stay there until both parties are able to move into data and logic. You can't use analytical processes to deal with emotional issues! (See Figure 7.2.)

Lead from the Heart, Follow with the Head

If I were to compile a composite of all the speeches I have heard executives present to layoff survivors, it would go like this:

> Our ROI has eroded to the point where the security analysts have expressed concern over the value of our stock to the shareholders. As you may know, our gross margins have also been declining over the past six quarters and reached a point last quarter where we suffered a pretax loss. Based on recent market research, we have confirmed the fact that we are losing market share in the United States and are facing increasingly stiff competition in Europe. The quality

Figure 7.1. Head-Heart Mismatch

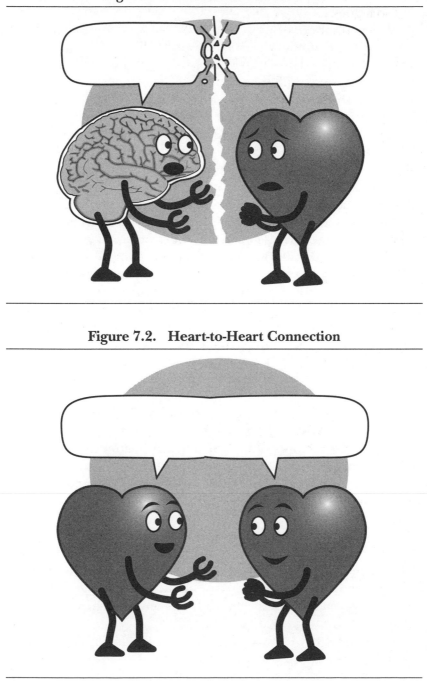

Figure 7.2. Heart-to-Heart Connection

indicators we installed last year show that we are not making the
gains we had planned, and our revenue per employee has declined.
We have no alternative but to implement a downsizing effort at this
time if this organization is to remain a viable economic entity. It is a
straightforward economic decision. Any questions?

Of course, there are no questions, and the shell-shocked victims
shuffle, glassy-eyed, back to their desks.

All the points in this typical speech are valid causes for downsizing. However, it is a communication of abstract ideas, and initially layoff survivors are not ready for "head" communication.
They are anxious, fearful, mistrustful, and in crisis, even if they
appear controlled or unemotional. They need to be reached at the
heart level, not the head. Logical, analytical, rational data do nothing for them. They need something more personal and human.

Managers communicating layoffs are presiding at a funeral, not
an M.B.A. class on financial analysis or analytical decision making.
Conducting a funeral requires an empathetic touch, the naming
and sharing of a feeling, and a grieving for our common human
vulnerability. Imagine the outrage and sense of violation survivors
would feel if a participant in a wake for a loved one launched into
a fact-filled dissertation on actuarial tables, mortality projections,
and the need for death in order to prevent overpopulation in the
world.

Managers who deal with people in crisis must lead with the
heart and follow with the head. The head is important too, but
people in crisis are not ready for it. They must attend to their emotional needs before they will have room for more cognitive communications. With a little practice, managers can begin with the
heart, not the head. Indeed, they can often deal with the cognitive
issues in the same meeting if they pay attention to the heart first.
The change from head to heart is a high-leverage change: a small
amount of effort will lead to a large gain in authenticity and empathy. I have often been humbled when, after what I perceive as
sophisticated interventions, clients tell me that the one thing I did
that helped the most was to teach them the heart-head timing of
communication.

If the executive's speech announcing layoffs had begun with
the heart, it would have sounded like this:

I know you are feeling sad and concerned about your friends who have gone. I know this because that's the way I'm feeling too. It is really hard to see people who have helped build this organization get laid off! I've talked to some of you, and I know you're anxious about your own future and concerned that you may also have to go. I'd like to be able to assure you that won't happen, but the fact that I can't foresee the future and honestly make that commitment makes me even sadder. These are tough times, and things are not easy for any of us. I think we are all going to have to struggle through and make the best of it. It helps if we can be honest and share our feelings. Ultimately it will help if we can move the organization to be leaner, more flexible, and market focused. It is sometimes helpful for me to think of the forces that cause us to have to resort to layoffs. Our ROI has . . .

It is easy for organizational leaders to see and feel the power of the heart-and-head approach. But convincing them that they have the skills to use this approach and that it is all right for them to share their feelings openly with employees is often more difficult. The examples of the layoff speeches illustrate three main points:

Heart and Head Learnings

- The approach of leading with the heart and following with the head is a model for all survivor interactions. Survivors are in crisis. Acknowledging their underlying emotions is a necessary first step for any meaningful communication.
- Heart-head communication liberates the sender as well as the receiver. Organizational leaders who share their feelings before retreating to analysis experience the cathartic effect of authenticity.
- The risk is worth the reward. A small gain in using and communicating feelings can reap large rewards for managers. This is a high-leverage intervention.

Tell the Truth, and Never Say Never

George was a general manager for a semiautonomous research and development division of a large West Coast–based corporation. Many of his division's engineers and technicians were in their mid-forties. They had been with the division for a long time, many since college, and like their organization, they were slightly out of date. Most of them were now in administrative or quasi-management roles.

All the hooks of the old employment contract were operational. The organization was the primary social outlet for many employees through a network of company-sponsored recreational activities such as softball, golf, and bowling leagues; social activities such as dinner dances and trips; and a number of special-interest clubs. Most of the old-timers had grown up together in the division and formed friendships there. The fringe benefits were great, much better than the market, and the pay was high for the work done. Even the new engineers, of whom there were too few, were already in a codependent relationship with the organization.

Turnover was very low, so payroll costs increased each year, even though productivity did not increase, and the margins of George's division continued to decline. The old employment contract was performing admirably; it was acting as a magnet, pulling the employees in and causing them to define themselves in terms of where they worked, not who they were. At the same time as they were being drawn in by the old contract, they were coming closer to the new reality. The division was merely drifting along, with a market advantage created by an earlier patent breakthrough. When the patent protection expired, the result was predictable: a violation of the old contract and devastating layoffs.

The men and women in this organization, both survivors and victims, displayed various cultural trinkets with pride. During the exit interviewing process, nearly every male victim was wearing his gender's version of the organization's tenure trinket: a tie bar coded silver for five years and gold for ten years, with various colored stones inserted in the center for further five-year increments. The preferred tenure trinkets for women were key chains or earrings, and many women also continued to display these trinkets. It is a sure sign of the strength of the old employment contract when layoff victims wear trinkets designed to celebrate tenure on their way out the door.

This division had all the preconditions for layoff survivor sickness, and it was no surprise that it was experiencing early symptoms. George was working to establish developing authentic communication and had a strong desire to tell the survivors that the downsizing was over. The pressure on him to make this reassuring statement was enormous. His direct reports were saying, "We've done the hard things, made the cuts, got the workforce down to where it should be. Let's tell them it is over, and get back to work." A related theme was, "*They* can't go through that again; *they* need to hear it's over," which meant that the management team really wanted George to tell *them* it was over. (This form of projection occurs often with top managers.) In fact, everyone, at all levels of the organization, wanted to hear it was over so that they could go back to the old ways. The desire to turn back is a natural reaction to change, threat, and uncertainty. Children want to travel back in time during loss or hurt, nations want to turn the clock back during economic or social flux, and organizations suffering layoffs want to be told the downsizing is over, that things can go back to the way they were.

George may also have wanted to tell himself the layoffs were over, even though deep down, he knew they weren't. So despite my advice (and I was not suffering George's tremendous stress and anxiety), George told employees the downsizing was over. He did a lot of other things right, though. He talked to the employees in groups and thanked each group for their courage, acknowledged their fears and survivor feelings, and owned up to his own feelings. He then talked about the new vision. This was good stuff. However, he committed that fatal mistake made by many organizational leaders when he told them it was over. He also used the old "if only" theme: if only you work hard, embrace the vision, are more customer focused, and embrace quality—if only you do these things—we will have a bright future together, and there will be no more layoffs. I could see a physical relaxing and almost hear the sighs when the groups heard this. The boss was a hero! He said, "No more layoffs." They were thinking, *Things will be better; we can forget this nightmare. He said we wouldn't have to go through it again!*

But at one level, no one really believed it. The employees were all intelligent adults and knew what forces were at work in the world economy. But on the public level, they were reassured, or at least had a shared fantasy of the kind everyone buys into at some time in his or her life: the boss said it would be okay. Work hard and you will get your reward. The bad guys never win. Vote for me, and the economy will turn around, and there will be no tax increases. Racism and sexism do not really exist in my city. The predictable happened: six months later, there was another round of layoffs, and

George, who had once been the hero boss, became the villain and is now working hard to regain his lost credibility.

The example of George's mistake illustrates three profound points for organizational leaders to brand into their memories:

Truth-Telling Learnings

- Leaders feel tremendous pressure from all parts of the organization and from within their own psyches to say, "It is over!"
- But it is never over. This is as close to a law as anything I have found in the study of layoffs. The forces of the economy, the dynamics of technology, and the reality of the new employment contract make any kind of a long-range employment promise an illusion.
- Telling oneself and other survivors the truth takes tremendous courage, foresight, and tough love. The truth is the exact opposite of what survivors want to hear. Nevertheless, layoff survivors need to take individual responsibility for their job security and face the probability that they cannot count on their current jobs to last. In the articulation and understanding of this truth lies the path to a more authentic, less codependent employment relationship.

Two Denial Traps

For reasons of psychological comfort, short-term orientation, and a need to displace their anxiety with any form of action regardless of its value, managers often deny the reality of what is going on around them. I call these denials *traps* because they are short term, illusionary, and trap the managers into taking actions that will not help them or their organizations increase the odds of survival. Here are two examples.

Denial Trap 1: Spurious Self-Actualization

A medical technologies firm whose specialty medical device had captured a large percentage of a narrow market niche had grown from fewer than thirty to just over five hundred employees in less than six years. At about the same time as the competition caught up with this firm, a number of quality problems surfaced in the firm's cash cow product. As a result, sales declined, earnings were depressed, and the venture capitalists who had originally bankrolled the company became jumpy. The firm had had one minor layoff in its manufacturing operation and was planning a large and comprehensive "restructuring."

The firm's human resource vice president was serious about wanting to "do it right" and invited me to help with planning the process issues. She believed she was acting in accord with the desires and objectives of her boss, the president. It was clear that the employees were deeply concerned, fearful, and anxious about their future. The members of the top team had been selected for their technical skills, not their management or leadership skills, and communication, which had been tenuous in the best of times, had virtually ceased in the past two months.

The first clue that a denial trap existed in the form of spurious self-actualization was that neither the president nor any key staff member was willing to take the time to talk with me. They were too busy, out of town, or had conflicting meetings. This, to a consultant, is always a sign of resistance and suggests that the top team may not be serious about dealing with the issues. The human resource vice president organized a time to discuss layoff planning and the restructuring during the top team's weekly staff meeting. The meeting revealed an atmosphere of frenzied excitement. The chief financial officer was deeply involved in seeking new funding alternatives, and the manufacturing vice president was studying new processes and a number of subcontracting options. The president was looking at a strategic alliance and was in the early stages of a mating dance with a merger partner. The organization was in a crisis, and the top team was playing save-the-company. They were fatigued, tired, and stressed, but they had never before felt so challenged or relevant. They had a feeling of self-actualization, but this fulfillment would turn out to be spurious.

When I told them the rest of the organization was slipping into the initial stages of layoff survivor sickness and that they needed to do something about it, they responded that they didn't have time. They wondered why they could not delegate that "soft" stuff to the human resource people. (As a result, I fired myself as this organization's consultant.) Nine months later, the "merger" became recognized as an acquisition, and the organization was in dire straits. A few months after that, the president was fired, and the organization became a small division of the acquiring organization.

Learnings About Spurious Self-Actualization

- There is frequently a gap between the activities of top management and the rest of the organization. In times of crisis, top managers engage in the exhilaration of playing a save-the-company or save-the-division game. They may feel almost messianic in this mission. In the heat of the challenge, they have little empathy or understanding for the rest of the organization.
- Spurious self-actualization is widespread in organizations.
- Spurious self-actualization is short term and delusionary. It is based on the macho and isolationist principle that a small group or an individual can "save" a large number of others. But no one can save an organization attempting to hide behind the old employment contract (the market will see to that), and the days of the Lone Ranger riding in and saving the town are long gone. Collaboration, human bonding, and teamwork are the tools that save modern organizations, not a separation of the top from the rest of the organization.

Denial Trap 2: Myopic Mergers

Many layoffs are triggered by mergers. In a description of useful prescriptions to combat postmerger survivor sickness, Mitchell Marks and Phillip Mirvis (1992, p. 18) point out that survivor sickness "infects employees even in the best of deals." In my experience too, the myopic merger denial trap is often a complicating factor in survivor sickness. Ten working principles illustrate why the attitude that "they'll leave me alone; I'll leave them alone" is a denial trap:

- The difference between an acquisition and a merger is control.
- The organization that has the control calls the transaction an "acquisition."
- The organization that does not have control calls the transaction a "merger."

- The acquiring organization has a built-in compulsion to install its people, systems, and policies in the acquired organization.
- The acquiring organization often denies its nature, fights against its compulsion, and promises autonomy.
- The acquiring organization eventually follows its compulsion.
- The merging organization colludes with the acquiring organization and buys into the promise of autonomy.
- Deep down, the merging organization knows it will be taken over, its systems replaced, redundant people laid off, and identity diluted.
- Both the acquiring and the merging organizations are deeply psychologically invested in maintaining their mutual denial.
- The primary intervention in these situations involves straight talk and honest communication within and between the two entities.

Organizational leaders must work through this interlinked denial trap. Although most postmerger layoffs occur in the merging organization, there are cases where survivor symptoms have bled over into the acquiring organization, usually owing to a long and confusing series of false starts in the relationship. Bleed-over is minimized when quick, decisive planned action and communication take place. But before this can happen, management must take the time and have the honesty to develop a clear joint vision and implementation plan. Unfortunately such honesty and time taking is rare.

Process Research

Most layoff survivor research has focused on process issues (factors that have an impact on survivors and can be managed before, during, and shortly after layoffs) as opposed to longer-term individual and systemic solutions that might provide a more permanent immunization to layoff survivor sickness. This research has also tended to be laboratory-based studies of controlled student populations and extrapolations from other theories as opposed to field-based, face-to-face interactions with survivors in their workplaces. Nonetheless, it is an important and growing body of knowledge that supports field-based studies and practitioners' experience. The major themes in this process research are survivors' needs for fairness, equity, participation, caretaking, and prior notification.

Fairness

Like beauty, what is fair is often in the eyes of the beholder. Therefore, the perceived fairness of not only the reason for a layoff but also the process for selecting those who leave is an important factor for survivors. The practical implications of this survivor need are that communication must be clear and honest. Open discussions are needed about the rationale for the layoff and the way layoff selections were and will be made. The key ingredients are trust and authenticity. Without the lubricant of trust, layoff processes will grind out anger and fear and polarize groups within the organization.

Equity

Do the layoffs include top management? What is the difference between their exit pay and the severance of average middle and lower managers? Survivors are concerned about sharing the burden. Layoffs that include a disproportionate percentage of middle managers and workers exacerbate normal survivor symptoms. Even if the number of layoffs is fairly distributed across the board, severance equity will remain a major concern. Newspaper reports and proxy statements that tell of multimillion-dollar deals for departing top executives leave survivors feeling abandoned and outraged.

Participation

Did the organization consider alternatives: voluntary retirement, special severance bonus payments, full time changed to part time or to job sharing, pay freezes and cuts, or long-term leaves of absence? Research that has applied the concept of procedural justice to layoffs has found (unsurprisingly) that people were more satisfied with the process when they were given control in establishing the conditions of a layoff, such as the selection process, the period of advance notification, and the processes for determining severance pay. Such participation is rare in organizations owing to distrust and management's need for control; nevertheless, those are not insurmountable barriers. I know of two organizations that put similar ideas into operation. A large manufacturing operation actively involved employees in exploring alternatives to layoff, and a relatively small service business involved employees in establishing criteria for those who would be laid off. In both cases, it took courage and conviction on the part of one employee to bulldoze these ideas through a resistant system. Unfortunately, most second act layoffs are taking place without employee participation, and neither the organizations nor the employees are benefiting from the lessons of the past.

Caretaking

The way layoff victims are treated is a survivor hygiene factor. Their severance pay, efforts to help them find other employment, and the dignity and respect granted them by the organization are parts of this factor. Horror stories such as rumors that victims have been told of their fates by an administrative assistant when the boss is out of town, sent an e-mail, or phoned by a human resource person whom they have never met tear through survivor organizations with amazing speed, whether the stories are true or not. In one division of a large organization, stories were told of layoff victims' being given no advance notice, asked to clean out their desks, and then escorted to the human resource function where they were "read their rights," given a severance payment, and escorted to the door by a security guard. Indeed, these incidents did take place—but in another division two years earlier! There is power in management's publicizing what is being done right, and great harm, for many years afterward, in management's tolerating practices that rob layoff victims of dignity.

Prior Notification

The longer the advance notification, the better. Public corporations in the United States must work within the constraints of the legal issue of materiality. Corporations with material news that will affect the price of their stock must make internal and external announcements of this news simultaneously. However, many organizations take secrecy far beyond this constraint. Well after an initial public announcement in divisions far from corporate headquarters, organizations remain concerned that layoff rumors are leaking and organizations often maintain elaborate security, holding secret meetings and formulating elaborate need-to-know communication plans. This intricate web of secrecy is based on assumptions about negative employee reactions, not on Securities and Exchange Commission concerns.

Enlightened practice would argue that the longer employees know their fate in advance, the more they are put in control, can plan their own futures, and are able to face and manage their own anxieties. Companies argue that employees who know too much in advance will spend all their time looking for jobs and will not be productive. The fact is that once layoffs are announced, the survivors' focus will shift from the job to their survivor symptoms in any case, and without preparation and adequate notice, the shift will be much more intense and substantial rather than less so.

Ethics is also an issue here. A manager who knows that he or she is going to "do something to" another person, who also knows that advance notice would be helpful to that person and nevertheless withholds that notice for purposes other than strictly legal ones, is not going to win the ethics-in-business award.

Finally, most organizations have a key constituency that requires advance notice: the employees the organization wants to keep. They may be high potentials, key managers, or key technical employees. They need to hear that management values their contributions and will do its best to keep them. This needs to be said in the right tone, with the right disclaimers. Managers do not know for sure that they can keep anyone, and if they are honest, they do not even know about their own longevity. They can, however, communicate intentions.

Middle managers who will be asked to administer the layoff also require advance notice. They are the implementers, who should not be too far removed from the planners. The layoff timing, numbers, and processes and the communication process all need the ownership of this group.

Learnings and Implications

Layoff processes have important effects on survivors. Authenticity, congruency, and empathetic communication are primary level 1 interventions. All of us—top executives, middle managers, and individual contributors—erect traps to control and manage the information and emotions that should be spontaneous and free flowing.

In order to be relevant to ourselves and our fellow survivors, we need to go against the grain and resist our tendencies to control and deny. We need the courage to engage in straight talk with ourselves and others.

Dealing with survivors' perceptions of fairness, equity, and caretaking and permitting prior notification and participation in decision making are other important level 1 interventions.

Process interventions are tactical. Though important, they serve only to stop the bleeding; they do not promote healing. Healing itself begins with emotional release, or grieving. Second-level grieving interventions are explored in the next chapter.

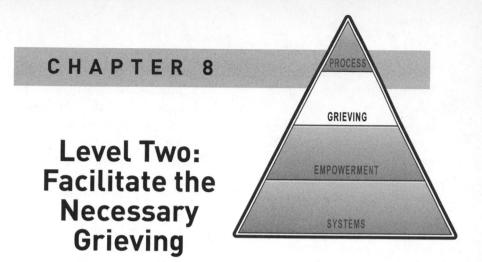

CHAPTER 8

Level Two: Facilitate the Necessary Grieving

"Some of the people are ushered out of here coldly, like it's all over and you can't even say good-bye to your friends. They come in here and clean off their desks at night. All of a sudden, the desk is clear; it's gone. They've disappeared."

In the best of times, organizations don't like the word *grieving*. It sounds wimpy, whiny, too much from the pop psychology self-help books, and to suggest its necessity is perceived as an indictment on the myth of a rational, logical, emotion-free, business-only organizational culture. In times of organizational trauma, organizationally sanctioned grieving is most often seen as an expensive, time-wasting, touchy-feely distraction from the macho, "suck it up and move on" postlayoff environment.

The reality, however, is that most organizations may be able to "suck it up," but they clearly can't move on with an organizational system that is gridlocked with employees who are angry, anxious, depressed, and fearful. Since the evidence is overwhelming that these survivor symptoms exist despite the norm of denial, organizations that want to weather the storm and survive in the new reality have no choice but to deal with them. A foundation of the theory of psychotherapy is that unarticulated, internalized, unprocessed emotions such as anger and anxiety bleed over into more serious forms of mental health issues such as depression. It is obviously neither feasible nor desirable to turn managers into unlicensed therapists. Neither, however, is it useful or conducive to their long-term survival for organizations to adhere to policies or perpetuate organizational cultures that cause employees to repress and bottle up feelings and emotions. Like it or not, organizations that want to weather the second act and prosper need to find ways to help their employees vent their repressed emotions.

One way to help organizations overcome the bind this norm of denial puts them in is to simply label venting and grieving sessions as something else. This chapter presents examples of grieving interventions not as rigid, prescriptive recipes but as examples of how the use of sessions labeled as "team building," "communication," or "planning" can be configured to address the necessary grieving. As a consultant, I have helped organizations engage in many dimensions of grieving, but I seldom use that word when I am publicizing and organizing these sessions.

Level 2 interventions help organizations unblock repressed feelings. Even in the best-handled layoffs, survivors feel violated. Some survivors do avail themselves of private therapy, and others have support systems that allow them to sort out their feelings, but the vast majority of layoff survivors repress their feelings and have no personal or organizationally sanctioned outlet for externalizing their anger and fear. The metaphor of the surviving children in Chapter One is once again instructive. Imagine the energy the surviving family expends to repress their strong and toxic emotions and go about their daily routines. Unfortunately, organizations too are filled with survivors slogging through bleak days, repressing their feelings of violation and, as their anger turns inward, sinking deeper into the funk of survivor guilt and depression.

The bad news is that repressed anger and other emotions are widespread. The good news is that the intervention process is not difficult to start, managers don't need to engage in therapy to facilitate it, and once it is started, the feelings do come out. The organization may have to use outsiders to begin the process. In the long term, management should integrate a process for facilitating survivor grieving into the organizational system.

The Burden of a Heavy Bag

Gunnysacking is a term for storing up hurt feelings, anger, affronts, and unresolved conflicts. Organizations are filled with employees carrying some pretty heavy rocks in their bags (Figure 8.1). It is hard for employees weighed down with the burden of these bags to muster up the energy, creativity, and commitment necessary to help organizations rebound. When the weight of the psychological gunnysack becomes too heavy to bear, as inevitably it must, survivors create even more problems for themselves and others by unloading it, usually to an inappropriate degree in an inappropriate context, and in response to what is often seen by others as a trivial issue.

Figure 8.1. The Survivor Burden

We all gunnysack to some extent, but most psychologically healthy people find ways to keep their bags relatively light. Unfortunately, many layoff survivors operate in an environment where they have neither the personal resources nor the organizational permission to lighten their loads. One way to conceptualize grieving interventions is to visualize them as a means to help employees empty their bags (Figure 8.2). Although individual sessions are helpful, I have found group work the most effective and efficient method of bringing survivor emotions to the surface and lightening psychological gunnysacks. This chapter presents some examples to illustrate the variety of ways organizations can engage in these interventions.

Figure 8.2. A Lighter Load

I will discuss a successful team intervention, a not-so-successful systemwide process, a small business visioning process, and a departmental wake.

A Team Intervention

The client: A director of support services in a recently merged health care system and her surviving managers.

The situation: Two large hospitals merged. Sarah's unit was responsible for providing central services such as accounting, information services, training, human resources, records, maintenance services, and other administrative and technical services for the new organization. Before the merger, there were two managers for each of these services; after the merger, there was one survivor. Not only had many managers lost their jobs, but the remaining organization was rightsized, which meant another 20 percent reduction in Sarah's department. Nearly nine months after the layoffs, the productivity and morale of the group had declined to the point that it was clear to Sarah that the group was suffering from layoff survivor sickness.

The intervention. Sarah and her family, the group of survivor managers who reported to her, participated in a three-day retreat. We called it a team-building session to eliminate anyone becoming hooked on words like *grieving* or *venting*. The meeting objectives, which they stated in health care language, involved "diagnosing and developing a treatment plan" for what ailed them.

The retreat started at noon, and by dinnertime, with the aid of the metaphor of the surviving children and other exercises, some participants began to express their survivor feelings. Everyone was then given an assignment of writing his or her survivor story. Story ground rules required the use of feeling language and a personal focus; escape to abstraction was not allowed. The next day, with a great deal of facilitation and support, the managers told their stories: first individually, then combined with the stories of others in small groups, and finally as part of the entire family story. Before the merger, both hospital systems had self-perceptions of being kind and nurturing. However, the story that emerged at the retreat was a sad one, filled with blaming and perceptions of betrayal.

That day was filled with tears, anger, and touching occurrences of emotional support. Over dinner that evening, the intervention switched from the heart to the head. The group viewed a slide show of the symptoms of layoff survivor sickness. The participants were then split into two groups and given an assignment to develop a one-act play—a tragedy based on the group's story.

The next morning, the groups presented their plays, which turned out to be more humorous than tragic (this shift seems to be typical in similar groups). Then they spent the next few hours discussing how their efforts could be turned into inspirational plays. Sarah, who had previously been either a participant or a silent observer, led this discussion. In the early afternoon, two new groups were formed with instructions to write and act out an inspirational play that could serve as a new vision for the team. These two plays were presented after dinner with Sarah as the "judge," armed with several humorous prizes. The plays had humor, power, and passion. Sarah, overjoyed and somewhat tearful, told the groups that the performances "knocked her socks off." (I have seen several versions of this exercise and am always amazed at the participants' creativity, intensity, and optimism.) Sarah told the group they never could have done this without the "agony" of the past two days.

The next morning, the entire group talked about ways of transferring the learnings to their organizations, established some ground rules as to how group members would relate to each other back home, and planned two future meetings.

Team Intervention Learnings

- In a relatively short time, most natural work teams, or *"families,"* can make a great deal of progress in unblocking and addressing their survivor feelings.
- Because of the importance of having someone involved who knows how to deal with feelings in a positive and productive way, this intervention should not be attempted without an initial diagnosis, a supportive boss, and a skilled facilitator.
- Often survivor feelings must be teased out through metaphor, structured exercises, and nontraditional processes such as drama.
- Layoff survivors express powerful and passionate feelings easily when given the opportunity. Conversely, survivors' suppression of these feelings takes an enormous toll on productivity and on simple human authenticity, day after day, week after week, and often year after year.

- Interventions must deal with the head and heart—and feet too! "Mono–body part" events have poor results. Working at the emotional level (heart) is extremely important but alienates participants if overdone. Working only at the cognitive level (head) is also important, more so than many behavioral practitioners realize, but it also alienates people if overdone. Action planning—doing something with what has been learned (feet)— is a priority for busy managers. But action with no emotion or theory behind it is a self-delusion and, unfortunately, the intervention of choice for many organizations and used by too many managers to avoid or sabotage real learning.

- In successful group interventions, the extent to which even sophisticated and psychologically aware leaders and managers are reluctant and ashamed to own up to their own survivor feelings is often experienced as a collective "Aha!"

- Nearly every group, even one working over a very short time frame, yearns for a galvanizing vision. For this reason, groups should seek a new vision even in their early getting-the-feelings-out cathartic sessions.

- Participants and facilitators must take symbolic survivor feelings literally. The exercise of developing and performing a play is a literal acting out or purging of survivor feelings.

- Facilitators should involve the "family" head. Sarah's team must continue to function when the outside facilitator is long gone; therefore, it is important not to create any dependence on the outsider. (Nevertheless, transference and, if the outsider is not careful, countertransference often do occur, even in relatively short sessions.)

- One-shot cures do not work. Even when they have fully positive immediate results, short-term fixes do not take. Sarah had a strategy of multiple sessions. There are always ups and downs in multiple sessions too—the earth did not move at all of Sarah's subsequent sessions.

An Attempted Systemwide Intervention

The client. The new CEO of a spin-off division of a high-technology communications company.

The situation. As a part of a corporate restructuring, a large product organization spun off a specialty division. The former division general manager became the new operation's president and CEO. In order to make this operation show sufficient short-term profit to satisfy the demands of the venture capitalists who helped fund the spin-off, an across-the-board workforce reduction of about 10 percent took place just before the formal spin-off. Six months later, another substantial layoff took place. At this point, the vice president of human resources convinced the top management group that a systemwide intervention to "revitalize" and "re-recruit" the workforce was needed to pull the new organization out of its continuing decline.

The intervention. The initial step constituted what was labeled "off-site planning meeting" for the top team. In the new president's words, the team's objective was to "plan" ways to "increase the productivity" of the workforce. (Language is a lens to a culture: the health care organization had a "retreat" to "diagnose" and develop a "treatment" plan; the business organization went "off site" to "plan" an increase in "productivity.") The results were far less dramatic than those of the health care group. There was much denial; the president was particularly resistant, often becoming directive and outspoken and stifling dialogue. However, the team's survivor feelings did get discussed, and the tragedy plays yielded insights for the president, as both groups portrayed him as the arch-villain. On a scale of 1 to 10, this intervention would rate a 5. That score is about par for the first time a top team goes through this kind of session because the higher the organizational level, the greater the denial, and the greater the difficulty of staying out of the head and in the heart.

The next step was a series of one-on-one meetings with the top team members. As any change agent will agree, it is crucial that systemwide change have ongoing top management involvement. I continued to help individuals vent their emotions during these sessions. Team members had a great deal of anger at the parent company for spinning them off with no choice. They also blamed the president for "selling them out" and for bad leadership, each other for not pulling an equal amount of weight, and the employees in general for not following directions, for failing to be "grateful" that they had a job, and for not appreciating the extent to which team members were "working their asses off to meet the payroll." The president was disturbed by the feedback he had heard, and he blamed the top team for not understanding his vision. He also was anxious to "do" something and was impatient with me and my internal colleague, the human resource vice president, for not implementing his ideas to increase productivity and "raise morale."

The third step was another meeting with the top team. Originally scheduled for one afternoon, it lasted nine hours. This was not a popular meeting. Most consultants occasionally reach a point at which they must take a stand, and I was prepared to abandon the project if team members did not face their own issues before attempting to "do" something "to" the rest of the employees. After that, they heard the collected themes from their one-on-one meetings: the anger, the blame, the hurt that employees did not recognize top management's efforts to save the business, and the institutionalized anxiety that they were ineffectively attempting to escape through a quick-fix orientation. This time they were able to both own and work their data. By the time they adjourned, they had not only made an initial pass at dealing with the group's layoff survivor symptoms but had also formulated a systemwide intervention strategy that was to be integrated with the management structure. The integration had the following steps:

Step 1: Require all managers to attend a "revitalization" workshop, which would help them examine and confront their own survivor feelings. They were to attend in "stranger" groups rather than in groups with managers working for the same supervisor. They then were trained, or often refreshed, in basic helping skills: listening, giving and receiving feedback, and responding to feelings.

Step 2: After managers attend the workshop, require them to meet with each of their employees, focusing the discussion on the layoffs and asking about employees' feelings. (Managers would have an outline and a structured checklist to facilitate this discussion.) Although many managers were not experienced in conducting such interviews, the top team felt that the managers were the natural organizational communicators and that any discussion of survivor symptoms, regardless of how clumsy, was infinitely better than no discussion.

Step 3: Plan a communication and team-building program to take place over the next year to build commitment to the new vision.

The program got off to a positive start. However, less than three months into implementation, the board, which included venture capitalists who had little empathy for layoff survivors and no buy-in to the intervention strategy, fired the president. The new CEO promptly instituted another round of layoffs, in which one of the top management team's key supporters of the program was let go. After that, the program fell apart for lack of funding and support.

Systemwide Intervention Learnings

- Systemwide interventions are difficult to sustain within organizations experiencing significant flux and change. Coalitions and management support do not hold together over time.
- Survivor groups should be met where they are, not where the intervenor wants them to be. The initial language and intervention strategy need to be formulated in a way survivor groups will understand and accept. Confronting them in the first ten minutes with their repressed survivor symptoms and blaming behavior will only get the external intervenor thrown out and leave the layoff survivors without any help.
- A time comes, however, when the intervenor must confront survivors and, in order to help them, run the risk of losing them.
- Involving line managers is the only natural way to implement a systemwide intervention.
- Something is better than nothing! Not all line managers are gifted at teasing out survivor symptoms, but even the most awkward management intervention can have a positive effect. Help is defined by the helpee, not the helper, and employees suffering from survivor sickness seem appreciative if anyone tries to help.
- Even limited success makes a difference. Some groups in this organization continued to work, albeit without any corporate support, on their revitalization issues.

A Small Business Visioning Intervention

The client. Josh, the president and son of the founder of a small specialty furniture manufacturing and sales company.

The situation. This family-owned business suffered from the classic one-two punch especially common to small, labor-intensive, thinly financed U.S. companies.

The first blow was the need to shift manufacturing overseas—in this case to China—to reduce labor costs and remain competitive. The second punch was the ripple effect of the subprime lending debacle, which for this firm meant the drying up of its credit line and inability to adequately finance its inventory and overseas manufacturing costs.

Most of the manufacturing workforce was gone, and the few survivors, working in final assembly and shipping, were waiting for the ax to fall. The professional staff was made up of the president, two underemployed manufacturing supervisors, a small sales force, and a two-person administrative and accounting group. The total professional staff, including the president was fourteen people. There were fewer than ten full-time employees in manufacturing. In what they described in their regional drawl as "the good ole days," the workforce was about 150.

The company was facing a major crisis in direction and purpose, as was the president. He had taken over from his father during boom times when his firm was viewed by the community as an exemplary corporate citizen, contributing to local charities and often taking the lead in improvement projects. Now they were scraping to find funds to meet the payroll, with nothing to spare for the community. As was the case with many other old-line manufacturing companies in the South, entire families—fathers, mothers, sons, and daughters—were part of the manufacturing work force. So when the layoffs hit, it was quite literally a family affair. When I met him, Josh thought he had let them all down: his father, the community, and his employees. His was a particularly virulent, "Why was I chosen to preside over a funeral?" form of survivor sickness.

The intervention. We labeled the intervention *visioning,* and the first vision we worked on was Josh's. This was a series of one-on-one sessions designed to help him realize that it wasn't his fault that U.S. labor costs had escalated higher than an interconnected world economy could swallow and that he wasn't personally responsible for the greed-driven, irresponsible lending and financing practices that had ignited the fires of a global economic meltdown. These were not easy sessions but eventually Josh began to let go of his repressed anger and guilt and replace it with a new, more relevant personal vision. Rather than seeing himself as the paternalistic head of a regional manufacturing company with his contributions denominated by the number of people he employed and the level of his community contributions, he saw himself leading a smaller, more efficient technology-based marketing and distribution business. There was sadness that he was unable to provide manufacturing jobs and that he could not index his self-esteem on his financial commitment to the local community, but there was also realism and a liberating form of acceptance that in his industry, this economy, and this country, that was just not in the cards.

The next step was a visioning session with all fourteen professional staff members. We began with Josh as president explaining his new vision. He was excited, and his expectations for buy-in were high. But he was soon brought down to earth. The group had been together a long time but had never really met to talk about how they worked together. Because of the stress of the business downturn and the perceived lack of structure for the session, they felt authorized to surface long-repressed issues with each other and the president. Despite Josh's initial disappointment, this was an important and necessary session. All change requires letting go of the old before embracing the new. At the end of the first session, after much venting, emotion, and airing of repressed issues, there was a collective sense of relief and the group was ready to look at a new vision.

In many organizations, the creation of vision statements is a waste of time, money, and energy. The products of these sessions end up in binders, gathering dust on bookshelves. When properly done, however, vision creation can result in a shared picture of the future that serves to align an organization and create excitement over a desired future. It is all a matter of the commitment, motivation, and sincerity of those who craft the vision.

Josh and his professional staff spent three additional sessions working on their vision, and it is still a work in progress. They continued the theme of letting go and holding on and discovered how difficult it is to let go of the familiar, yet unproductive, old and grasp the frightening, yet exciting, new. Part of their letting go was to externalize their own survivor symptoms; part of their holding on was to take a collective risk on a desirable future. Josh and his team now have an aligning vision and a new business plan. They returned to profitability two quarters after the initial session. But their visioning was not without casualties: neither of the manufacturing managers had the skills or motivation to make the transition, and they are no longer with the firm.

Small Business Visioning Learnings

- Layoff survivor sickness is found in all types of organizations: large, small, public, private, for profit, and nonprofit.
- The recovery process for small businesses, particularly those that are family owned, is inexorably intertwined with the recovery of the owner or head person.
- If approached with sincerity and commitment, the creation of a galvanizing, energizing, future vision can be an effective intervention for overcoming survivor sickness.
- Moving forward as an individual or an organization requires letting go of strategies, assumptions, and self-images that may have been appropriate in the past but don't fit the new reality. This letting go is the first step in overcoming survivor sickness.

A Departmental Wake

The client. The corporate human resource department of a defense contractor.

The situation. The defense contractor had suffered continuing significant layoffs over a three-year period. When the vice president of human resources left, the new vice president differed in values and education from her subordinates. Margaret had a doctorate in counseling psychology and had worked in education prior to joining the company. She was also the company's only woman at the level of vice president. Margaret quickly diagnosed her department as "burned out" and unable to "let go of the past." In this case, the past had included high growth, lots of "fun" projects, and relatively high job security for this industry. Margaret wanted her team to move from a controlling, "rules administration" role to a "helping" role; she wanted her group to perceive employees as "clients."

The intervention. After I held a series of diagnostic interviews and small sessions that we called "discovery group sessions," it was clear that members of this department did indeed have a death grip on the past and were extremely angry about organizational changes and their diminished role. Those who had spent time conducting exit interviews and dealing with layoff victims' pay and benefits engaged in the rationalization and justification behavior described in Chapter Six.

The initial intervention for this department was a version of the family workshop. Due to a large degree to Margaret's sensitivity and group process skills, this was a powerful and helpful session in terms of both expressing emotions and identifying a new vision. One successful activity that evolved during that session and that I have used successfully in other organizational settings was a departmental wake, culminating in an actual burial.

Rather than participate in the small group plays described earlier, the entire group decided to hold a wake, complete with candles, music, and testimonials. Individuals wrote out the old-system ideas and activities they needed to let go of, read their lists, tore them in half, and placed the torn-up paper in a large cardboard box draped in black. Then each person, including Margaret, stood in front of the group and read from a list of his or her fears. This list too was torn up and placed in the box. Some people "said words" over the box. Although this has not happened in other groups, Margaret's team joined hands around the box and sang "We Shall Overcome." The session ended when the group symbolically buried the box by putting it in the dumpster behind the conference center. (Once, another group actually buried the torn slips of paper in a vacant lot beside the group's facility.)

This intervention and others that followed had dramatic results. The organization bonded around a new image of service and, with Margaret's continuing facilitation and support, successfully navigated a number of wrenching changes.

Departmental Wake Learnings

- Symbolic acting out has power and value. Even organizations that initially perceive this exercise as strange and "touchy-feely" find potency and meaning in it. My most resistant group reported this exercise as the most meaningful when they looked back three months later. At some level, the burial is real, and the wake, like its real-life counterpart, serves as a symbolic way of letting go of the past and allowing survivors to move forward.
- Confession is cathartic and bonding. Team members stood in front of their peers and owned up to a wide range of survivor feelings. People learned, to their surprise, that others harbored the same set of feelings. Therefore, the process of confession

led to sharing and acceptance. Survivor feelings were accepted as a natural consequence of what individuals had been through.

- The intervention is easier when the boss has good interpersonal and group-process skills. For those who are less skilled in human relations than Margaret, the process is more labored and needs more outside facilitation. Nevertheless, the results are still positive.
- Organizational survivors easily make the connection between the grieving process and their survivor symptoms.

Empowering Leaders Through Models of Change

The examples in this chapter are not intended to present an unchanging methodology but to illustrate the wide number of options and latitude for creativity available to intervenors. Interventions can be facilitated by helping professionals or skilled managers from inside or outside the organization. However, because internal managers and staff are also survivors, are part of the system, and at times are in a codependent relationship with the system, initial interventions typically work best when done in partnership with an outsider. In addition, level 2 interventions should not be started without a diagnosis of the organizational culture and the depth and breadth of layoff survivor symptoms. The most productive diagnostic process involves a partnership between someone outside the system, such as an external consultant, and someone inside the system, such as a line manager. If line managers play roles in the intervention itself, they should also have guidance from a trained helping professional.

These caveats do not mean that organizations should forever rely on outsiders for level 2 interventions. To the contrary, such reliance on forces outside the system to solve the system's problem creates an unhealthy dependency and disempowers managers. The need for level 2 interventions is so widespread that the best gift an outsider can give any organization is the capacity to continue the process long after the outsider has ridden off into the sunset. One natural way organizations accomplish this transference is by developing a cadre of trained internal intervenors. This cadre usually comes from staff groups such as human resources or organization development.

Although empowering these staff groups to help deal with survivor issues is very helpful, a second level of empowerment is necessary to complete the job. This level comes into play at the interface between employee and boss. The most effective level 2 work takes place at this interface. Two straightforward interventions are of great assistance when an organization wants to spread helping skills throughout the natural management structure: train managers in the helping skills that are relevant to their new-paradigm role and give them a model for grieving.

Helping Skills

Ask any old paradigm manager and, sadly, many of today's business schools to define the manager's role, and their description will usually be some combination of the trite and dusty "-ings" of the machine age: planning, organizing, directing, coordinating, evaluating. Most of these old paradigm managerial functions involve data that can be generated by a computer and handled directly by the employee without any management interaction.

The real role of managers in the new paradigm is helping. Managers with basic helping skills are powerful tools in a survivor workforce. No one likes to be directed, organized, coordinated, or controlled. When these things are done "to" employees, they turn around and do them "to" someone else. The result is a manipulative, codependent workforce bonded around everything but good work. Level 2 interventions require helping, empowering, coaching, and listening skills. I am always amazed at the rapidity with which line managers (even those who see themselves as bottom-line-oriented, hard-boiled, or tough-minded) can learn and use basic helping skills (Figure 8.3). A helping skills workshop for all managers and organizational reinforcement of new paradigm skills and behaviors through the performance appraisal and compensation systems can be powerful tools for ushering in new paradigm behavior.

A Model of Grieving

Consultants perform an important transference intervention when they help organizations develop the internal capacity to facilitate

**Figure 8.3. Changing Old Paradigm "-ings"
to New Paradigm "-ings"**

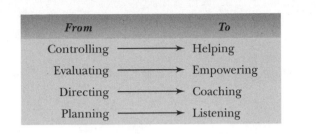

From		To
Controlling	⟶	Helping
Evaluating	⟶	Empowering
Directing	⟶	Coaching
Planning	⟶	Listening

survivors' catharsis and grieving. Consultants should also give organizations a good theory or model to support their work with survivors. In my early work, I was oriented toward skills, not theory. I thought managers were more interested in doing than in theories of why they were doing. Since then I have discovered the power of Elisabeth Kübler-Ross's model of the stages of grieving (Kübler-Ross, 1969) and have learned that managers like theories and models.

The Kübler-Ross theory both legitimizes survivor feelings and provides a common language for facilitators and survivors to use when they discuss previously repressed survivor feelings. The Kübler-Ross model has five stages:

1. Denial
2. Anger, including rage, envy, and resentment
3. Bargaining
4. Depression, which includes sadness, gloominess, pessimism, guilt, and feelings of worthlessness
5. Acceptance, which is not equated with happiness

The Kübler-Ross model presents a frame of reference that many managers find useful for understanding and legitimizing survivors' grieving processes. In the following list, I have connected Kübler-Ross's stages to the experiences of layoff survivors and layoff victims in order to help intervenors stimulate head and heart communication.

Layoff Victim

Stage 1: denial

"It can't happen to me."

Stage 2: anger

"It's not fair."

"I can't act out my anger and rage."

"I resent those who stayed."

Stage 3: bargaining

"I'm better than some who are staying. Keep me."

"Can I get longer notice or better terms?"

Stage 4: depression

"I feel sad and pessimistic."

"I'm not worth keeping."

Stage 5: acceptance

"I'm cut out of the system."

Layoff Survivor

Stage 1: denial

"That's the way businesses operate."

"I'm not a victim, not emotionally involved."

Stage 2: anger

"I can't act out my feelings of anger."

"I feel guilty and angry that I remain employed."

"I feel separated—I'm a victim too."

Stage 3: bargaining

"How can I negotiate my own safety?"

"Can we look at options other than laying off my colleagues?"

Stage 4: depression

"It's bound to happen to me sooner or later."

"I've lost my joy in work and spontaneity."

Stage 5: acceptance

"I'm not the same—I've been violated."

Learnings and Implications

Today, most layoff survivors are suppressing strong, toxic, and debilitating survivor emotions. Level 2 interventions help them express these feelings and get them out on the table so they can be dealt with. Emotional release and the necessary grieving over the layoffs and a lost way of life are prerequisites to healing. Facilitating the release and the grieving is a key management role.

In order to help others, organizational leaders must first help themselves. They must confront their own survivor feelings and get past their natural repression and shame. They must discover that

it is okay to feel bad, that survivor feelings are a natural consequence of old paradigm conditioning carried over to the new reality. But it is not right for anyone to avoid dealing with survivor
sickness. Repression of survivor symptoms is hazardous to individual and organizational health.

Dealing with repressed survivor feelings and facilitating grieving is not the end of the intervention process. But the catharsis that
occurs during level 2 interventions is a milestone along the road
that will lead to individuals' breaking organizational codependency
and becoming self-empowered. Third-level interventions, which will
help individuals reach this goal, are the subject of the next chapter.

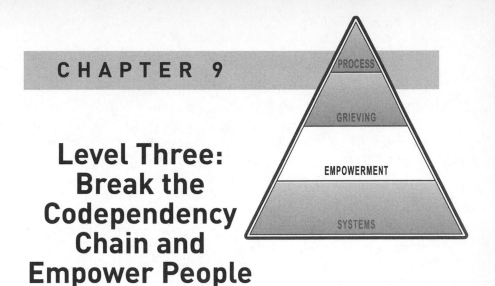

CHAPTER 9

Level Three: Break the Codependency Chain and Empower People

"It isn't necessarily a commitment to the company; it's a commitment to the kind of work that I do. So it's a commitment to my own self, and it's a commitment to my department too, but not necessarily a commitment to the company."

Third-level interventions represent a basic shift in focus from earlier interventions. Levels 1 and 2 react to existing layoff survivor symptoms; level 3 offers the possibility of preventing survivor symptoms in the first place. Level 3 interventions are both more complex and more hopeful than levels 1 and 2. They are complex because they are played out within each person's human spirit. They are optimistic because they have the potential to help people move from being victims to being adventurers in control of their own identity, happiness, and creative powers. The field of codependency research and treatment offers both a language and a frame of reference that can help managers and employees understand how to bring about this optimistic transformation.

Dagwood's Prescient Stand

Cartoonists, particularly those with staying power, offer uncanny insights into our collective psyche and social values. Nearly two decades ago, on Sunday, September 6, 1992, millions of Americans awoke to find new paradigm behavior unfolding in the comics of their morning paper. After more than fifty years in an abusive, manipulative relationship, Dagwood Bumstead, the prototypical old employment contract employee, walked into his boss's office and, standing tall, with fists clenched and a resolute expression, told Mr. Dithers that he was quitting. Not only was he quitting, he was going to work for his wife, Blondie, in her catering business. What may have seemed one small step for a cartoon character was a giant leap forward in symbolic terms: Dagwood had broken the chains of organizational codependency.

Art does imitate life. Back in 1992, the nature of the employment contract represented by the relationship of Dagwood and Mr. Dithers was beginning to unravel, but in many quarters, it was still powerful. Cartoonists Dean Young and Stan Drake illustrated something beyond the obvious easing of the old stereotypes and their unnecessary limitations. They showed the personal courage an employee must have to break out of an employment relationship that is hazardous to his or her self-esteem and personal authenticity. When Dagwood Bumstead got mad as hell and wouldn't take it anymore, he not only walked away from the J. C. Dithers Company, he walked away from organizational codependency and toward personal empowerment. That, I suspect, is why many of us cheered him. Alas, two weeks later, we opened our Sunday papers and found our hero had fallen. He returned to J. C. Dithers Company, crestfallen, having been fired by Blondie for eating the catering business's profits.

Dagwood's brief flirtation with empowerment demonstrates three realities of organizational codependency: (1) risk taking and courage are necessary to break out of a codependent employment relationship, (2) it is easier to become empowered than to remain empowered, and (3) codependency is a disease in and of itself. Dagwood, as a personality archetype, is hard-wired to be a permanent victim.

Codependent Relationships

Humans beginning with Adam and Eve have had codependent relationships. The term, however, was first used only in 1979, and to describe the relationship of a significant other with an alcoholic (Beattie, 1987). The initial, and relatively simple, idea was that people who deny their feelings, alter their identity, and invest a great amount of energy in the attempt to control an alcoholic share the alcoholic's addiction: they are codependent with the alcoholic. The idea has been expanded to cover many other forms of addiction, and some social scientists think that codependency is an underlying primary disease in itself.

Third-level interventions help individuals break organizational codependency and lead a self-empowered life. When individuals are self-empowered and have personal control of their self-esteem and sense of relevance, they are immune to layoff survivor sickness.

A vivid example. A feminist colleague uses this story to illustrate one dimension of codependency and the way self-esteem and identity are held hostage in a codependent relationship:

> A woman was swimming alone on a secluded beach when she was caught in a riptide and swept out to sea. Luckily a lifeguard happened to see her from a distance, sprinted down the beach, and eventually pulled her from the water. She was in bad shape, and initially he thought she was gone. But miraculously, after a lengthy period of artificial respiration, she eventually came around. By this time, a crowd had gathered, and one inquisitive bystander bent down and asked her, "We almost lost you. What did you think about when you were on the brink?"
>
> She coughed, spit up some saltwater, looked at him, and responded, "As I was dying, my husband's whole life flashed before my eyes!"

Organizational Codependency

Here is how I use the concept of codependency in an organizational context. Just as a person can exist in a codependent state with another person in relation to an addiction, a person can also be codependent with an organizational system. People who are organizationally codependent have enabled the system to control their sense of worth and self-esteem at the same time that they invest tremendous energy attempting to control the system.

People are the carriers of organizational codependency. The network of organizational codependency can be visualized as a series of chain links, from bottom to top and across all levels, as though a chain-mesh fish net covered the organizational pyramid, with each link a reciprocal codependent relationship. The people in these relationships are ensnared in a collective Abilene paradox: they are all conspiring to be collectively something that they do not want to be individually.

Relationships that are free of unhealthy control and dependency are fun, spontaneous, and creative. The same is true of organizations. Organizations that are free of codependency are vibrant, open, and productive. They are filled with employees who are invested in good work and managers who are competent in helping skills. Although they too may have layoffs, their survivors are largely immune to survivor sickness because the survivors (and those laid off) index their self-esteem and sense of personal worth not to the organization but rather to their own good work. Layoff survivor sickness is dealt a double blow in these organizations: employees are virtually immune because they are not unhealthily dependent, and the organizations tend to be much more productive and competitive because employees' immunity frees up employee energy and creativity. Thus, the incidence of layoffs is reduced.

A primary symptom of codependency is that the codependent's sense of value and identity is based on pleasing, and often controlling, not himself or herself but someone or something else. Codependents make themselves into permanent victims. People suffering from layoff survivor sickness are similar full-time victims. Survivor symptoms are caused by survivors' surrendering to organizationally imposed values and organizationally imposed identity. The primary level 3 intervention brings about the effort that will break this codependent relationship.

Breaking any codependent relationship is a struggle requiring a personal act of courage. That is why we admired Dagwood Bumstead's effort. Even though he failed, he tried to rid himself of what—despite the humor and stereotyping—in real life would be an unhealthy and manipulative employment relationship. Blondie too made and implemented a courageous decision when, over Dagwood's earlier protestations, she started her own business. I hope Blondie and Dagwood hang around the cartoon strips for another fifty years. It will be interesting to see how they fare. Living free of any form of codependency is a lifetime effort. Each individual's goal is to live life as an adventurer, not as a victim.

To break the organizational codependency chain, individuals must maintain internal control, keep their personal power, and love themselves without making this love conditional on organizational approval. They must maintain their authenticity, without obsessively and schizophrenically attempting to both please and control the system. The organizational goal is empowered employees working with minimal control. They work because they are invested in the task and interested in a quality product, not because they need to control or please others to maintain their self-esteem. Like individuals' efforts, organizations' efforts to maintain a culture that allowed empowerment and shuns codependency must be unending.

Several common codependency treatment strategies can be effectively translated into level 3 survivor interventions: detachment, letting go, and connecting with a core purpose.

Detachment

In codependency treatment, detachment is a facilitating strategy. Without detachment, the codependent cannot take actions that promote personal autonomy and healing. In classic codependency treatment, the object of this detachment is the addicted other. Codependents must detach themselves to the point where they no longer index their self-esteem and identity to the behavior of this other. Detachment is also necessary to break organizational codependency. If who you are is where you work, you will do almost anything to hang on. If employees derive their sense of identity, self-esteem, and uniqueness from pleasing the boss and remaining in an organizational system, they are in an organizationally codependent relationship. They have given up their uniqueness; their focus and energy are external, artificial, and bent on pleasing.

Good Work

The quest for good work is the most important task any of us undertakes in our work lives. It means finding work that is a manifestation of our human spirit—work that is in congruence with our individual uniqueness, sense of purpose, and relevance. It doesn't need to be lofty, cerebral, or antiseptic. If serving others is our unique gift, good work can be plain, gritty, and humbling. Discovering our core purpose and grounding our self-esteem in work that is congruent with that purpose is the foundation to an organizational detachment strategy because we index our self-esteem on our tasks and our work, not the organization where we happen to perform those tasks. Good work always starts internally and is the outward expression of our unique gifts and talents. In its essence, good work is internally goal driven, not externally relationship driven. The purpose of good work is to produce something or to accomplish a task of internal value, not to please the boss or impress the system. Pleasing the boss or impressing the system may happen as a consequence of good work, but these consequences are not the primary intent of good work. Good work is a basic component of the new psychological employment contract, which is short term and task oriented. When Paul Hirsch (1987) calls for "free agent management" and advocates loyalty to self as opposed to organizational loyalty, he is advocating the new employment contract. Because this contract is grounded in good work, not in pleasing relationships, it promotes detachment. Conversely, because it was grounded in relationships and pleasing, the old psychological contract stimulated codependency.

The Seductiveness of Person Capturing

Organizations of the past have been very good at sucking the autonomy from employees and fostering institutional codependency. The seductiveness of the process is illustrated by the budget presentation of a human resource director in an old employment contract organization that was just beginning to feel the ascendancy of the new paradigm.

Brenda began by outlining a number of the strategies the organization had in place to meet the "continuum" of employee "needs."

These strategies included benefit plans, recreation programs, group travel benefits, day care, tuition reimbursement plans, and a comprehensive career planning system. Brenda finished her presentation with details of a new "talent management system." Her concluding statement was that these strategies served to "tie the employee to the organization over the long term" and helped to "capture the total person." However, this organization's difficulty was that it had already captured too many people and tied them in too well. It needed to untie many. It had too much talent that was too expensive and too many people managing that talent. The last thing it needed was a new talent management system.

"Person capturing" is an old-paradigm strategy. For example, career planning in Brenda's organization took a long-term view of employees. Career paths had been laid out by the organization during its days of stability and predictability. However, because employment in the new paradigm is neither predictable nor stable, this organization's career planning was irrelevant to the new reality. Worse, the implied promise of long-term planned careers had created employee dependency. The implied promise had been effectively shattered during the heavy layoffs that had recently plagued the organization. However, organizations typically hold on tenaciously to the assumptions in the old contract long after their utility has disappeared. The idea of holding on to employees in order to be prepared for a predictable future is seductive and hard to shake.

Despite its recent layoffs, Brenda's organization approved her budget, and the old strategy carried on for one more year, even though the real need was for management to communicate the impending reductions and develop strategies of detachment that would enable people to take individual control over their career planning, rather than trust that vital task to an institution. As the recent global financial meltdown has painfully proven, the world economy is too complex, interconnected, and volatile for anyone to trust that any one organization can "take care of them."

Diffuse Root Strategy

Despite increasing evidence as to the disutility of the old strategy, many organizations continue to delude themselves, and many of their employees, by attempting to tie in the employees. In these cases, the employees must untie themselves.

The detachment process begins with an individual's decision not to rely on an employer to nurture all aspects of his or her life. The basic change that must occur can be most easily illustrated by comparing two plants. One plant gets all its nourishment from a single taproot, just as an employee's self-esteem, identity, and social worth can all be nourished by a single organization (Figure 9.1). When this is the case, the codependent will manipulate, cajole, control, and scheme simply to hang on. Considering the option, manipulating and controlling make sense. What happens if that single taproot gets cut? If who you are is where you work, what are you if you lose your job?

Another plant may have a diffuse root system, reaching out to different areas of soil. Emotionally healthy individuals reject the

Figure 9.1. Taproot Strategy

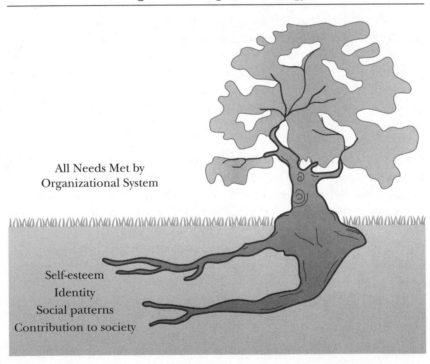

All Needs Met by
Organizational System

Self-esteem
Identity
Social patterns
Contribution to society

Figure 9.2. Diffuse Root Strategy

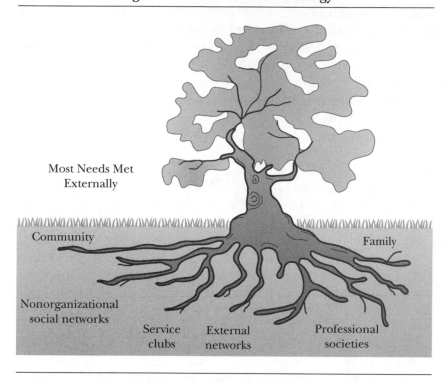

simplicity and seductiveness of having all their needs nourished through a taproot into the organizational soil. Through planning and effort, they develop a diffuse root system (Figure 9.2). They establish a nondependent relationship, so that if the organizational root is cut, they can still grow and thrive. It is simple and effective for managers to ask employees to diagram their own root systems. Many employees are surprised to find that they have a virtual taproot into their organization. Their discovery can stimulate them to cultivate other options, and diffuse roots.

Although detachment is a primary intervention in all codependency, achieving detachment is a continuing battle for many. One view of codependency is that it exists both in relation to a specific situation, alcoholism, for example, and as a disease in itself. This means that those with the illness of codependence who are left untreated will go through life moving from one codependent situation to another. Dagwood went back to Mr. Dithers, and we have all seen employees who seemed to have broken the codependency chain move into organizational situations that have restored their codependency. Both the specific situation and the underlying disease must be treated. Level 3 interventions deal with the specific codependency situation. However, since employees spend the majority of their waking hours in working situations, these interventions may also contribute to the solution of the underlying disease.

Letting Go

Codependents feel compelled to control others. "We nag; lecture; scream; holler; cry; beg; bribe; coerce; hover over; protect; accuse; chase after; run away from; try to talk into; try to talk out of; attempt to induce guilt in" the other person (Beattie, 1987, p. 69). When they are controlling another's behavior, codependents often operate outside reality. If you are a codependent, you will try to "force life's events to unravel and unfold in the manner and at such times as you have designated. Do not let what's happening, or what might happen occur. Hold on tightly and don't let go. We have written the play, and will see to it that the actors behave and the scenes unfold exactly as we have decided they should. Never mind that we continue to buck reality. If we charge ahead insistently enough, we can (we believe) stop the flow of life, transform people, and change things to our liking" (p. 71).

In the second act, as I did in the first, I see employees of all ages and generational stereotypes desperately trying to retain control of a decaying and nonproductive work environment. They are often consumed in acting out a play that closed long ago. The old employment contract is dead, and holding on to it is toxic to the human spirit. Despite this reality, workers and unions continue to cajole and demand job security and higher wages for unchanged work and productivity. The newer generation Y employees, who grew up expecting immediate gratification and in an educational system that sought to protect them as much as possible from experiencing failure, seek simple answers to complex problems, looking for someone to blame and seldom looking within themselves or the system. Middle managers set up elaborate control systems to artificially maintain managerial influence in the face of information technology that makes their information exchange role outdated. Top managers cling to fantasies of organizational permanence and long-term decision making. During crises such as layoffs, controls are intensified, information is managed, the truth is feared, and straight talk is driven underground by control talk.

The paradox of codependency is that the controllers are always controlled; that is what makes them codependent. The alcoholic dances a control dance with the codependent other, but the alcoholic always leads. Organizational codependents are ultimately controlled by the organizational system. The more they try to turn back the clock, manage the natural flow of honest information, ignore the facts in favor of an artificial reality, or suppress their own needs and feelings, the more they dance to the very tune they are attempting to control. They become focused on controlling reality rather than helping the organization be productive within the real world. The journey from organizational codependency to autonomy and independence involves moving away from an organizational identity to one of personal relevance and meaning (Figure 9.3).

Organizational codependents need to admit the folly of their attempts to control an uncontrollable situation and then let go. They must trust their own perceptions. This puts them in a bind.

Figure 9.3. Moving from Organizational Codependency to Autonomy and Independence

From	To
Who you are is where you work.	Who you are is what you do.
Social network revolves around the organization.	Social network is external to the organization.
Self-esteem is grounded in organizational affiliation.	Self-esteem is grounded in one's profession or skill set.
Contribution is indexed in organizational approval.	Contribution is indexed in one's self-evaluated good work.
Strategy of controlling and manipulating.	Strategy of letting go and detaching.

Codependents tend not to trust their perceptions unless they are validated by someone else (Schaef, 1986). However, because codependent organizations are made up of interlocking webs of codependent relationships, and no one in these organizations trusts his or her own perception about the emperor's lack of clothes, validation is hard to come by. That is why the nondependent outsider, or an insider with the courage to speak up, is often the one who breaks the logjam. In fact, speaking what to an organization is the unspeakable is often what the organization perceives as the best use of an outsider intervener's skills. I call this a *straight-talk intervention*. Such interventions do not always work, but when they do, they are dynamite. An example of the liberating power of straight talk took place at a firm I will call XYZ Company.

The Agony and the Ecstasy of Straight Talk

The top management team of XYZ, a small professional organization, met one weekend at a resort to work on a strategic plan, which they visualized as a formal document that would be distributed to all employees. The organization had lost a large contract and as a result had a significant revenue shortfall. The members of the top team were contemplating a significant cutback of professional staff, even though they prided themselves on never having laid people off in the past. Prior to the meeting, the top team engaged in abstractions and speeches on the subject of the lost contract, but team members did not discuss what the organization was going to do about the revenue shortfall. When I pressed the issue during interviews before the meeting, the conversations grew strained and stilted.

During the morning of the first day of the planning meeting, the team members developed an elaborate procedure to outline their external and internal environment, formulate their "driving force," develop a series of strategic goals, relate the goals to their mission statement, and draw up short-term action steps. On the surface, they were working well and doing a good job of developing a traditional strategic plan, but the event had an artificial feeling, like a play with bored actors going through the motions.

That afternoon, it was clear that something was fundamentally wrong. The group had no energy, the plan was just a series of words on flip charts, and no one had even addressed the revenue shortfall. When the group reconvened after dinner, I confronted them with straight talk. I fed back the themes of the premeeting interviews and my observation that some norm was preventing people from talking about the immediate financial problem and that the meeting thus far was a victory of form over substance. I asked, "Why is it not okay to discuss this issue?" I was persistent, but what was even more important was that, beneath the surface, the group wanted to get the issues on the table.

Eventually there occurred what a group member graphically called "squeezing the boil." The issues all came out, as he said, in "one gooey wad!" The trigger was one person taking a risk: having the courage to speak his mind and tell the truth. His straight talk revealed a number of issues that were creating group paralysis. The managing partner, new in his role, did not know what to do and was afraid of looking bad to his colleagues. He was so consumed with controlling his image and hiding his fear that he repressed the financial issue. The others, knowing there would have to be a reduction, were protecting their own staffs. They did not want to raise the issue and be the ones to trigger the cutback. The administrative vice president was afraid for his job and felt sure that if there were reductions, the nonprofessional staff would be the first to go. The culture of the organization was conflict averse and nonconfrontational. Essentially the top team was hoping that if it controlled the organizational reality, the problem would go away.

Straight talk begets straight talk, and by the end of that planning meeting, team members had come to grips with their revenue issue, giving each other honest feedback for the first time and beginning the long and painful path toward authenticity and letting go.

Shedding covert control needs is not a one-shot proposition, and this management team is still in process after holding a number of what the members now call "straight-talk sessions." The company did experience a small layoff, but the top managers were able to deal with their bottom-line issue primarily through stringent cost control, including a salary cut and a bonus moratorium for the top team.

"If Only"

The career of an industrial/organizational psychologist exemplifies the way an individual codependent holds on to codependency. Edith had emerged from a Ph.D. program at a midwestern university as a classic "dust bowl empiricist." To her, there was no knowledge except that which could be quantified, statistically analyzed, and measured. Her need to see the world in terms of predictable, and therefore manipulatable, data points predisposed her to the control orientation that was to paralyze her later in her organizational life.

After a brief flirtation with academia, she went to work in the human resource function of a large organization. It was a traditional old employment contract organization, still in the growth phase, unaware that disaster was lurking just around the corner. Edith became the queen of measurement. She did test validation, performance management studies, employee attitude surveys, training evaluation studies, and anything else that could be quantified, measured, and reported to upper management. When the first round of layoffs hit, she was managing a small group of three other psychologists and a support staff of five.

Edith's boss was abusive and sexist, and he took personal credit from top management for much of Edith's excellent work. She spent a lot of energy managing (controlling) her relationship with him through a wide range of controlling behavior: denying what was happening, telling him what he wanted to hear, hiding the abusive relationship from her staff by meeting with him only one-on-one, and threatening to go to top management unless he changed.

She also controlled her staff and her colleagues. She was a perfectionist, wanting all her reports in a format and context predetermined down to the color and size of the paper. When she worked on cross-functional task forces, she wanted people outside her function to understand her data the way she did and was frustrated if they came to other conclusions. She spent much energy attempting to control their interpretation, often through overwhelming them with data. She played the "if only" game: if only they had enough information, they would react the way she wanted them to react. She did not see this as a question of whether they could have their own opinion. For her, it was simply a process of moving them to the "correct" conclusion—hers!

Edith's top management interactions were also marred by the if-only game. When some executives, in order to avoid Edith's data overload, requested Edith's employees to make reports, she coached the employees in ways of controlling interpretations, thus killing two birds with one stone; she overloaded and controlled her subordinates and top management at the same time.

Her reaction to layoffs was an extended if-only game. She entered into a massive internal advertising and public relations campaign designed to communicate the message, "If only you understood the good things I am doing for the organization, you could come to no other conclusion than to retain me and my staff!" Her boss, colleagues, and top management received reports, charts, graphs, and personal presentations, all suggesting her irreplaceability. When, despite her efforts, she was ordered to terminate her support staff and all but one psychologist, she redoubled her efforts to prove her value. When the inevitable happened and she too was "taken out" of the organization, leaving only her former subordinate in place of her entire department, she was shattered.

The happy ending of this story is that Edith's termination served as her wake-up call. Through a combination of therapy, career counseling, and an ongoing support group, Edith has come to grips with her codependent control needs. Now a partner in a very small consulting firm, she considers herself "a recovering codependent."

The examples of the XYZ Company and Edith are by no means extreme cases. They exemplify the common holding-on behavior found in most organizational systems. There are six learnings from these examples.

Letting-Go Learnings

- Not telling the truth, repressing reality, and holding back feelings and perceptions are forms of denial. These controlling behaviors actually shift control from the self to the other (in those examples, to an organization). These behaviors are contagious, and as illustrated in the XYZ example, they can result in a collective disavowal of reality. If unchallenged, they can result in organizational failure.
- Truth telling is a powerful letting-go intervention. It usually is an act of individual courage since it often violates a strong cultural norm. Truth telling too is contagious and frequently results in freeing up people's energy so that they can deal with fundamental organizational issues.
- Attempting to control others so they do what the controller wants them to do or be what the controller wants them to be, as opposed to what they want to do or be, is a futile and manipulative effort. Its predictable results are a movement of control

from the would-be controller to the other; the loss of personal power, autonomy, and self-esteem; and the interminable and draining investment of energy to control the uncontrollable.

- Controlling, whether through denial (repressing individual perceptions of the truth) or overt manipulation (attempting to induce others to think, do, or act the way the controller wants them to), is a major cause of organizational codependency and increases susceptibility to layoff survivor sickness.

- Letting go of the need to define oneself through others' behavior and reclaiming individual control of self-esteem is the major antidote for self-destructive control needs. Letting go is not easy. It requires constant struggle, feedback, and support at both the individual (Edith example) and organizational (XYZ example) level.

- Letting go is an act of faith. It is often terrifying because as crummy as things are, at least you know what they are. A venture into the unknown has been compared to moving through a series of trapezes. In order to maintain momentum, you have to let go of one and have faith that there will be another to take its place. There is a terrible moment of fright when you have let go of the old and the new is not yet there to grab. Such is the nature of personal growth. If you do not let go, you will have absolute control, but you won't go anywhere. You will be hanging, alone and isolated, in control but hollow and separate. If you take the leap of faith and let go, you will continue to move, you will still be in process—there is always another trapeze out there—but you will have the adventure of recapturing your destiny. It is a paradox with no respite on either side. Letting go frees you to grow, but growth forces you to accept a continuing disequilibrium. Holding on offers predictability, but you cannot hold on forever. Eventually fatigue will cause you to drop into the void of continued codependency. It is far better to undertake the adventure, frightening though it may be.

Connecting with a Core Purpose

The third set of organizational codependency immunization activities involves tapping into a core purpose. This is a powerful yet elusive quest, for it is a spiritual journey. In traditional codependence parlance, this is the twelve-step program originally developed for alcoholics. It requires the recovering person to surrender and give himself or herself over to a greater power. The twelfth step reads, "Having had a spiritual awakening as the result of these [eleven previous] steps, we try to carry this message to alcoholics, and to practice these principles in all our affairs" (Beattie, 1987, p. 189). Today the twelve-step program is used in treating all manner of addictions, including codependency. The program has a natural position in the flow of third-level interventions: individuals must first detach, then stop controlling, and finally awaken to unifying purpose and identity. Detachment and letting go are about removal; connecting with a core purpose is a putting back.

Connecting with an underlying purpose or mission has a spiritual dimension that may or may not be formally religious in nature. Each person must determine his or her unique purpose in life. In many organizations, this purpose is difficult for people to discuss since these organizations have norms against talking about spirituality or personal meaning. Since most organizational leaders now realize that business organizations are the social systems in which people spend large parts of their lives, these norms are unproductive holdovers from the old paradigm. Part—perhaps the most essential part—of the human condition involves our quest for meaning and relevance in the universe. To assume that we set aside this basic human pursuit when we enter the workplace is to deny a basic reality.

Don't Place Your Spiritual Currency in the Organizational Vault

Under the old paradigm, a great deal of people's sense of relevance and purpose was provided by the organization, which behaved somewhat like a religious institution. A small consumer finance organization that had been acquired by a larger financial services institution is a good example. There was a hierarchical all-male "priesthood" that culminated in a charismatic founding father who was deified by the employees and responded by dispensing gifts (a year-end bonus and promotions) to the loyal. This organization had its catechism in the form of a belief system that customer service was supreme and a demand that personal needs be subordinated to an overarching organizational loyalty, with the ultimate reward of continued employment and the honor of being part of the team.

This organization had other characteristics of a formal religion: a regular Saturday morning meeting (service), with stories of sales and quota achievements followed by applause, handshakes, and affirming smiles (testimonies), and a pep talk by the founding father (sermon). There were rewards (gift certificates for dinners for two dispensed to some who had done an extra-good job) and symbols (a watch commemorating fifteen years of membership in the congregation). The organization did not have a company song, but it did have a number of mottos and slogans tacked to office walls. I learned some things they did not teach me in graduate school from this organization. First, this structure did not feel contrived, and it worked: the organization was highly productive and efficient. Second, the organization was essentially a spiritual place. Employees derived a sense of purpose, worth, and value from it. Unfortunately, because the organization was newly acquired, it then experienced a layoff and was the unwilling recipient of a number of policies and procedures that stripped away its uniqueness.

That, of course, is the moral of the story. It is not healthy to place one's spiritual currency in business organizations' vaults. The organization cannot guarantee that currency's safety. This view of the organization as a religious system is not limited to small firms with a hands-on, charismatic leadership. A study of the history of IBM, just one example of large organizations, reveals ceremonial rites of passage, revival meetings (100 percent clubs), and strong spiritual cultlike norms of conformity. When the first act took place, the spiritual bond it once had with its employees cracked, the congregation became confused, and the organization had to reinvent itself.

People need a more personal, more secure, and less organizationally dependent sense of purpose or spirit. This does not mean that they cannot or should not attempt to find meaning or purpose within business organizations. It does suggest that the origin of an individual's purpose and spiritual meaning ought to start within the individual and spill out into organizations. Purpose should not be a property of the organization, flowing from the organization to the employee and conditional on continued "membership."

Core Purpose Exercises

The pilgrimage to seek personal meaning and purpose does not lend itself to prescription. However, the pilgrimage is often started by a wake-up call. Wake-up calls may result from layoffs as well as from attention-getting devices: heart attacks, deaths of people close to us, and divorces, for example. Such intensely emotional events cause people to ask deep and searching questions. For this reason, the trauma surrounding organizational unraveling provides excellent teaching and learning opportunities. The following exercises are of value in seeking a core purpose:

- *Write a personal mission statement.* Individuals can also be asked to share their statements with significant others in and out of the organization. This sharing results in feedback, provides a reality check, and stimulates communication. Individuals often find great value in this experience. For example, one manager had his wife and children sign his mission statement, which he now displays in his office.
- *Develop a lifeline.* Individuals prepare graphs outlining their personal highs and lows from birth to the present and then project this lifeline to their projected date of death. They must also predict their cause of death. People are always shocked when they look at actuarial tables and family histories and discover how few good years they have left. Next, they outline what they want to accomplish during the remaining years. Sometimes they write their own obituaries and have others read them. This is a serious, introspective, and powerful experience that often leads to clear values and basic spiritual insights.
- *View the organization as religious institution.* Following a discussion of symbols, artifacts, and belief systems, individuals write a story of their organization as a temple, synagogue, mosque, church, or any other formal religious structure. Afterward they examine the degree to which they derive spiritual satisfaction from the organization and then write another story in which they are "excommunicated." Alternatively they can be asked to pick the symbols, rituals, and belief systems that are most important to the organization and imagine what would

happen in a takeover by another religion with opposing belief systems and rituals.

- *Define good work.* In this guided imagery process, participants explore what for them, and uniquely for them, constitutes good work. They explore periods of extreme joy in work, work spirit, and personal satisfaction; contrast these experiences with opposite experiences; and attempt to distill the core components of their personal good work.

Exercises such as these are short-term, relatively canned experiences. By themselves, they will not provide a long-term, fundamental sense of purpose or individual mission. They can, however, stimulate the quest for this purpose. Organizational survivors who take these exercises seriously can achieve an impressive depth of self-discovery in a relatively short period of time.

Regardless of how this third component of breaking organizational codependency is accomplished, it is at the heart of the personal empowerment that prevents layoff survivor sickness. Possession of a personal sense of purpose and mission enables employees to retain internal control and accomplish good work in their lives, regardless of organizational boundaries.

Learnings and Implications

Organizational codependency is seductive. Its current manifestation is the result of more than fifty years of post–World War II organizational strategies designed to tie employees in for the long term. It is easy to be lulled into a pattern of pleasing and controlling. We must have the courage to engage in detachment, stop defining ourselves in relation to our organizational affiliation, and resist the simplicity of putting a taproot into organizational soil. We need to stop controlling and manipulating the system and let go. Above all, we need to connect with something bigger than ourselves, with a personal core purpose. The result will be a rebirth of spirit, self-control, and a work relationship centered on good work, as opposed to manipulation and control.

Breaking organizational codependency is essentially an individual effort. The individual detaches her or his identity from the organizational culture. Organizations too need to detach, let go, and discover their core purposes. Organizational struggles mirror individual efforts, and it is difficult for organizations to detach from their paternalism. Moving away from employee control and toward true employee empowerment means letting go of an attitude rooted in history. Searching for a new purpose and vision in the face of global competition and world economic parity involves the pain of creating a new identity. However, for both individuals and organizations, the gain is well worth the pain. The payoff is survival and relevance in the new paradigm. Reformulated organizations have the opportunity to create systems and processes congruent with the new employment contract and form a new partnership with empowered employees who have broken the chain of code-pendency. This partnership is the subject of the next chapter.

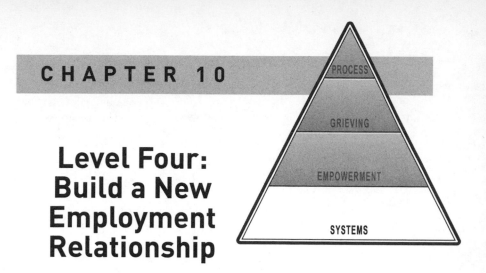

CHAPTER 10

Level Four: Build a New Employment Relationship

"I am committed to my customers. I am committed to the people who use my services, and it doesn't make any difference where I work; it's the people that I work with that I really enjoy, and I really want to do a good job for them."

Level 4 interventions create systems and processes that structurally mitigate layoff survivor sickness. These interventions grow out of the new psychological employment contract. Tables 10.1 and 10.2 outline the implicit assumptions, strategies, and outcomes of the old and new employment contracts.

Table 10.1. Old Employment Contract

Implicit Assumptions (Based on Old Environment)	Strategies	Outcomes (Based on Current Environment)
Employment relationship is long term.	Benefits and services that reward tenure	Older workforce
	Employee recognition processes that reinforce long-term relationship	Demographically narrow workforce

(continued on next page)

Table 10.1. Old Employment Contract, Cont'd.

Implicit Assumptions (Based on Old Environment)	Strategies	Outcomes (Based on Current Environment)
Reward for performance is promotion.	Linear compensation systems	Plateaued workforce
	Linear status symbols	Demotivated (betrayed) workforce
	Fixed job descriptions	
	Static performance standards	
Management is paternalistic.	Excessive and duplicative support services	Dependent workforce
	Long-term career planning systems	
Loyalty means remaining with the organization.	Approved career paths only within the organization	Narrow workforce
	Voluntary turnover penalized	Mediocre workforce
	Internal promotion; discouragement of external hiring	Nondiverse workforce
Lifetime career is offered.	Fitting in	Codependent workforce
	Relationships	

Table 10.2. New Employment Contract

Implicit Assumptions	Strategies	Outcomes
Employment relationship is situational.	Flexible and portable benefit plans	Flexible workforce
	Tenure-free recognition systems	
	Blurred distinction between full-time, part-time, and temporary employees	

Table 10.2. New Employment Contract, Cont'd.

Implicit Assumptions	Strategies	Outcomes
Reward for performance is acknowledgment of contribution and relevance.	Job enrichment and participation	Motivated workforce
	The philosophy of quality	Task-invested workforce
	Self-directed work teams	
	Nonhierarchical performance and reward systems	
Management is empowering.	Employee autonomy	Empowered workforce
	No "taking care" of employees	
	No detailed long-term career planning	
	Tough love	
Loyalty means responsibility and good work.	Nontraditional career paths	Responsible workforce
	Policies that don't penalize employees for leaving or returning	
	Employee choice	
	Accelerated diversity recruiting	
Explicit job contracting is offered.	Short-term job planning	Employee and organization bonded around good work
	Not signing up for life	
	No assumption of lifetime caretaking	

The Global Context of the New Reality

The old psychological contract was forged in the post–World War II culture, where big was better, relationships were long term, and the United States enjoyed a historically derived competitive advantage. Today we live in a global, technically interlocked economy, and many of the old contract's assumptions and strategies are played out against far different realities. As Friedman (2007) points out, technology has leveled the playing field, and the United States now is but one, albeit a key player, in the world economy.

The global epidemic of layoffs is unfolding within diverse economic and social contexts. In North America, the United Kingdom, and parts of Australasia, despite a significant cultural lag from the old psychological contract, the new "free agent" concept is beginning to take root. In much of Western Europe and Scandinavia, the socialist-oriented infrastructure and government regulation of the employment process is based on outdated assumptions of organizational permanence and employment continuity. As these countries experience the economic reality of the second act, layoff survivor stimulated anger will be directed not just toward individual firms but to governmental institutions and political philosophies. In Russia, Eastern Europe, and parts of Central Asia, the old psychological contract never unfolded, and the disappointment of a thwarted dream generates anger and frustration. These feelings are compounded by the return of many guest workers where, in more prosperous countries, they acted as a buffer to better-paid full-time employees. The United States and other Western economies fueled a boom in China, India, Vietnam, and other Asian countries through massive exportation of cheaply manufactured products. With the financial meltdown, Western countries are no longer importing products; they are exporting layoffs. The oil-denominated prosperity of the Persian Gulf is showing the inevitable signs of erosion. Saudi Arabia, for example, is attempting to protect Saudi nationals by sending expatriate workers back to their home countries. Japan, the poster child of the old psychological contract, is desperately struggling to hold on. In Japan and a number of other countries in both Asia and Europe, even though contract, or "guest," workers may have been employed for a number of years, they are not seen as "real," permanent, full-time employees.

These second-class contract workers who constituted a ring of defense to protect "real" employees have been dismissed, and those "real" employees are themselves feeling vulnerable. Because of the high-context, group-oriented Japanese culture, there will be a particularly virulent form of survivor sickness when the inevitable layoffs hit.

The inexorable global shift to the new psychological employment contract will unfold differently within each country and regional culture, but it will indeed unfold. Managers, employees, unions, business owners, and governments will need to adapt to this irrevocable paradigmatic change and adjust to a reality that runs contrary to values conditioned over long periods of time. The differences between the old and the new employment contracts are best understood as a series of shifts from what was to what is.

From Long-Term to Situational Employment Relationships

Organizations operating under the old contract assumed employees would be there over the long haul. They rewarded tenure with trinkets such as tie bars, watches, wall plaques, recreational services, and benefit plans that increased in value with employee tenure. Today organizations are reaping what they have sown. Because of the success of these strategies in establishing long-term commitment, many organizations, public and private, now have an aging, nondiverse, locked-in workforce. This is true throughout the world, but particularly apparent in Western Europe and Japan. As the recession deepens, many will defer retirement, and their survivor sickness will linger with them. Attempting to affix blame is not helpful; we are collectively experiencing the outcome of demographic, cultural, and worldwide competitive changes. Organizations operating in the new paradigm do not need an aging, locked-in workforce. They need just the opposite: a flexible, diverse, and situational employee population. Older, experienced employees offer exceptional value to organizations, and their career options should not be limited because of being financially or emotionally tied to just one organization or because of invalid stereotypical assumptions that lead to age discrimination.

From the employees' perspective, being tied in is confining and no longer feels comfortable. In many countries, employees feel trapped by health insurance plans that cannot be duplicated or afforded outside the organization and pension plans that have a heavily weighted payoff for employee longevity. Many employees are locked into organizations that do not want them and where they themselves want to leave. What are needed are systems compatible with the new reality.

Flexible and Portable Benefit Plans

People's need for adequate and affordable health insurance that is not tied to the place where they work requires a change in national policy in the United States and other countries without optional plans. This change is a priority for both the health of citizens in these countries and the efficiency and competitiveness of their organizations. Although pension plans are portable in some professions—education, for example—pensions remain a difficult and complicated issue, one that tends to lock in rather than free up employees. Government and private sectors must cooperate to solve the problem and develop flexible and portable benefit plans.

Tenure-Free Recognition Systems

Revamping recognition programs is something organizations can accomplish without government assistance. Although it makes no sense to celebrate employees' tenure in an organization attempting to be situational and flexible in the way it employs people, the idea of changing organizational symbols and rituals is hard to sell in organizations where top management has risen up through the ranks and has a great deal of cultural identity invested in honoring tenure. Nonetheless, looking for events to celebrate that are more consistent with the strategy of the new employment contract is an important intervention. It is a relatively small effort with the potential for a large payoff because changing organizational rituals is dramatic and makes a strong statement about the new culture. Here are three suggested changes:

- *Deemphasize and, if possible, discard inappropriate trinkets.* Tie bars, cufflinks, bracelets, wall plaques, and other public symbols that celebrate employee tenure give the wrong message when an organization requires a flexible, situational employment relationship. (Employees in one organization tell the survivor horror story of a well-liked production supervisor who received her ten-year bracelet on a Monday and was laid off that Friday.)

- *Celebrate achievement.* Catch people doing things right, and find a way to publicly reinforce their achievement. There is nothing wrong with using trinkets, dinners, theater tickets, or public pats on the back as rewards as long as they celebrate desired behavior. New employment contract organizations find ways to celebrate goal achievement, excellence in customer service, and good work. They do not have a use for unauthentic relationships based on pleasing others and do not value time spent in the organization.

- *Celebrate departures.* Under the new employment contract, an employee's leaving is a cause for celebration, not lament. If the organizational goal is a just-in-time workforce, one that is situational and available when appropriate good work is needed, the organization will have a continuing flux of arrivals and departures. Leaving will be a planned event, a celebration of achievement. The leaving ritual should be more than a quiet departmental lunch. It should be an organizationally sanctioned event and a rite of passage.

Blurred Distinctions Among Full-Time, Part-Time, and Temporary Employees

Many old employment contract organizations built walls and made clear distinctions among various categories of employees. Full-time, so-called permanent employees were at the top of the scale and temporary part-timers at the bottom. When the organizational goal is a situational employment relationship, the strategy has to develop a much more fluid workforce. In some organizations today, it is impossible to tell whether an employee is a "temp," a "contract," a "part time," or a "full time." This is the trend of the future. Evidence of the demand for the flexible employee is the growth of contract employment firms and temporary help agencies that fill both traditional clerical and newer managerial and technical temporary jobs.

Difficult though it may be in countries such as Japan or those that rely on contract or guest workers as lower-status buffers, it is necessary to develop a truly flexible just-in-time workforce. Organizations must remove artificial pay, benefits, and status distinctions among employee classifications. Given what has been happening in many organizations for the past few years, full-time permanent employees are a rare and endangered species. All employees are now temporary, and artificial status, pay, and benefit differences based on how temporary employees are do not fit into the new paradigm. Organizations that continue to maintain sharp differentiations among employment categories not only cut themselves off from a growing and fresh source of new people and ideas, they put unnecessary barriers in the way of the crucial flexibility they need for future survival.

From Rewarding Performance with Promotion to Rewarding Performance with Acknowledgment of Relevance

A fundamental old paradigm assumption was that the basic reward for employee performance was promotion. In reality, many organizations used promotion to reward factors other than performance, such as loyalty, fitting in, and length of service. Under the old employment contract, organizations developed compensation systems that were hierarchical in scope and linear in design. The way to get more money was to get promoted. Status symbols such as office size, reserved parking spaces, and accessibility to special dining areas were also linked to employees' hierarchical levels. Job descriptions were linked to levels and, in classic Weberian bureaucratic fashion, were arrayed hierarchically, like a pile of blocks. Performance standards, in turn, were linked to these static job descriptions. There was nothing inherently wrong with this arrangement. It served organizations well, given conditions of continued growth, advantages to being large, and long-term predictable planning horizons.

The world, however, has changed. To survive now, organizations are shrinking, accepting short-term planning horizons, demanding employee flexibility, and becoming nimble and responsive to global changes. New paradigm organizations have flattened, or delayered. As Bardwick (1986) pointed out, promotions in these flatter firms are far and few between, and a large percentage of the workforce is structurally plateaued. This plateaued workforce often feels betrayed because it was taught the old paradigm assumption that promotion is the reward for performance, yet organizations cannot deliver on this promise. Promotion was the currency of the old realm. The new realm offers task investment, job enrichment, participation, and a shared vision. The outcome of this new currency is a workforce motivated by task investment in good work. There are several new paradigm strategies that help to create this motivated workforce.

Job Enrichment and Participation

Job enrichment is an old idea whose time has come. The clear linear chain of promotions that characterized the old-employment contract depended on static jobs, but today's organizations need adaptable employees. Organizations should expand jobs laterally, empower employees to make decisions, and form structures to facilitate job enrichment. Job enrichment does not mean simply adding the duties of departed employees to the job descriptions of those who remain; such tactics overwhelm employees and increase their survivor symptoms. True job enrichment eliminates nonessential tasks and invests employees in relevant, useful, achievable work. In the new paradigm, the opportunity to do good work in an enriched, participative environment replaces promotion as a motivator. Employee participation could not grow in the soil of the old paradigm, but within the new, it is a key component of empowerment. Good work is accomplished through employee voice and choice.

The Philosophy of Quality

The total quality movement is another concept that could not flourish in the structured, control-oriented soil of the old paradigm. One of the reasons a total quality movement often starts with a flourish but stalls as it approaches the top of the organization is that those at the top often carry the cultural baggage of the old paradigm into the new reality. To borrow a phrase from an old Chrysler advertisement, "Those at the top had better lead, follow, or get out of the way." The philosophy of quality fits the new employment contract.

It is necessary to separate the bureaucratic wrappings from the essence of the quality philosophy to appreciate the fit. Total quality is not about programs: slick announcements and slogans, hierarchical checking, and patching quality goals onto the existing system. Measurement is important, but only as a means, so quality is not about Pareto charts and histograms. Customer orientation is a total quality core value, but not just because it provides a service focus. A customer focus also gives an organization a structural immunity to the internal relationship focus that leads to organizational codependency.

Separated from its techniques, total quality is about empowered people performing good work that serves others. This theme runs through the basic philosophies (as distinct from the techniques) of all the quality gurus. Whether you follow Philip Crosby, W. Edwards Deming, Armand Feigenbaum, Kaoru Ishikawa, or Joseph Juran, the central idea is the same: the philosophy of quality is empowered people, linked together by good work that serves others. This idea is the essence of the new employment contract.

Self-Directed Work Teams

Another tool that was blunted by the paternalism and control orientation of the old paradigm is good work performed by empowered family, cross-functional, or nonhierarchical teams. Although a number of good techniques are available to help managers develop and empower these teams, it is necessary to separate the techniques from the essence. Self-directed work teams are important in the new employment contract because they require managers to take a helping, facilitating, and coaching role while the empowered teams bond around good work, uninhibited by unnecessary old paradigm controls.

Redirected Performance and Reward Systems

Organizations must make their performance and reward systems relevant to the new paradigm. This may seem obvious, but in many organizations, these systems remain linked to the dying paradigm of the past, a fact that explains the continuing frustration of most managers and employees. Managers need to be appraised and rewarded for new paradigm behaviors, not old paradigm control. If coaching, facilitating, helping, and empowering are the tasks of new paradigm management, the reward system should reinforce these behaviors. *Performance management* describes a number of healthy and productive new approaches that are systemically based and consist of explicit contracting and employee accountability, but the term itself smacks of the old paradigm. *Managing* another person's performance suggests controlling that performance. Far better to name it *performance facilitation, performance empowerment,* or even *performance contracting.* The shift in terminology does not mean that new paradigm performance systems let anyone off the hook. On the contrary, they promote employee responsibility and accountability and free managers to be creative and strategic.

Nonmanagerial employees should be rewarded for networking, teamworking, participating, and producing good task outcomes. Task and accomplishment is the name of the game. The time has come to bury trait-rating systems forever. Organizations must now implement compensation systems that may have seemed radical, illegal, or administratively difficult in the old paradigm. Examples include empowering self-directed work teams to set compensation policy for team members, moving away from monthly and weekly pay increments and toward task-specific payments, and implementing group performance appraisals and rewards.

From Paternalistic to Empowering Management Behavior

Once when I suggested to an organization's management committee that a good start toward the development of an empowered workforce would be to undo some of their paternalistic management practices, they almost threw me out of the room. "Who us, paternalistic?" they exclaimed. "No way! We're a modern organization; we're into participation and total quality! How can we be paternalistic?" However, they eventually discovered that they were indeed paternalistic, and paternalistic managerial behavior does not stimulate empowerment. Instead, it has the opposite effect: creating a dependent, compliant workforce.

Most organizations do not like to think of themselves as paternalistic or, as a female chief operating officer once retorted, "At least call us maternalistic!" But regardless of the label, the reality is that most organizations take pride in "taking care" of their employees. Employee caretaking was an integral part of the old employment contract and is very difficult to reverse, even in the harsh light of the new paradigm. However, organizations must give up caretaking, because employees taken care of by the organization no longer find it necessary to take care of themselves, and their dependency is hazardous to their health. Dependent employees lose skills they must have to thrive in the new paradigm. The result is akin to the fate of wild animals that are taken care of in captivity and then suffer when they are returned to the wild because they lack the skills to fend for themselves. The difference, of course, is that wild animals cannot take charge of their fate. People can: they can learn or relearn needed skills, and organizations must foster this learning.

The roots of the compulsion to take care of employees go deep into human history. Primitive tribes had clear and binding roles and reciprocal obligations of hunting, food gathering, and providing security. Leaders of early settled groups rewarded warriors with land as the spoils of battle. Medieval serfs pledged a portion of their harvest to the nobleman who took care of them by providing protection and land. This idea of taking care of people in exchange for their loyalty and labor was carried on by the old employment contract.

Both employers and employees now find themselves at an interesting place. Modern power holders and employers are unable to maintain their end of the bargain. Their "armies" are merging, and many of their loyal workers are being laid off. History seems to have evolved to the point where the employers are discovering their codependence with an ineffective and artificial system. The belief in the "God-given right" of certain people singled out by their gender, family, or race to rule (or manage) others is eroding, as is the belief in the shackling and growth-limiting obligation to take care of those "less fortunate." An exciting and potentially liberating part of the new employment contract is that all employees can have the opportunity to develop the skills and perspective to take care of themselves, increase their self-esteem, and break the limitations of inappropriate and outdated codependent relationships. Organizations can facilitate this new paradigm by encouraging autonomy, letting employees plan their own careers, and applying the principles of tough love.

Promote Autonomy and Stop Taking Care of Employees

The first step organizations can take to promote employee autonomy is to recognize that the old employment paradigm is in its death throes and that autonomy is the best strategy for employees and the organization. Managers who have come up through the old employment contract ranks not only have difficulty perceiving that their behavior is paternalistic but also resist changing the system even after they recognize their caretaking. Thus, the price of their action is often trauma. The top management wake-up call is frequently rung by competitive disadvantage, mergers, and layoffs. There are two key lessons for organizations:

- *Do not condition employees to be dependent.* If leaders expect employees to be responsible adults, they will behave responsibly. Most organizational leaders have experience with teenage children. Teenagers need guidance, limits, and, most of all, trust and independence. And at some point, parents need to let go. This may require a nudge or something stronger, even a push. Just as it is not healthy for families to create unnecessary dependence, it is not in the best interests of organizations to attempt to hold on to employees.
- *Eliminate unnecessary support systems.* Health insurance and retirement plans are a burden on organizations, such as those operating in countries like the United States that have no national plans yet. However, organizations cannot simply abandon these obligations. The government, insurance carriers, pension-funding groups, and employees themselves must take more responsibility in this area. A start has been made through the increased cofunding of health insurance, driven by costs. Also, employees are making more of their own choices about the levels of health care their insurance will cover and the levels they will cover personally. Organizations should also scrutinize other employee support systems. A good rule is that if the community provides the service, the organization should think carefully before it duplicates that service. For example, employees should not depend on the organization that provides a paycheck to also provide organized recreation such as social clubs and sports leagues. Other unnecessary and so-called no-cost support services involve group purchasing power. These services include group travel programs, co-op purchasing plans, and various organizationally sponsored discount plans. On the surface, there is nothing wrong with these plans; everyone likes to get a good deal. The problem is that they are another link

in the dependency chain. Empowered, independent employees will find their own discount plans. Many organizations also actively promote social interaction through employee clubs, organizationally sponsored dinners, family picnics, or other services and events that provide socialization at the organizations' expense and, as it now appears, the employees' hazard.

Resist Detailed Long-Term Career Planning

Organizationally specific long-term career paths are artifacts of the old employment contract. Job planning, not career planning, is the stuff of the new paradigm. In the past, employees wanted to know the experiences and education that would, over a career lifetime, get them to the top of a particular organization. Organizations responded with detailed, often elaborately prepared, graphically illustrated, and professionally packaged prescriptions for the tickets employees needed to have punched to rise to the top. In the new paradigm, organizations are flat, growth is not hierarchical, systems are temporary, and careers are short term and situational. Detailed long-term career planning makes no sense because organizations can neither guarantee employment continuity nor forecast the situational and rapidly evolving skills needed over a thirty-year career.

Why then do organizations persist in offering internal career planning? This too is a legacy of the old employment contract. Employees seek comfort in asking for a career prescription. Organizations collude and write one, even though they cannot deliver on it. In the end, such collusion serves only to create false expectations and leads to a lose-lose relationship between the individual and the organization.

The E-Word Demands Tough Love

The word *empowerment* carries a lot of emotional and definitional baggage. One human resource executive, concerned about his line managers' reaction to the word's perceived softness, refers to it as the *E-word* and does not use it during management meetings. His managers do not see the E-word in its true perspective. Without accountability, *empowerment is* just a fuzzy word. But true empowerment is the stuff of the new paradigm. Truly empowered employees are also accountable. One cannot happen without the other.

It requires great courage to accept that control is an illusion and to create an independent, self-reliant workforce—an empowered workforce. Organizational leaders must have the strength to let go, to replace controlling with coaching. They need the tenacity to tell people what they do not want to hear: that there may not be a long-term career for them, that the future is unclear, that there is no guaranteed permanence in organizational systems. Managers need the coaching skills that empower employees to accept personal free-dom, take self-responsibility, look for opportunities for good work, relish the task and not deify the system, and maintain personal con-trol of their lives and careers.

Empowerment requires tough love. Leaders must show "love" for employees not by caring for them but by believing that healthy, autonomous individuals have the capacity to take care of them-selves. These leaders must let go of their control needs and require employee responsibility and accountability.

From Toxic Fidelity to Healthy Self-Responsibility

As part of a significant across-the-board multidivisional layoff, an organization was seeking to lay off one thousand people, primar-ily professionals and middle managers. The organization was in turmoil, the first stages of layoff survivor sickness had set in, and the members of the top management team were desperately seek-ing a galvanizing vision to hold onto while the organization as they had known it was disintegrating. In the middle of this chaos, the director of marketing resigned. At the top management meeting to work on the vision, the dinner conversation turned into a group lamentation over the loss of such a key player. It was true that the marketing director was considered a high-potential employee and had high visibility since he was only one level below the top man-agement group; however, there were a number of qualified inter-nal replacements. Nevertheless, people attacked his loyalty: "How could he be so disloyal as to leave the organization during this cru-cial time? Just think of all this company has done for him!"

The next morning the group was challenged to define *loyalty* as part of reaching their new vision. The question they faced was this: If the organization saw a continuing need to "take out" man-agers and entire layers of the organization, and if managers were smart enough to read the cards, what was disloyal about any employee, including those in the room, who looked for a job outside the organization? In fact, wouldn't it be in the best interests of both the organization and the employees if every employee was given a regular opportunity to look at other options with the help of outside job placement professionals and with no guilt attached?

It was clear that a raw nerve had been plucked and a norm had been challenged. Almost all the top managers had come up through the ranks. Those who were rising had never admitted even thinking about leaving. If they had done it at all, it was in secret, for fear of invoking the organization's anger. As happens in all cases where a value is questioned, the managers dug in their heels and initially rejected these ideas. In fact, they were angry at the consultant for raising the ideas. This example illustrates three barriers that organizations must deal with as they shift to the new paradigm:

- A deep-seated value in many old paradigm organizations is that leaving the organization—or even thinking of leaving or engaging in exploratory interviews—is a sign of disloyalty. In these organizations, employees test the external employment market in a climate of secrecy and organizationally engendered guilt.
- Organizations carrying this value into the new paradigm are unnecessarily burdened and restricted. Helping and encouraging employees of all levels to leave, whether or not they are on the high-potential list, is often the best strategy for both the organization and the individual. The individual gains revitalization and a sense of responsibility; the organization creates mobility, gains flexibility, and reduces costs.
- Managers operating in the crosscurrents of a paradigm shift have difficult and painful jobs. They must often discard values and belief systems that made sense to them on their way up the organizational career ladder. This act requires great personal courage.

Two basic tenets of the old employment contract for the individual were, "I am grateful for my job" and "I will plan a career within the organization." The two reciprocal organizational strategies were, "We will take care of our employees" and "We will promote only from within." The new employment contract realities are, "Organizations cannot keep their end of the bargain and thus create mistrust," and "The result of promoting from a limited and internally conditioned labor pool is a narrow workforce that is not responsive to the new paradigm." The new paradigm demands the level 4 intervention strategies of legitimizing in/out career paths and recruiting for employee diversity.

Legitimize In/Out Career Paths

It is unrealistic for an organization to expect a lifetime commitment from an employee and unhealthy for employees to collude with organizations in creating this expectation. In the new paradigm, employees should be encouraged to move in and out of organizations as their and the organizations' needs dictate—what I call an in/out career path. When they are move on, they can gain experience from related employment in other organizations, further their education, try something completely new, or consult. When they are in, they can focus on a specific time-bound assignment where they are task oriented and able to do self-fulfilling work. When they are out, they can become revitalized. When they are in, they can focus on good work. Of course, transitions in or out of organizations may be painful, take time, and involve uncomfortable changes. They often require struggle at the financial, interpersonal, and organizational levels. Such transitions are, however, necessary and constitute a major activity in the new paradigm. There are at least three actions organizations can take to facilitate in/out career paths:

- *Eliminate penalties for returning.* Despite all the evidence that a new paradigm is operating, some organizations still will not rehire employees who leave on their own. Organizations that do rehire often penalize employees by making them restart benefit waiting periods or vacation accrual. It is vital that organizations stimulate rather than discourage in/out career paths. Benefits and other support services should not discriminate between those who stay and those who leave and return. These services should be available to help support all employees.
- *Develop processes to stimulate leaving.* Organizations should consider a mandatory career review at fixed-time increments—for

example, every three years. This is not a normal performance appraisal. Rather, it is a time when employees can review their life and career options in a safe, objective manner. Career reviews work best if outside experts such as financial advisors and outplacement specialists assist employees during the reviews. The result of a review may be a decision to "reenlist" in the same job, explore different options internally, or leave the organization, either in the short term or at a planned future date. Regardless of the decision, it should be guilt free for the employee and sanctioned by the organization. Although processes using outside experts can be expensive, their cost needs to be weighed against that of keeping a nonproductive employee or, worse, that of future layoffs.

- *Tell the truth up front.* Employees should be told the truth, beginning with the initial employment interview and again during the new employee orientation process. The truth is that the organization cannot guarantee that if employees do a good job, they can count on a job until they retire or choose to leave. New employees can be offered opportunities for learning; performing good, challenging work; and working in a safe, clean environment. Any opportunities beyond that are speculative in the new employment contract. Other truths employees should hear are that employees need to set boundaries, establish a diffuse root system, and establish a nondependent relationship with the organization.

Many organizations resist suggestions that they tell the truth up front because they assume that it will be counterproductive. "You want me to tell them *that* the first day?" shouted an otherwise enlightened top manager. "How will they ever stay motivated?" But the organization did tell employees "that," and they not only stayed motivated, they appreciated the honesty. True motivation comes from investment in a task and the joy of good work, not from colluding in the old paradigm concept of loyalty that both the employee and the organization know, deep down, is false and irrelevant.

Accelerate Diversity Recruiting During Tough Times

Employee diversity is the fuel of the new paradigm organization. The external market is diverse, fragmented, global, situational, competitive, and demanding of service and quality. The internal skills to handle and relate to this new market rely on diverse perspectives, new ideas, and fresh approaches.

Successful new organizations will have a continual inflow of people of diverse work experience, gender, age, ethnicity, and data-gathering and decision-making style who will create the organization's competitive edge. The only way to acquire and maintain this needed competitive edge is through external recruiting. Old paradigm organizations that promote only internally have an increasingly narrow pool of very similar people from which to select. The diversity grows ever narrower as one moves toward the top of the pyramid. The reason members of top management teams are often perceived as all looking the same is that they often are the same. In many old paradigm organizations, they not only look the same in terms of age, gender, race, and dress, but through culturally conditioned inbreeding they often think alike, gathering data and making decisions similarly. In the new paradigm, such homogeneity is the harbinger of a going-out-of-business curve.

When societies are relatively stable, as U.S. society was in the post–World War II era, organizations can get by with the inherent arrogance of a homogeneous perspective. In today's less predictable, globally networked times, organizations need new voices and heterogeneous perspectives. It is very difficult to bring new and different people into organizational systems that are in trouble. It is even more difficult to empower them and listen to them. But it is vital that organizations make this effort.

From an Implicit Career Covenant to an Explicit Job Contract

The play *How to Succeed in Business Without Really Trying* (1962), set at the apex of the old paradigm, was based on the premise that the hero would "play it the company way," and whatever the company told him, that was okay. That is really the way it was in the old days. The employee would behave in accordance with the culture, and the organization would offer him, or less often her, a permanent career. It was a long-term win-win relationship, and it enabled the employee to make long-term personal plans (financing a mortgage, serving in the local community, and keeping children in the same school system), while the organization could count on a stable, manageable, culturally conditioned labor force. The common denominator for these plans was continued organizational growth and global competitive dominance. Unfortunately, the growth resulted in bloated organizations, many of which found their lunch being eaten by foreign competition that was more responsive to customers' changing needs, less bound by work rules, and able to manufacture quality goods at much lower prices. The result was a painful dissolution of the old understanding between employees and business organizations with not much to take its place.

What is beginning to emerge now is a shorter-term and more specific employment contract. The relationship is still win-win, but it is more equal. The employee does not blindly trust the organization with his or her career. The organization does not assume an unassumable burden. The tremendous energy once required to maintain relationships can be turned to doing good work. The common ground, the meeting point, is not the relationship but the explicit task. This task-focused relationship is healthier for the individual and the organization. It also facilitates the diversity necessary for future survival, since the emphasis is on the task, not on the gender, race, or traits of the person performing the task. The new employment relationship is much more explicit than the old and may involve specific formal contracts for tasks.

Despite its benefits, the new employment relationship is often confusing and frightening to organizations and employees alike. It goes far beyond the current standard relationship with temporary or contract employees. To help readers understand the concerns of managers facing level 4 interventions, this chapter ends with excerpts recorded from a brainstorming session in which five U.S.-based executives addressed the employee contracting concept. I have included it to provide a real-world perspective and stimulate further discussion and dialogue. The session began this way: "Our task is to talk about what we think are advantages to establishing a contractual relationship with all employees, regardless of level or tenure in the company would be. The rules of brainstorming apply: no evaluation, just ideas." Here are the comments, divided by topic:

Employee Contracting Advantages

- "It would clearly be a way of differentiating pay for performance. If you would have specific parameters for time and cost and task, you would have pay for performance much more clearly linked [to outcome] than we have today."

- "It would require increased responsibility on the part of the employee in the relationship with the organization."
- "Since expectations would be clearer up front, there would be fewer surprises and feelings of disappointment and betrayal."
- "There would be greater emphasis on power of the professional contribution as opposed to power of position based on titles, office, other supporting things."
- "It would respond to the needs of the individual in terms of career change and career flexibility. We would be similar, by way of model, to what the sports industry is doing, what the acting industry is doing, what the academic community is doing."
- "It fits with the just-in-time manufacturing concept, so that the organization will have the right number and types of people for the duration it needs and can quickly change that when necessary."
- "It could make the task of human resource planning possible with a shorter turnaround time and responsiveness to acquiring the kinds of people you need."
- "It would force our very senior managers to be much more strategic and much less transactional and remote, because their job would be to manage a whole series of interlocking contractual relationships around implementing a strategy to which they agree."
- "It would eliminate not knowing from one day to the next whether you have job security. You have a limited amount of security for a defined period of time. Security could be extended more than year to year because the contract could be self-renewing."
- "[As there is in] marriage, there is a desire for continued active commitment and recommitment and not taking the relationship for granted, so that both employee and employer see this as a partnership in terms of continuing to be a viable business entity, rather than assuming everything will be taken care of."

Employee Contracting Disadvantages

- "[It would be a] complex administrative process . . . an administrative nightmare."

- "[It would require] a great shift in thinking and expertise on the part of both employees and managers."
- "It would require a great deal of change in attitude for those who are uncomfortable with anything new and innovative."
- "It goes against the need for connectedness and affiliation."
- "It treats people like things and will probably get people to act like things—*commodities* is a better term."
- "If the economy goes bad in society as a whole, rather than organization's sharing responsibility for the welfare of [society's] citizens, it would be an everybody-for-themselves environment."
- "In some way [success] would depend on other parts of business and industry [doing] similar things, in order to accommodate the coming and going of professionals."
- "[It prevents] the advantage of having a built-in core labor force that is loyal to the organization, that can be counted upon."
- "[It] would encourage the mentality of portfolio management vis-à-vis employees. Bring 'em in, kick 'em out, whenever necessary."
- "We could end up without the necessary talent if everybody didn't renew their contract."

What Contracting Would Look Like: Some Scenarios

- "If you had a typical office—let's say fifteen administrative assistants, two middle managers, sales managers, and a general manager—my vision is that the assistants would have a relatively standard contract that renewed itself every year, that spelled out terms and conditions of employment, their attendance, their severance pay if they leave. The next level, the supervisor, might have a two-year contract that doesn't automatically renew itself, with some clear performance standards relative to productivity indexes. The senior person would have possibly a four-year contract with termination provisions in the middle of it and with very clear financial goals. If [the senior person] didn't meet those, the contract would not renew itself. The sales managers would have different goals, almost like our current sales incentive plan."
- "I see what you're saying. For example, let's say that the organization wants a management development system. It would define if it means all managers going through certain pre-

scribed training courses despite where they work. If that's my initial mission, then someone gives me a contract to do that, it would certainly make my job much easier and their job much easier because they've already contracted, they've paid me to do it so you wouldn't get a lot of, "What was that objective again?" It would be much more clear going in, in terms of the outcomes. I would say, 'Fine, I'll give you a system. It will take three years. I need ten people and I need $3 million, and I need to have a facility. Here are the benchmarks. . . . At the end of those three years, here's what we'll get.'"

- "There's difficulty there. If you make the contracting relationship so hard that it goes beyond one-on-one, with our current management process, you've got to get zillions of people to agree on something."

- "It certainly does put a priority on the planning function. Let's say that you contract with a person to build you an executive succession planning system. The first thing you have to have is a clear shared vision of what the completed executive succession planning system process looks like, which forces communication. Second, you have to have some benchmarks of what it's going to look like in January and March and June, so that you can check it. You wouldn't just want to wait for the two-year period and have it not happen. So it really does put a premium on shared goal setting and on benchmarking."

- "The thought would be the same as when we go out and hire headhunters. Half the time the headhunter coming in is saying, 'Okay, you've got to pay me anyway. What are you looking for again? And why do you want to hire this person outside? And what are the specs? You've got to pay this much money to get that person.' We'd say, 'We don't want that.' What happens is, by going through the contracting process, you end up having a lot clearer values. The same thing [is true in] the example. If someone wants to hire someone to build us an executive succession planning system, [the person hired would say,] 'It's going to cost us $1 million, it will take two years, here's what it's going to look like—okay?' It would force the company to really think through its commitment before launching. Something else it would do is take all the garbage and junk out that you end up getting involved in. Things would be clearer."

- "One flaw to all that is the rest of the world is not in tune with it. Take the manager in his midfifties. He says, 'Where do I go now?' And there's no support system to help him out of that nest he's now in."
- "Part of what I'm thinking as we talk about this is that we're getting down into a whole lot of unrealistic stuff, and that stretches our thinking. But on the other side, I'm getting a greater sense of comfort that what we're talking about is an employment relationship that, in a more structured way, introduces these elements which probably should exist today but do not. So that we're almost bringing in contractual terms and just using them in our current situation."

Employee Contracting Thoughts

- "I'm encouraged because . . . it addresses aspects of issues that we are troubled by right now. Second, I think it has a plausibility. In fact, it only seems to require a shift in what we're already doing."
- "It would cause people to rethink the work relationship. I think in the short term, the headaches would outweigh any benefits to be gained from it, so I think there is a short-term cost. And short term is probably the first three to five years."
- "We have to be sensitive to where people's heads are today. I think people's heads are in every bit as bad a spot as our survey data indicate. So I think we should do something. Clearly, plateauing and lack of commitment, all the things that we are talking about, are an issue to all organizations. I'm for explicit employee relationships. I'm for a more explicit relationship relative to development and renewal than we have today. So I think there is meat here."
- "We are heading in a direction that is the next logical step in employment relationships within America. It is strategic in its responses to strategic issues. I think that it is exciting in the sense that it builds on existing tools, but with an important difference. Traditionally we have focused our tools on the starting of jobs, on the starting of relationships—things that need to be done. We are now also adding to that to focus [up front] on the ending of jobs . . . through contingency."

Figure 10.1. A Model of Employee Contracting

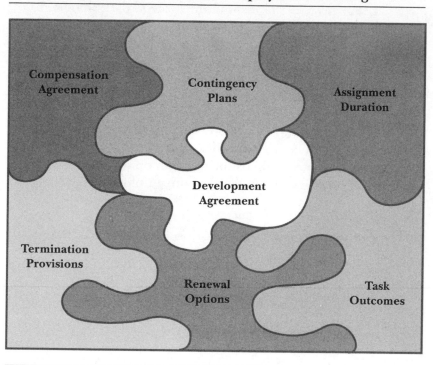

Compensation
Agreement

Contingency
Plans

Assignment
Duration

Development
Agreement

Termination
Provisions

Renewal
Options

Task
Outcomes

Elements of Explicit
Contractual Relationships

Figure 10.1 illustrates a model of employee contracting. It contains
the seven elements that organizations should include in contracts
with employees:

- *Task outcomes.* This is a clear, unambiguous statement of the work
  to be done, along with task benchmarks and key indicators.
- *Assignment duration.* This is the agreed-on time for the task.
  If the task is a project, the time frame extends to the completion date. If the task requires an ongoing process, the time
  frame extends to the date the agreement expires and renewal
  does or does not take place.

- *Contingency plans.* These are the "what ifs." What if unanticipated changes take place at either the organization or individual level? Contingency plans often lead to the termination provisions.
- *Compensation agreement.* This spells out how the person is to be compensated for her or his work. It should be as flexible as possible to meet the individual's needs. A cash payment could be made up front, individual monthly payments could be agreed to, or a completion bonus could be developed. Compensation could be in cash, stock, or enhanced benefits.
- *Development agreement.* The contract spells out the effort the organization will make to develop the employee's skills for the current task or new skills for jobs inside or outside the organization.
- *Termination provisions.* These provisions specify what happens when the contract ends and there is no other work in the organization. It covers what financial and other help the organization will provide.
- *Renewal options.* These options describe the results that must happen, for both the employee and the organization, before the contract can be renewed.

Learnings and Implications

Level 4 interventions are the supporting and complementary systems changes that will promote the climate that invites individual empowerment and autonomy. These new paradigm systems changes can foster the individual acts of courage necessary to break organizational codependency. Level 4 interventions are chicken-and-egg situations. It is hard to say which comes first, the change in the system or the change in the individual, because the two changes are totally interdependent. In today's multicultural global economy, neither is easy or lends itself to a prescription or a quick fix. Moreover, the need for change is no one's fault; it is a systems issue. The implicit assumptions in the old employment contract fit the competitive and social environment of their time, but the same seeds that blossomed in the soil of the old reality sprout weeds in the new reality.

The mismatch that comes from old strategies played out in a new environment does not feel right from either the organizational or the individual perspective. Those who manage and lead organizations must make the same accommodations to the new reality as those in nonmanagement roles. In addition, top managers have the challenge of keeping the system together during a time of fundamental change. They need the skills, courage, and survival sense to take whatever risks are necessary to align organizational systems with the new reality and wrest control away from a paradigm in its death throes.

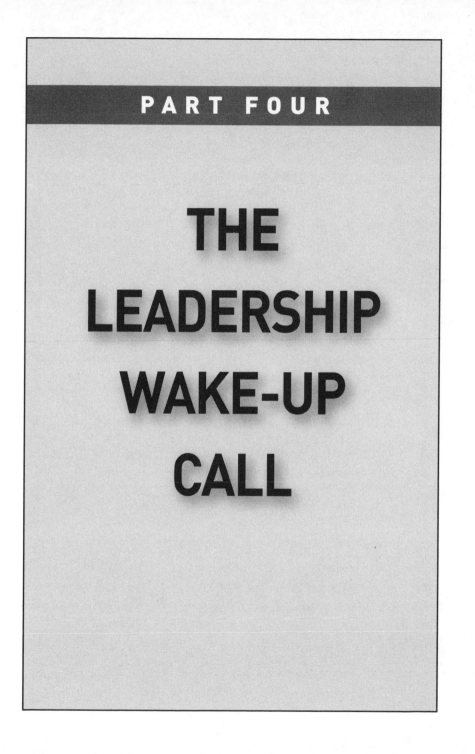

PART FOUR

THE
LEADERSHIP
WAKE-UP
CALL

CHAPTER 11

Requisite Leadership Competencies They Don't Teach in Business School

"It was a hell of a lot more fun building this outfit up than what we're doing now: ripping the guts out of it."—Financial services executive

"We practice 'Apache management.' We ride the horses until they drop; then we eat the horses. They don't teach that in business school."—Marketing manager

The quotations that begin this chapter come from two organizational leaders who find themselves in the frenzied heat of an all-too-familiar battle to save their organizations in the midst of a global economic meltdown. It is exceedingly more frustrating and difficult leading organizations in decline than those in ascension. Both of these leaders have M.B.A. degrees and have discovered that neither the analytical tools nor the behavioral theories they learned adequately equipped them for the ambiguity, turmoil, and gut-wrenching choices they deal with daily in the new reality. The evolving field of emotional intelligence (Goleman, 2006) begins to address some of the needed competencies, but academic models don't come close to an adequate description of the pain, anguish, and stress experienced by leaders attempting to hold organizations together in the second act. In this chapter, I discuss important competencies that most business schools and leadership development programs don't cover.

Choose the Right Wolf to Feed

In order to be relevant to helping people and organizations survive the new reality, leaders must first make a conscious, fundamental choice of how to be. This existential choice is illustrated by a story a hiker on the Appalachian Trail told me:

> One evening, an old Cherokee told his grandson about a battle that goes on inside people. "The battle," he said, "is between two wolves inside us all. One is Evil: it is anger, envy, jealousy, sorrow, regret, greed, arrogance, self-pity, guilt, resentment, inferiority, lies, false pride, superiority, and ego. The other is Good: it is joy, peace, love, hope, serenity, humility, kindness, benevolence, empathy, generosity, truth, compassion and faith." The grandson asked his grandfather, "Which wolf wins?" The old man replied, simply, "The one you feed!"

The power of this story is in its profound simplicity. Leaders are also employees and must overcome their own survivor sickness. I have found that the higher one resided in the organization before the meltdown, the greater was the temptation to wallow in self-pity in its wake. In order to be relevant to their organizations, their employees, and ultimately to themselves, leaders need to feed the right wolves. Here are four worth feeding.

The Wolf of Service to Others

In order to feed this wolf, leaders need to starve its evil twin: self-absorption, selfishness, and cynicism. Once they remove the blinders of self-pity, they are able to see people struggling with the devastating effects of layoffs and insecurity. After meltdown, organizations do not want for opportunities to help others. No matter how bad leaders think they have it, there are always others in worse shape and with less control. When leaders reframe their role from a controlling to a helping relationship, magic happens: they automatically feel better about themselves, employees feel better, and productivity improves. This is a leadership wolf worth feeding.

The Wolf of Stewardship

Stewardship involves resisting cynicism and manipulation and, even though each day seems filled with bad news and disappointment, mustering up the necessary optimism and working to make the organization a better place because of your leadership. That means you can't just go through the motions while sitting on the sidelines worrying about your own stock options, organizational safety, and potential severance pay. That's a passive, selfish, and ultimately self-destructive wolf that doesn't need feeding. Sitting on the sidelines won't make things better for your organization and is hazardous to your self-esteem. Feeding the wolf of stewardship is not a spectator sport. Organizations of all types need leaders committed to making things better if they are to thrive in the new reality.

The Truth-Telling Wolf

In many organizations, fear of making mistakes, the need to appear in control with all the answers, and discomfort with dealing in feelings and emotions stop leaders from authentic communication with employees. In peer relationships, competition and fear of looking out of control often cause managers to swallow the truth. In upward communication, truth becomes tangled with pride, power, and political correctness. These wolves need to be starved. In order to help people and organizations through the trauma of downsizing, leaders need to take personal responsibility to break the gridlock and stimulate authentic communication. The creation of an environment of open, compassionate, and honest dialogue is a core task of successful leaders in the new reality.

The Wolf of Positive Role Modeling

People in positions of power and influence are always on stage— and more so than many realize. What they do and say, and how they do and say it, has an enormous impact on others, particularly in times of stress and trauma. The boss who preaches openness and participative management but then engages in temper tantrums and controlling behaviors is feeding the wrong wolf. Employees are looking for hope and seeking light at the end of the tunnel. Leaders who respond to this need with cynicism and pessimism are not only feeding the wrong wolves; they are engaging in a self-fulfilling prophecy that will ensure their own demise.

Avoid Layoff Leadership Traps

Having confided in me that the current layoff provided a good opportunity to get rid of those "overpaid, do-nothings" in marketing, the newly appointed general manager stood on a table in the employee cafeteria and addressed his new employees. This is a paraphrase of his comments: "Since you were lucky enough to keep your jobs, I expect you to work extra hard to make this organization lean and mean. This won't be the last layoff, I'm good at cost control, and I personally intend to monitor everyone's performance." Pausing and looking over the mute and stunned audience, he sternly continued, "I won't tolerate any bitching or whining. Now let's stop wasting time and get to work."

As a consultant, I had the unenviable, and impossible as it turned out, task of convincing him that lean and mean strategies often translate to angry and unproductive employees and that he had become the poster child for three classic traps that prevent leaders from revitalizing downsized organizations.

The Gunnysacking Trap

Gunnysacking is a term I introduced in Chapter Eight for storing up hurt feelings, anger, affronts, and unresolved conflicts and, when the weight of the psychological gunnysack becomes too heavy to bear, unloading it, often to an inappropriate degree in an inappropriate context. We all gunnysack to some extent, but most psychologically healthy people find ways to keep their bags relatively light. Unfortunately, organizational managers are not immune to gunnysacking. I have discovered that a surprising number operate for many years under the oppressive burden of a heavy bag and use a crisis mode of operation as an authorization to unleash long-repressed feelings of anger and frustration by figuratively beating their fellow employees about the head with their overloaded gunny-sacks. In layoffs, this takes the form of those in power "getting" both functions and people that frustrated them in the past but were pro-tected by a more tolerant organizational culture.

Gunnysacking is unhealthy for both the leaders who practice it and the prognosis of organizational survival. If you see it happening, help those wielding those heavy bags find better ways to lighten them. If, in the heat of the battle for organizational survival, you are tempted to form a coalition to "get" a person or a function for the wrong reasons, resist it. If you find yourself the victim of gunnysack-ing, don't try to get even, because that only compounds the prob-lem. Try to discover what past event lies unresolved in the leader's bag, and muster up the courage to confront the issue directly.

The Cost-Cutting Activity Trap

An activity trap involves becoming so enmeshed in a task that one loses sight of more important, fundamental objectives. Leadership gurus such as Peter Drucker have long warned leaders of the haz-ards of getting caught in activity traps. However, in times of eco-nomic chaos, many action-oriented leaders, uncomfortable with complexity and ambiguity, are driven to do something personal, immediate, and tangible. They become heavily involved, often obsessed, with line item budget cuts and the layoff process. At the very time when their perspective, wisdom, and creativity are needed to help the organization survive, they succumb to the seduction of micromanagement. In today's environment, cost cutting and lay-offs are sobering and necessary realities, but that's not how true leaders spend their time. We need leaders to give hope, inspire, and, difficult though it may be, navigate a strategic course that will ensure organizational productivity and survival.

The Repeating What-Got-Me-Here Trap

Leading organizational growth is much easier and requires a different set of skills than leading organizational decline. Most defi-nitions of management include the classic "-ings": directing, orga-nizing, evaluating, and controlling—and most leaders of public and private organizations got where they are by excelling in these.

However, in many years of working with organizations going through downsizing, I have yet to hear employees describe their best boss as one who excelled at directing, evaluating, or controlling. During troubled times, the best bosses are seen as those who are good listeners, straight communicators, and have the ability to form empathetic relationships. Helping skills, not controlling or evaluating skills, are the leadership currency of the realm during troubled times. That doesn't mean that leaders are absolved of the responsibility to make hard decisions or can magically alleviate the pain of organizational restructuring. It does mean that revitalizing organizations requires re-recruiting demoralized employees, and that is not accomplished through excessive control, evaluation, or direction. It is done through the leadership "-ings" of listening, empowering, and coaching.

Behave Courageously

Courageous leadership is not about naiveté or false bravado. It involves feeling fear, anxiety, and uncertainty; facing it; and moving forward. Organizations in all countries and of all dimensions— small, large, family, public, private, government, nonprofit, military—need responsible, coherent, courageous leaders to help them through the morass.

To be an effective leader in today's world requires something significantly more fundamental than mere technique or skills: it requires the courage to move beyond simple answers, the paralysis of fear, or the safe anonymity of the sidelines in order to help make things better. Here are four dimensions of the courage necessary to leadership in today's world.

The Courage to Resist Cynicism

It is easy to succumb to anger, blaming, and cynicism in tough times. Effective leaders, however, are able to face their frustrations and anxieties, maintain a positive perspective, and work to find answers. Leaders who allow their cynicism and anger to affect their followers are ineffective. They not only don't help make things better, but they pass their own anger and cynicism on to those they are attempting to lead. If there is one thing layoff survivors don't need, it is an angry and cynical leader. That is a situation that will only compound their symptoms.

The Courage to Help Others

The old adage is profound and simple: If you feel bad about yourself, find someone who feels worse and help him; you will feel better, and he gets helped. In times of stress and confusion, leaders who make a difference have the grit to put their own issues aside and make themselves available to others. A person who is struggling with fear and an uncertain future doesn't need a leader who is too caught up in her own issues to focus on others' problems. This person needs someone who has had the courage to face her problems and the focus to be present for others.

The Courage to Engage

One response to the problems we face today is to hunker down in the trenches, avoid risk, and hope things improve. Given the magnitude of the problems, it is easy to understand why many leaders end up just going through the motions; they limp through each day, not of much use to themselves or to those seeking their leadership. Courageous leaders get up in the morning and choose to engage. They certainly feel the fear and anxiety, but they choose to make a difference. Rather than adding to the problems, they seek to help solve them.

The Courage to Look in the Mirror

Courageous leaders are made, not born. They have the ability to learn from their mistakes and from feedback. If they discover themselves becoming cynical, blaming, and withdrawing from optimistic engagement, they have the fortitude to change. Lots of people get feedback, but not everyone has the ability to hear it and the courage to take action. Leaders who make a difference have the ability to look in the mirror and the bravery to do something about what they see.

There is no magic formula for developing courage. It comes down to a matter of choice. Those who have the courage to help make things better consciously decide not to let their frustrations and fears disable them. They instead choose to rebuild, not accept defeat. The bravery of the leaders we desperately need to help us through uncertain times is found not in flashy speeches but in their steady, quiet, and unrelenting efforts to make things better. These people we need to rebuild our organizations, our nation, and our world.

Let Go of Outdated Managerial Commandments

Anyone who has seen a child swinging across monkey bars or has personally experienced the adult equivalent in a military obstacle course knows that in order to get from one end to the other, you need to grab a bar with one hand and, while maintaining your momentum, grasp the next, let go of the first, and continue the process of holding on and letting go until you reach the end. There is a moment where you need to take a leap of faith by letting go of one bar without the absolute assurance that you will be able to grasp the next. If you don't take that risk and hold on to any bar too long, you lose your momentum and eventually drop to the ground.

This image of letting go of certainty in order to move forward provides a powerful metaphor for new paradigm leadership. There are some leadership bars that may have been useful in the past but need to be dropped in order to let us move forward. Our grip on these bars has been formed by leadership commandments that do not fit the new reality.

Let Go of the Need to Have All the Answers

In many old paradigm organizations, the boss is endowed with an aura of infallibility. Even if the boss is wrong, the culture conditions employees to nod, smile, and accept the wrong answer. This semi-deification of the boss varies with culture but is particularly valid in Asian, Middle Eastern, and Latin cultures that researchers have described as having high power distance (Hofstede, 1997). It is also widespread in a number of more traditional organizational cultures throughout the world. Many leaders were conditioned to accept this role as they ascended the managerial ranks. The result was that they were expected (by themselves and others) to have all the answers, know what was going on, and communicate irrefutable facts. Many organizations with this culture have a policy that all communications flow through the manager, and they have strong norms against employees skipping managerial levels when sending or receiving information.

In times of organizational chaos, confusion, downsizing, and reorganization, no one really has all the answers; moreover, because of the smoke and dust surrounding the heat of battle, no one knows what is going on at any given time. The cultural commandment that requires managers to have all the answers and be "right" causes them to shut down at the very time their empathy, understanding, and nonjudgmental, unscripted communication is most needed. In one organization, a director of engineering actually called surviving employees into his office and read them a script that the corporate legal department had approved. Stilted, controlled communication, however, is the exact opposite of the sharing and empathy necessary to help employees move on. It is not only acceptable for leaders to tell employees they don't know everything that is going on and don't have all the answers, it demonstrates their humanity and facilitates the necessary empathy. Leaders definitely need to let go of the "I need to know all the answers" bar, or they will be left hanging, irrelevant to the needs of their organization and their employees.

Let Go of Unquestioned Conformity and Unquestioned Acceptance of Spin

In a past consulting project, I encountered a feisty, creative branch manager whose firm had just been taken over by a large corporation. The only adornment in his spartan office was a large, framed caricature of a cow on the wall behind his desk. What made the drawing even more unusual was the label. In large block letters directly under the cow was the word "HORSE" followed by the new corporate logo. His explanation was, "I use it to remind myself and my employees that no matter what kind of a spin those . . . [I won't quote his string of picturesque adjectives] people at headquarters put on things, we need to trust our own judgment, believe what we see, and make up our own minds."

A managerial commandment of many previously stable bureaucratic systems was, "Don't rock the boat." Rather than being perceived as useful and leading to better outcomes, suggestions and disagreements were seen as toxic and disloyal. In organizations experiencing rapid and wrenching change, autonomy, independent judgment, and reality checking are essential managerial roles. Although I am not advocating the divisive approach of the manager in this example, effective leaders in times of change do need the freedom to question, debate, and challenge decisions. Organizations need to create cultures that will allow boat rocking. Otherwise they will strand their leaders on noncreative bars that will only hasten organizational decline.

Let Go of the Myth of Rational, Analytical, Antiseptic, Managerial Methodology

I once asked a group of managers to draw a picture representing the leadership style of their CEO. They drew a gigantic hourglass sitting on a small desk with the CEO standing at a blackboard, calculating the rate of flow and listing people to blame. "He's great at analyzing what's happening and placing blame," they said, "but his solution is to keep changing the location of the hourglass. He needs to understand that no matter where he puts it, he can't reverse the passage of sand. He has to accept that inevitability and find creative ways to keep this organization afloat. He's analyzing us into oblivion."

Management as a profession of scientific, clear, and antiseptic methodology was a myth even in the early days of Fredrick Taylor's scientific management. Now it is totally irrelevant to the needs of downsizing organizations. Many new managers, particularly newly minted, inexperienced M.B.A.s and undergraduate business majors, come to the business world with the expectation that it is a place of rationality, subject to objective analysis and thoughtful, quantitatively based decision making. This is a result of both their own naiveté and of being subjected to the teaching of management professors who have spent their entire lives in classrooms—from grade school through graduate school, then into the role of teacher—and have never actually worked in a business. During the good old days, when organizations had money for management training programs, they colluded in perpetuating the rationality myth by offering courses in management "science" and brought in speakers with the latest prescriptive "how to do it" fads.

Today's organizations are filled with the warm, messy, thick goop of human emotions, not the clear, rarified air of objective analysis. Raw emotions are rampant. Employees at all levels are struggling with dashed hopes, bruised egos, fear, anxiety, and mistrust. In order to help rebuild productivity and commitment, leaders need to let go of the rung of analyzing and prescribing and grab hold of the warm, slippery rung of empathy and responding to emotions. Here are four thoughts:

- As safe and sterile as it may seem, you can't analyze people out of their pain. You need to connect with them at the heart, not the head.
- When employees are in the midst of a crisis of identity and purpose, they are not interested in strategic analysis, demand curves, or decision trees. They need high touch and low tech.
- Planning and objective analysis are essential management tools, but without people to carry out plans, they are just academic abstractions that will gather dust on unused bookshelves while the company goes bankrupt.
- Once the rational, analytical commandment is put into perspective, managers can learn basic helping skills, combine them with their analytical tools, and truly help the organization move forward in this chaotic world.

Let Go of Win-Loss Competition

We learn it in sports when coaches tell us that two players are competing for a starting position. We learn it in elections when two candidates compete for one office, and we learn it in business when two peers compete for one promotion. The commandment of healthy competition, where one person wins and the other loses, is ingrained into the management psyche at an early age and played out within organizational cultures. This is a particularly strong commandment in countries and regions with highly individualistic cultures such as the United States, Canada, Australia, Scandinavia, and Western Europe. It is not as prevalent in many Asian, Latin, and Middle Eastern cultures that have been described as more collectivist in their cultural orientation (Hofstede, 1997).

When organizations are imploding and people are terrified of losing their jobs and stuck in the crosscurrents of organizational turmoil like deer paralyzed by headlights, "healthy competition" is decidedly unhealthy. "I'm safe; you're not" barriers are erected. At times, they wall off necessary teamwork between entire departments or functions as in the classic line-staff differentiation: "We're a line department; we bring in revenue. You are a staff function and an unneeded expense. We're okay. You're not okay!" In trauma-filled organizations, healthy competition soon turns unhealthy, unhealthy completion turns sour, and sour competition becomes toxic to the teamwork and collaboration necessary for organizational renewal.

Organizational leaders have achieved their status to a large degree by developing excellent, persuasive debating skills. They have the ability to sell their ideas and prevail over other viewpoints. The downside of debates is that there are winners and losers, and the last thing traumatized, hypersensitive employees need is more fragmentation. Stress can polarize groups into paralysis by triggering "I'm right, you're wrong, and the only way to do it is my way" camps. What organizations most need in times of turmoil is the ability to learn, and research on organizational learning has emphasized the importance of replacing debate with dialogue. Dialogue involves working with others for a better, more synergistic solution rather than dogmatically selling or forcibly imposing a single point of view.

The ability to engage in constructive dialogue and not destructive debate is key to organizational learning and systems thinking. Leaders seeking to create an organization that will survive in the new reality need to let go of the bar of "I'm right, you're wrong" debate and grab the bar of constructive dialogue that leads to organizational learning. They need to let go of "I" and "me" and grab hold of "us" and "we." It is amazing how much trust can be established and how much progress organizations can make when leaders roll up their sleeves, stop making speeches, and work collaboratively with employees to make things better.

Don't Listen to Chicken Little

The origins of the fable of Chicken Little date back to Indian Buddhist folklore, and there are many variations of what is now a classic children's story. The financial meltdown that triggered the second act began in 2008, and the global tipping point occurred in 2009. In the Chinese calendar, that was the Year of the Ox. Given the state of the economy, a more fitting representation for that year would be a chicken, as in the fable when Chicken Little panics and sets off to warn the king that the sky is falling. In the story, she misinterprets an acorn falling on her head, alarms friends such as Ducky Lucky and Turkey Lurkey, and in many endings winds up being eaten by Foxy Loxey. Here are four perspectives that will help organizational leaders see acorns for what they are and, in a metaphorical sense, avoid Chicken Little's fate.

We All Share the Same Sky, and It's Not Going Anywhere

It is the same sky all over the world, it's not falling, and it will be here long after we are gone. We live in difficult times, and the jobs of organizational leaders are exceedingly stressful. Difficult though it may be, leaders need to rise above the turmoil and gain perspective. This perspective will lead to wisdom, which will lead to much-needed optimism that they can bring back to their organizations. We will get through this. The economic system will survive, and we will emerge stronger with new learnings. We have already discovered the magnitude of the interconnectedness of the world's financial infrastructure. Leaders, regardless of their skill and power, have limits, and when they exceed them, they end up doing more harm than good to their organizations and themselves. Organizational leaders can be concurrently comforted by the reality that no single organizational system got us in this mess and sobered by the realization that no matter what they do, they are only a small, incremental part of the solution. Like it or not, it is going to be a long, global, systematic fix that can't be solved by one industry, one region, or one country. It will require patience, perspective, self-sacrifice, wisdom, and optimism from all leaders.

We Have a Choice of Opening Out or Closing In

Psychiatrist Robert Jay Lifton (1993) points out that people who are facing trauma either open out or close in. If they open out, they connect with others, form supportive communities, and develop the psychic capacity to reconcile themselves to new, and perhaps unsettling, paradigms. If they close in, they become isolated, rigid, self-absorbed, and trapped in futile attempts to simplify complexity and control the uncontrollable. People have a remarkable capacity to survive almost anything if they open out, but they wither, shrink, and fade away if they close in.

In a time when people are being hit on their collective heads by the acorns of layoffs, erosion of their savings, deferment of their dreams and hopes, and the prognosis of a prolonged sickness in the financial system, leaders need to guard against a closing-in reaction because if they choose this path, they become part of the problem, not the solution. Opening out is a strategy that will protect their own mental health and equip them to help others. A wise and humble person once told me, "When you feel bad about yourself, find someone who feels worse and help them. You get a double win: they get helped, and you feel better." In times of organizational trauma, employees need leaders' help and compassion. Leaders who withdraw from the fray and don't engage in a helping relationship pass on the message that the sky is indeed falling. Feeling sorry for themselves and walking away is a closing-in strategy that will leave employees stranded and shrivel leaders' souls.

When People Think the Sky Is Falling, They Need Leaders Who Are Helpers and Enablers, Not Blamers and Micromanagers

In both public and private organizations, people are increasingly being perceived as costs to be reduced, not human resources to be developed. That reality, however, does not mean that effective leaders are those with an obsession with cost cutting, micromanagement, and overcontrol. Controlling expenses is a necessary management task, but one that is not central to leadership. Leaders need to re-recruit organizational survivors, help them conjure up the necessary risk taking and innovation to ensure future success, and empower them to serve customers, not hunker down in the trenches for fear of getting laid off. Unfortunately, to paraphrase Warren Bennis (2003), most organizations going through downsizing are overcontrolled and underled. Blaming and scapegoating become a substitute for team building and empowerment. Cutting costs and managing expenses are essential in today's economy, but true leaders facilitate the establishment and monitoring of goals, get out of the way, and find ways to help people feel good about themselves in the process. Micromanaging and overcontrolling are closing-in tactics that result in less productive, fearful, risk-averse employees who collude to give leaders the illusion of control by telling them what they want to hear as opposed to what they need to hear.

We Can Turn Acorns into Alarm Clocks

There are a lot of acorns falling in this economy, and we can't duck them all. Leaders can, however, help employees, by using the impact as a wake-up call as opposed to Chicken Little's panic call. Job loss is often traumatic, but it has also caused many people to reassess their life and career plans and move into fields that may not pay as well but are much more satisfying and provide more balance between work and family life. Those in leadership roles too can turn an acorn bump into a midcourse career correction. In my consulting and executive coaching work, I am continually surprised by the number of people in managerial and leadership roles who didn't like their jobs in good times and really don't like them now. Many explain that they were seduced by money, power, and status early in their careers and feel trapped by debt and an expensive lifestyle that now seems artificial and meaningless.

All traps are painful, but with enough sacrifice and persistence, most can be sprung. Leaders and employees alike have a choice. They can close in, become angry and cynical, accommodate the trap, and lead a life of pain, constraint, and suboptimization. Or they can reframe their experience as a wake-up call and move toward the light. As any novelist knows, character revelation takes place in times of conflict and turmoil. We learn more about ourselves when things are difficult than when they're easy. For some, today's tough times have triggered a rediscovery and affirmation of core values and spiritual grounding.

Learnings and Implications

Leadership in an environment of organizational turmoil and downsizing in the context of economic decline and global financial instability is significantly more stressful and complex than during normal times. It is much harder to lead on the way down than on the way up. Unfortunately, many of the skills, values, and perspectives necessary for relevant leadership in times of organizational trauma are not found in undergraduate business schools, M.B.A. programs, or company-provided management development programs. Leaders must have the courage to challenge and drop some of the basic management commandments that got them where they are and adopt new, often uncomfortable, approaches.

Helping organizations survive the trauma and upheaval of the new reality is both an opportunity and a developmental challenge. The opportunity is great, and the stakes are high. If ever organizations needed relevant leadership, they need it now. What is at stake is nothing less than organizational survival. The developmental challenges are equally significant. In order to be effective, leaders must abandon the safety of past objective, rational, analytical models and techniques. They must engage employees in the warm, messy, unpredictable arena of raw emotions, frayed nerves, and deferred dreams. The only tool that really works is their own authenticity and ability to engage in empathetic, helping relationships. In order to be truly relevant and engage employees in any meaningful way, leaders must drop their hierarchical, analytical defenses and become vulnerable to the power of human emotions.

CHAPTER 12

Thou Shalt not be
Seduced into
Dependence

Thou Shalt Take Care of
Thyself

Thou Shalt Continually
Network and Keep Thy
Skills Marketable

Thou Shalt Provide an
Environment That Lets
Thy Employees Motivate
Themselves

Thou Shalt be Empathetic
and Caringly Candid

Thou Shalt not
Place Thy Social and
Emotional Eggs in the
Organizational Basket

Thou Shalt not Expect
Long Term, Uninterrupted,
Employment Continuity
with a Single Organization

Thou Shalt Not Keep the
Wrong People for the
Wrong Reasons

Thou Shalt Facilitate
Employee Venting

Thou Shalt be Freed by
Unmasking Thine own
Vulnerability

Rethinking Loyalty, Commitment, and Motivation

The Long and Painful Birth of the New Reality

"Tell us something that sounds like it's coming from someone's heart and not from their ledger."

"My job is where the rubber hits the road in all this paradigm change crap."

The new employment contract is a product of a long and agonizing birth. The pains began in the first act (the late 1980s and early 1990s), and the financial meltdown beginning in 2008 triggered the final, agonizing delivery. For better or for worse, the new reality has arrived. We don't have to like it or even trust it, but if our organizations are going to survive, we have to deal with it. An example of the discomfort and frustration engendered by the change was evident when, at a transition workshop, an angry group of general managers who had caucused at the bar the night before came to a morning session ready to do battle. Our dialogue was short, pointed, and instructional.

"We don't buy into a lot of that stuff," snapped the spokesperson. "It takes away all the tools we have to manage!"

I said, "Yes, it does."

"It isn't fair."

"No, it isn't."

"The new way may not work either."

"It might not."

"It busts up the culture we've spent so long creating."

"Culture busting hurts."

"You're damned right!"

I remember this little dialogue because of its intensity and because it drove me to incorporate the term *culture busting* into my work. It is a powerfully appropriate term for the new paradigm leadership challenge. Culture busting *is* necessary, and it is painful. It is all the more so for the leader who must destroy that which he or she created in the past in order to make meaning for the future.

Ten Old Paradigm Commandments Reframed

The cultural conditioning of the old paradigm resulted in behavioral "commandments" that were ingrained in the way leaders and followers viewed organizational citizenship. Although we are well into the second act of the new psychological employment contract, it is a testimony to the power of these values that many organizations are still having trouble reframing some of them. Here, with their supporting rationale, are ten old-paradigm commandments that deal with loyalty, motivation, and commitment. Here also is the way, whether we like it or not, they must be reframed to accommodate the new reality:

First Commandment

- First Commandment: *Thou shalt make employees dependent on thy organization.* In order to control and direct employees, managers need to structure a long-term dependency relationship. The creation of dependency is often quite sophisticated and subtle, but without it, managers lose necessary power. The creation of a "mercenary" workforce is antithetical to management.
- First Commandment reframed: *Thou shalt not be seduced into dependence.* The skills to lead an empowered workforce are much different from those required to manage a dependent one, but there is a quantum difference in results. Employees who remain in organizations because they choose to be there, rather than because they have to be there, are much more creative and productive.

Second Commandment

- Second Commandment: *Thou shalt trust that the organization will take care of you.* Loyal employees trust that the organization will take care of them if they meet performance standards. If employees don't demonstrate this trust, managers conclude they are not team players.
- Second Commandment reframed: *Thou shalt take care of thyself.* By now employees should know that it is impossible for organizations to control conditions so that they will have the necessary resources to take care of their employees over the long term. Employees can be loyal to their task and their coworkers but know it is a bad bargain to trust the organization. Managers don't define team playing with abstract loyalty or trust.

Third Commandment

- Third Commandment: *Thou shalt not look for another job while still employed.* Loyal employees don't look for jobs while still employed. If managers discover that an employee is looking elsewhere for a new job, they conclude the employee is disloyal and factor that into their performance evaluation and future employment.
- Third Commandment reframed: *Thou shalt continually network and keep thy skills marketable.* In the new reality, everyone, including the manager, is encouraged to continually network and cultivate outside options. External networking and keeping skills relevant to the needs of the marketplace are indexes not of loyalty but of common sense.

Fourth Commandment

- Fourth Commandment: *Thou shalt motivate thy employees by bestowing rewards and delivering punishments.* Managers motivate employees by rewards and punishment. Rewards aren't always money; they can be psychological, such as recognition, but they are rewards nonetheless and are granted by the boss. Punishment is usually translated as lack of a promotion or a salary increase.
- Fourth Commandment reframed: *Thou shalt provide an environment that lets thy employees motivate themselves.* Employees are

capable of self-motivation, and this internal motivation is much more powerful than the externally imposed variety. In the new reality, the primary motivators are good work (see Chapter Nine) coworkers and the acquisition of valuable skills.

Fifth Commandment

- Fifth Commandment: *Thou must always be tough and brutally honest.* Managers must be tough, objective, and brutally honest, and they must never let feelings and emotions distract them from getting the job done. Touchy-feely management does not work in the real world.
- Fifth Commandment reframed: *Thou shalt be empathetic and caringly candid.* Feelings and emotions are the currency of the realm when employees are gridlocked by fear, anxiety, and depression. That's the "real" real world. The only way to move the organization back to productivity is to form empathetic, helping relationships. Truth telling is mandatory, but honesty should be caring, not brutal. Caring candor is helpful; brutal honesty is destructive.

Sixth Commandment

- Sixth Commandment: *Thou shalt be paternalistic to thy employees.* Paternalistic management is good. It results in employees who are loyal, committed, and motivated. It is therefore a desirable human resource strategy to provide as many services and programs as possible that tie employees' sense of purpose and social identity to the organization.
- Sixth Commandment reframed: *Thou shalt not place thy social and emotional eggs in the organizational basket. It shalt get dropped, and thine eggs shalt be broken.* Paternalism sends the wrong message in the new reality. It leads to unhealthy dependency and when, inevitably, downsizing happens, employees who overly rely on their organization for social and emotional support are set up for layoff survivor sickness.

Seventh Commandment

- Seventh Commandment: *Thou shalt promise a long-term employment relationship.* Employees need the promise of a long-term, stable employment relationship. Organizations provided it once, and they will be able to provide it again.

- Seventh Commandment reframed: *Thou shalt not expect long-term, uninterrupted, employment continuity with a single organization.* The last thing employees need is a promise that things will return to normal, including the old psychological contract. It is a promise that employers won't be able to keep and when, inevitably, it is violated, management credibility will suffer.

Eighth Commandment

- Eighth Commandment: *Thou shalt covet permanent, long-term employees.* Permanent, full-time, long-term employees are the glue that holds organizations together. A building filled with free agents is too unpredictable and will implode for lack of consistency.
- Eighth Commandment reframed: *Thou shalt not keep the wrong people for the wrong reasons.* Like it or not, in the new reality, all employees are "temps." That does not mean that under the right conditions, employees won't stay for a long time. When employers provide good work and empowering leadership, talented employees will stay for the right reasons, and they will tend to stay for as long as those two conditions are met. It is much more hazardous to organizational health when employees stay for the wrong reasons: because they are afraid to leave and have no marketable external skills. There is a far greater danger of organizational implosion because the wrong people stay for the wrong reasons.

Ninth Commandment

- Ninth Commandment: *Thou shalt not allow employees to whine and bitch.* Whining and bitching are bad, and managers need to stop it. In troubled times, employees need to suck it up and move on. Complaining serves no useful purpose and pollutes the workplace.
- Ninth Commandment reframed: *Thou shalt facilitate employee venting.* *Whining* and *bitching* are prejudicial words and serve only to reinforce norms that preclude employees from the crucial task of externalizing their disabling feelings. Properly facilitated, venting repressed feelings is an exceptionally powerful managerial tool.

Tenth Commandment

- Tenth Commandment: *Thou shalt be in control at all times.* Managers must be in rigid control at all times. In times of organizational trauma and turmoil, it is even more important that those in authority maintain an aura of stern unflappability.
- Tenth Commandment reframed: *Thou shalt be freed by unmasking thine own vulnerability.* In order to be relevant to the needs of their employees and reduce their own stress, managers give themselves permission to own and express their personal vulnerability. That reaffirms their humanity and frees their ability to form authentic empathetic relationships with their employees.

Putting the Pieces Back Together: Reintegrating the Busted Culture

Making sense of the new reality and incorporating it into the operational processes of organizations is a daunting task for employees and managers alike. As can be seen from the ten reframed commandments, it means assimilating a new set of values and perspectives that go against the grain of past cultural conditioning. Many initially react to the reframed commandments with a combination of anger and denial. Leaders face the necessary but arduous task of facilitating acceptance by helping organizations move past these natural reactions. Leaders need to help all levels of employees make sense out of these changes, and this means a new way of conceptualizing leadership as collective meaning making (Drath, 2001). Meaning making involves helping employees make sense of confusion, ambiguity, and new paradigmatic perspectives. Effective leaders facilitate this sense making by helping employees understand the change and integrate this insight into the way they view the world of work. It is a collective process because organizations need shared meanings of reality in order to work together productively.

Leaders, as makers of meaning, structure confusing and ambiguous environments toward a unifying purpose. This exciting concept defines leadership in terms of a process: any individual or group who can create a galvanizing meaning is exercising leadership, regardless of the individual's or group's formal organizational role. The basic task of new paradigm leadership is making meaning. Although anyone can, and often does, exercise leadership in a new paradigm organization, I have found it helpful in working with organizations to be more traditional and define organizational leaders as those whose primary responsibility is to facilitate meaning and, within that meaning, direction. (As a result, I do not differentiate here between leaders and managers.)

Those who occupy meaning-making roles in the midst of a paradigm shift enter into an adventure in confusion, ambiguity, and risk. Although it is sometimes terrifying, it is also sometimes exhilarating; most important, it is crucial to the survival of the organization. Not only is creating meaning out of the ambiguity accompanying the new employment contract an exceedingly complex and sometimes gut-wrenching job, it is also a chronically undervalued job. Even those who are doing it often depreciate the importance and difficulty of their role. Their self-doubts are fueled by outsiders. Nonpractitioners, including many behavioral scientists, have no experiential frame of reference with which to grasp the true level of stress and ambiguity facing leaders moving toward the new paradigm. These managers are envied, misunderstood, projected on, stereotyped, categorized, and often dehumanized by those who study them. For these reasons, line managers find themselves face-to-face with the paradoxes of the new employment contract with little support. One helpful way for them to visualize their meaning-making role is that it facilitates movement from the comfortable old to the paradoxical and relevant new. This movement can be broken down into six specific shifts that the manager needs to bring about (Figure 12.1):

- *From motivational strategies that promote dependence to strategies that promote independence.* It takes courage and creativity to buck the tide of many years of successful practice and untether the ties of organizational codependency. Often the new paradigm leader must go against both the tradition of the organization and the inclination of employees.
- *From the yearning for belonging to the necessity of autonomy.* In an age of transient relationships and increasing interpersonal alienation, people often look to organizations to satisfy their affiliation needs, but organizations' ability to do so is limited.

Figure 12.1. Leadership Shifts Behavior from the Comfortable Old to the Relevant New

From	*To*
Motivational strategies that promote dependence	Strategies that promote independence
The yearning for belonging	The necessity of autonomy
The organization as a primary social system	Employment as an economic relationship
The leader as savior	The leader as helper
The desire for permanence	The reality of transience
The leader as purveyor of objective reality	The leader as a maker of meaning

• *From the organization as an employee's primary social system to employment as an economic relationship.* The new employment contract is economic, not social, in nature. The employee engages in short-term good work, and the organization provides monetary compensation. It is impossible to interact within an organizational system, even over a short period, and not become part of a social system; forming relationships is essential to the human experience. However, new paradigm leaders know there is a real hazard in investing too much social currency in the organizational vault.

• *From the leader as savior to the leader as helper.* Many employees have a propensity to deify leaders, particularly the top manager. The boss knows all the answers. Got a problem? Need something resolved? Get to top management, and they will write a prescription for you! These are the unrealistic expectations that lead to layoff survivor blaming behavior. Organizational leaders are often linked both hierarchically and laterally in chains of powerless codependency. The boss cannot solve the economic, social, and organizational factors that led to the new employment contract. The boss can, however, put herself in a helping relationship with employees. Initially this often goes against the grain of both employee expectations and the temptation of the leader to play savior.

• *From the desire for permanence to the reality of transience.* The new employment contract is short term for all employees. The organizational leader must first deal with his or her own temporary status, then have the courage to work counter to culturally derived expectations in order to help employees understand the new contract's transitory nature.

• *From the leader as a purveyor of objective reality to the leader as a maker of meaning.* Leaders are not only expected to have all the answers; the answers are expected to be logical, rational, and objective. The great wake-up call for the new M.B.A. is that real-world decisions are not made behind desks using analytical models or rational processes; they are made in hallways or on elevators and are based on incomplete, fragmented, and conflicting data. New paradigm managers must deal with the dissolution of the old without any certainty of the new, yet they must also help others make sense out of change. This is their crucial task, and it is not a "soft" one. In a comment that has become a classic, Porter (1978, p. 3) captured the grit needed: "It takes courage and creativity to move into a situation and make something positive out of it. There is sure to be at least one hidden agenda in every pocket. People expect us to make them feel better, or they hurt and they want us to accept their diagnosis and give them the prescription they have decided on or they want us to eliminate all the symptoms. We may be the only person able to take a risk, to confront it, to ask the fools hard questions."

Learnings and Implications

The dawning of the new psychological employment contract has triggered fundamental changes in our culturally reinforced concepts of loyalty, motivation, and commitment. These culture-busting transformations have often generated anger and denial from all levels of employees.

Organizations are the arena in which the new employment contract is played out. If leaders are to develop systems that possess structural immunity to layoff survivor sickness, they must learn to use the skills and competencies that will facilitate the transition from the certain and comfortable old to the relevant but uncertain and confusing new. Leaders must make meaning in a time of profound change. They must stimulate the necessary culture busting.

There is a lesson to be learned from the culture busting that took place when the former Soviet Union dissolved and, with its former republics, moved toward a market economy. The same process, although in different stages of evolution, is taking place in China, Vietnam, Central Asia, and parts of Africa. These transitions require the courage and faith to move into the future with skills and perspectives honed in a past that may no longer be relevant. In these evolving economies, free markets are forming. Goods and services are beginning to be sold and valued in the light of market demand. The transition, although ultimately empowering and efficient, is filled with frustration, trauma, anxiety, and pain. In organizations implementing the new employment contract, market economies are also evolving. Individuals are moving toward an economic as opposed to a dependency relationship with their organizations. Just as was the case with Russia and Eastern Europe, as the old system unraveled, a new one did not automatically and flawlessly take its place.

The new reality is real, and like it or not, we must accommodate it. The task of organizational leaders is to help employees make sense of the changes in the basic commandments that regulate the connection between employee and organizations. This making of meaning is the most crucial task of new paradigm leaders.

CHAPTER 13

Developing the Right Leadership Stuff

"I can't say this in public—for sure not to my board—but to tell you the truth, I don't know what the hell we can do. Talk about no light at the end of the tunnel—I don't even know how to find the tunnel."—Small business owner

How do you acquire the skills, wisdom, and perspective necessary to perform a leadership role in this perplexing new world? How do you develop "the right stuff"? When thinking about this question, I always remember the profoundly simple answer a wizened professional writer (from whom I took a workshop years ago) gave to a question regarding how to be a relevant author. To paraphrase his response: live a long time and live intensely. Seek a variety of experiences and remember them. Retain your sanity, and tell the truth.

Developing Philosopher-Kings: Learning from Plato

There is much to be said for experience. An intriguing model is Plato's proposal for the development of philosopher-kings. After passing three successively more difficult examinations that would weed out all but a very few, the remainder of the candidates would be allowed to study philosophy. These candidates would be at least thirty years old and would spend five years in rigorous philosophical training. They would then return to society for fifteen years and earn a living with no special privileges. At age fifty, they would have the knowledge and experience necessary to assume a position of leadership.

Of course, this is not a workable way for us to train leaders today, but the combination of rigorous formal training and practical hands-on, mingle-with-the-masses experience does present a model. And as much as the Greeks needed philosopher-kings, our need for new paradigm leaders is far more crucial. Being a leader within the new paradigm requires taking unselfish responsibility for helping others wallow through continuing disequilibrium. In addition to the complex technical and functional competencies required of all general managers, there are three core relevancy skills for new paradigm leaders: intrapersonal insight, interpersonal competence, and a commitment to continuous self-improvement.

Intrapersonal Insight

In order to be relevant to others and facilitate collective meaning making, leaders must understand themselves, yet many do not have good insight into their effect on others, and some are not clear about their own values and motivations.

Valid Data

Leaders need ways to secure valid data about themselves and explore behavioral options. One way to begin this process is to participate in the kinds of training programs that provide feedback on their small group behavior and how others in the workplace see them. One potential problem is that it is difficult to justify spending money on leadership training when organizations are pinched for cash, but a deeper analysis reveals that the only valid tool for helping organizations overcome survivor sickness and return to productivity is the meaning-making competence of their leaders. Properly targeted, programs that help hone this tool are necessary investments. Of particular importance is 360-degree feedback, which allows leaders to compare their self-perceptions with those of their boss, peers, and employees.

Sensitivity Training

An exceptionally powerful feedback experience involves intense work within small groups whose members learn from their own data and give and receive feedback with the objective of opening themselves up to a wider set of behavioral options. This type of training, which I call *self-insight training*, is also known as *sensitivity* training or *T-groups* (the "T" stands for "training.") T-groups reached their ascendancy back in the 1960s and still carry baggage—some warranted—from those days. Because of a small number of nonprofessional trainers, sensitivity training was at times viewed as frivolous, "touchy-feely," and not relevant to the business world. The two ingredients that make this training live up to its potential are competent and healthy facilitators, who want to help participants achieve insight and not grind their own axes, and healthy participants, who are there to learn from their own data and are not seeking, or in need of, a group therapy experience. A criticism of T-groups has been that the personal growth and insight experienced in the group could not be transferred to the workplace. This was true in the old paradigm because there was no apparent connection between self-understanding and the leadership role. However, self-understanding and personal growth are key new paradigm leadership competencies. Through these competencies, leaders learn about themselves so that they can perform their primary function of helping others.

Structured Reality Checks

Although new paradigm organizational leaders are not therapists, much of what they do is place themselves in helping relationships. In order to perform this role, they must be self-aware and do whatever is necessary to achieve and maintain valid data on themselves. Wise leaders use processes such as upward performance appraisals, sensing groups, opinion surveys, and instrumented feedback to stimulate a flow of valid data. Personal feedback is not usually easy to hear, and it often shatters the mental scripts that leaders write about themselves and attempt to act out, but wise and effective new paradigm leaders accept the discomfort of burst bubbles as the price of relevance. Some organizational leaders have individuals who act as their reality checkers and designated feedback givers. This is an exceptionally useful role for a good human resource person who does not let the need for approval get in the way of saying what the boss needs to hear. However, this role can be also played by other people in the organization. I call these people "Petes," after an archetypal character I met in one organization.

Pete, the Professional Truth Teller

Pete's title was vice president of special projects. Although he reported to the organization's executive vice president and had a lot of influence in the top management group, I couldn't figure out exactly what he did until the first day of a team-building session when the boss opposed a clearly necessary change. His ego was so deeply invested in the current system that the harder the top management group pushed for change, the deeper he dug in his heels. In fact, he grew so irritated that the meeting ended early, and he and Pete went off to dinner by themselves. The next morning, the boss opened the session by telling the group he had thought it over and was wrong—the change should take place. This was an amazing turnaround, given his strong resistance the day before. When I asked one of the other participants about it, he just smiled and said, "Pete got to him."

Later it became clear that "getting to" the boss was Pete's only real function. Pete and his boss had once been contenders for the top job in the organization. At the time, both were about three years from retirement and were in their next-to-last jobs within that organization. When Pete was not selected, the arrangement they made was that Pete could remain in the executive suite, keeping his office and perquisites. All he had to do until he retired was to keep his ear to the ground and "tell the executive vice president the unfiltered truth." Pete was a personal truth teller, reality checker, and feedback giver to the top person. The boss didn't always agree with Pete's perceptions, but he took the time to hear them.

The arrangement worked because Pete was respected by the executive vice president and the rest of the organization, had no personal axe to grind, and did not manipulate the situation to increase his power and prestige. Not too many organizations can afford full-time Petes, or could find a person with the right balance of truth telling and humility even if they could afford a full-time Pete, but effective new paradigm leaders find ways to hear the truth, or at least another's perception of the truth. There are lots of part-time Petes out there, and even a few full-timers.

Interpersonal Competence

In his early, classic work on intervention theory, Chris Argyris (1970) introduced the term *interpersonal competence* as a prerequisite for what we now label *meaning making*. Today's leaders must be interpersonally competent in order to establish authentic employee relationships, facilitate meaning, and provide direction. The basic helping skills that make up interpersonal competence include the ability to give and receive feedback in ways that are constructive and reduce defensiveness, empathetic listening skills, the ability to reflect feelings, and the ability to confront others in a caring and nonjudgmental manner. These are Helping Skills 101, the basic communication and counseling skills that allow clarity and facilitate straight talk.

Top organizational leaders are often undertrained in these basic skills. In the new paradigm, a deficit in these competencies is akin to not possessing basic reading or math skills; leaders are simply unable to function effectively without them. There are several reasons that old paradigm organizational leaders have failed to fully develop the necessary interpersonal competency skills.

The Barrier of Macho, Controlling Cultures

In the old paradigm, "real" men did not reflect feelings, deal in empathetic dialogue, or ask for feedback. They made decisions, analyzed, and controlled. Similarly, in the old paradigm, women, who were culturally sanctioned to use helping skills, were undervalued. Although helping skills were clearly valuable, even in the old reality, they were not on the tickets that needed to be punched by either gender on the way to the top.

The Barrier of Left-Brain Bias

The right side of the brain controls our emotional and intuitive perceptions and behaviors. The left brain is involved in analytical, rational thought. In the United States and most other Western cultures, organizations have a strong left brain bias that results in an overemphasis on formal logic, analysis, and rationality. The new paradigm has more balance, but in most organizations, even with the increasing evidence of the utility of emotional intelligence, IQ trumps EQ (emotional quotient), and helping skills are much less valued than controlling and analyzing skills.

The Barrier of Management Science

The concept that management is a science is not "scientific management" as defined by Frederick Taylor (people can be taught to work systematically and can be factored into the production equation similar to machines). Rather, it has to do with the inferiority complex felt by business schools and management training institutions in relation to scientists and their subsequent overreaction as they tried to be "scientific." There was, and unfortunately still is in many institutions, the idea that you can study humans the same way you study rocks. Anything that was intuitive, feeling, or smacked of our unique human spirit was driven out of business education for fear that it would look weak and not seem scientific. Thus, entire generations of leaders grew up under the false assumption that there was an objective management science as opposed to what Vaill (1989), in a prescient description of new paradigm leadership skills, more accurately described as "management as a performing art."

The Barrier of Fear of Softness

At the zenith of the old paradigm was a reaction to anything that was deemed "soft": feelings, relationships, empathy, and anything that was "touchy-feely." If you think about it, this is a strange norm, because being alive and human involves relationships, feelings, and connecting with others. However, the value was facts and figures— "hard" stuff. Even though such rock-ribbed disciplines as physics now report that facts are relative, the bias continues. Organizations still talk about human resources and training as the "soft" side of management. But not only are people issues as real as financial and production figures, they require just as much skill and strength. In addition, they require authenticity and the risk of self-disclosure. This is much more difficult than hiding behind a memo or stack of figures. The good news is that despite all the reasons that organizations discount "soft" helping skills, a slow but steady revision is in progress. Organizational leaders are finding that interpersonal competence is in high demand in the new paradigm, and as they make this discovery, they are not only picking up useful skills, they are realizing a new sense of personal relevance as they discover new behavioral options and plumb the depths of their own repressed capabilities.

The Challenge of Continuous Self-Improvement

The primary meaning-making tool is the leader's authenticity and straight talk. All who truly want to lead in the organization of tomorrow need to go through whatever self-discovery is necessary to hone their own authenticity and candor and be as relevant as possible in dealing with the change that surrounds them. Continuous self-improvement is not easy. It takes courage to keep looking in the mirror and to assess what is there. Cross-paradigm leadership demands personal involvement and human interaction, and in the final analysis, the only tools that work here are each leader's own creativity, self-insight, and compassion.

Core Skills and Relevant Models

Although the new paradigm is a strange and confusing place, many analytical managerial skills can be transported from the old paradigm and used to illuminate dark corners of this new world. Some generic functional competencies such as marketing, financial planning, accounting, and strategy formulation can, with a tweak-in-time orientation, be carried over intact. Other dimensions of leadership require much more new skill development. These dimensions involve making transitions, creating visions, exhibiting congruent values, and understanding the significance of process.

Transition Facilitation Skills

Today's leaders must know how to accomplish individual and organizational transitions, but this competency is not taught in business schools or most executive development programs. It is not an abstract analytical process carried out in the sterile confines of the executive suite or the manager's office. It is a hands-on, dirty, sweaty, humanity-filled, emotionally laden, risky process. It puts the leader's skin in the game. It moves her or him from the role of detached observer and manipulator of the levers of power to full-fledged participant in the action. It is the most important arena in which a new paradigm leader can be relevant. The simplest and clearest job description for a relevant leader in the new reality is as a "transition facilitator."

In addition to basic competencies in helping skills, today's leaders need conceptual models of the transition process. Some consultants hold that one of the best organizational interventions is a good book. Similarly, I have found that one of the best gifts I can give to a client is a conceptual model. Models serve as a unifying frame of reference, a way to get everyone speaking the same language, and a path leading to shared understanding and commitment. Effective leaders do not have to be academic organizational theorists. However, they need a clear model for conceptualizing transitions. No one model is best, but the one selected should be clear, easy to communicate, and widely shared, so that the organization can create collective meaning. Of the myriad transition models available, I have found that three, somewhat classic models are of the most help in my work with organizational leaders. They are all stage theories, meaning that one stage of the model needs completion before moving to the next. Working managers like stage theories because of their clarity and action orientation.

Bridges's Transition Model

Perhaps the model that organizations find most useful when struggling through organizational and personal transitions is that outlined by William Bridges (1980). Bridges postulates a stage theory (events take place in a predictable sequence) in which the first event is an ending. This ending is followed by a "neutral zone," which is followed by a beginning.

What new paradigm leaders find most interesting in this model is the neutral zone. It is a time of floundering, a necessary period of ambiguity before a new beginning can be effective. If leaders rush the process, moving directly from an ending to a beginning without an intervening neutral zone, a true transition does not take place. Most layoffs move from reductions on a Friday to anticipated productivity gains the following Monday. One reason these gains do not take place is that survivors do not have the necessary neutral zone time and thus never make a true ending. Rebound marriages that do not last and rapid job changes after a layoff that leave survivors alienated and unfulfilled are examples of the ways people rush the transition process without having the patience to pass through the neutral zone. In survivor workshops, I often pass out copies of Bridges's first book (1980)— he has written others, but I prefer the simplicity, personal focus, and freshness of the first one—and then design exercises around it. I highly recommend it for all leaders experiencing personal or organizational transitions.

Lewin's Field Theory: Unfreezing, Moving, and Refreezing Model

This is a straightforward model based on Kurt Lewin's classic work in field theory (Marrow, 1969). It is a stage theory with a great deal of appeal to managers. A triggering event—such as layoffs causes the system to see things differently. It thus "unfreezes" the system. Once the system is unfrozen, it can be changed, moved in a different direction, and taught to perceive reality differently. Systems, however, demand some consistency and thus need to be "refrozen" after the change is in place.

Individuals move through transitions in the same stages. The old employment contract's failure, layoff survivor sickness, and global competition are triggering events for employer and employee unfreezing. Their movement is the implementation of the new employment contract. Their refreezing establishes the new employment contract as a system. This is a useful model for managers because of its long- and short-term versatility. Most organizations continually experience a limited number of longer-term and a larger number of shorter-term unfreezes, moves, and refreezes. This model's simplicity and versatility fit well into the new paradigm leader's volatile world. In workshops I often ask groups to draw Lewin's force field, a graphic representation of the current state existing in dynamic equilibrium between forces pushing for change and forces restraining change. They then brainstorm ways to reduce forces restraining change, which often leads them into the new reality.

Kübler-Ross's Stage Theory

Originally developed to deal with "death and dying," Kübler-Ross's stage theory (which I discussed in Chapter Eight in conjunction with grieving) outlines five sequential stages: denial, anger, bargaining, depression, and acceptance. I have used it successfully to work with groups to process their feelings in regard to the transition from the old to the new paradigm. It is a good way for groups to discover where they are stuck and work through ways to move forward. I have also discovered that "stuck" groups, in an effort to rapidly get on with business, have skipped stages. But groups that don't take the time to progress through the sequence of stages and deal with their feelings at each stop usually snap back and get stuck until they complete the business of the stage.

The Forgotten Four: Visioning, Value Congruence, Empowerment, and Process Wisdom

I have labeled these four skills and behaviors the forgotten four (Figure 13.1) because they are essential to the type of leadership needed in the new reality, but are often overlooked or underemphasized when selecting leaders or in leadership education. Here is an overview of each.

Visioning Skills

Leaders operating within the new paradigm need to stimulate the creation of a galvanizing vision—an idea that pulls the organization together. At the same time, they must guard against being seduced into the savior trap. The last thing organizations groping their way through the new reality need is a grandiose vision that flatters top managers' egos but has no value to the organization. Organizations need handles—pictures of the future that employees and leaders alike can hold on to and move toward. At times, a vision

Figure 13.1. The Forgotten Four

may simply be a shared picture of getting on with business after a layoff. Visions are not restricted to the end states of major strategic change efforts.

Leaders facilitating the crafting of visions do need to ensure that visions meet three tests. First, they must be visual, not verbal; they must be a picture of a desired future state, not just a series of abstract words. Next, they must be vivid and galvanizing, creating commitment and alignment toward a shared view of the future. Finally, they need to be dissonant, that is, significantly different from the current picture.

The creation of a vision is an act of collective meaning making, not simply the act of a single leader. Visions are collectively, not individually, owned. The visioning skills of top organizational managers can be the ability to hear and align the visions of others. In addition, it is a myth that visions must always be rosy and totally positive for everyone. A key task of new paradigm leaders is to help employees move toward something, but that something is not always immediately comforting. It could be the reality of short-term contractual employment with no long-term job security. An honest vision is better than no vision or a phony "bright future" vision.

Value Congruence Behavior

Value congruence is a term not frequently found in the literature of organizational change and development. I first encountered it a number of years ago as articulated by a former mentor, Dick Byrd, to describe the deceptively simple fact that effective change leaders need to walk their talk. I have since discovered it is an essential, and too often missing, quality in managers who are attempting to make meaning and facilitate movement into the new reality, engaging in creative culture busting.

In order to be effective in an environment of paradox and ambiguity, leaders must not only be visible and accessible to employees, they must be perceived as trustworthy. They cannot say one thing and do another. Their behavior must be congruent with their espoused values or they will lose their personal integrity. A new paradigm leader who has no personal integrity has no effectiveness. Value congruence is more of a behavior and way of being than a skill. However, skills such as the ability to hear feedback and the awareness that employees see only external behavior (which means that internal good intentions are invisible) help leaders adjust their behavior to match their words.

Empowerment Skills

Organizational leaders either live by the E-word or die by its absence. The new employment contract requires empowered self-reliant employees bound together by good work. In order to lead, managers must facilitate this empowerment, receive it, feel it in themselves, and distribute it to others. I call this *360-degree empowerment*. The manager creates a full circle of empowerment with boss, peers, self, and subordinates. These skills involve coaching, "catching people doing things right," sharing power, creating shared and mutual visions, and valuing diversity. Each leader has an invisible quiver filled with an unlimited number of arrows that contain a variety of behaviors that engender empowerment. Leaders use every interaction to discharge an arrow to all those they work with. Relevant leaders make meaning and distribute empowerment.

Process Wisdom Skills

Many years ago my friend and another mentor, Peter Vaill, made me aware of the concept of process wisdom when he wrote a book chapter titled "Process Wisdom for a New Age" (1984). At that time he meant that future leaders must be skilled at distinguishing, valuing, and participating in both means and ends, which are often tangled and difficult to distinguish. Once again, Vaill demonstrated his prescience. A critical skill for today's managers is being equally adept at leading (making meaning) both task and process contexts. A process-wise leader can be both a participant in an interaction and an observer. A process-wise leader knows that no two situations are exactly alike and resists the temptation to deal in pat, prescriptive solutions. In order to understand and help employees through the confusion and trauma of the new reality, leaders need to experience them individually, personally, and unfiltered by preconceived theories and abstractions. As much as leaders are tempted to experience others in the abstract, they must have the courage to interact with them in the moment. The new paradigm has many levels of reality and often presents irreconcilable paradoxes. The process-wise leader does not get hooked into a fruitless quest for the "one" answer.

The Global Context of New Paradigm Leadership

The employment relationship is more than what is defined by the "employing" organization; it also is shaped by national and regional cultures. The psychological contract between the organization and multigenerational employees (husbands, wives, sons, and daughters all working in the same plant), and living in a North Carolina "mill village," was certainly different from that of the highly employable software engineer working for a start-up during the boom days in California's Silicon Valley. It is a mark of the relentless advent of the new reality that the mills have closed, replaced by operations in China and other low-labor-cost countries, and that technology—and its fuel, venture capital—are now global commodities and by no means limited to Silicon Valley. The new employment contract will continue its inexorable global march, but the way it will unfold will be modified by regional subcultures, national cultures, and technology.

Much of the current knowledge concerning national cultural distinctions and their leadership implications is based on the seminal work of Geert Hofstede (1980). His research started with one seemingly simple question: Is the culture of a company (he used IBM) more important to employee behavior and values than the culture of the country where that employee works and has roots? He found that we tend to underestimate the impact of national cultures and that there are significant differences among national cultures. His initial study stimulated a stream of research that examined national cultures and their impact on leadership, coaching and communication (Hampden-Turner and Trompenaars, 2000; Rosinski, 2003). These and other studies have generated some additional ways of conceptualizing cultural differences. However, for purposes of examining the leadership challenges of global downsizing, I'll use two of Hofstede's original dimensions.

Collectivism Versus Individualism

This dimension deals with preferences for either individual achievement and recognition or that of a group. The United States, Australia, New Zealand, Canada, and the United Kingdom topped the individual list, with Scandinavia and Western Europe not far behind. Countries high in group values were in Asia, the Middle East, and Latin America. These rankings tended to hold true in subsequent research. Collective countries such as China, Saudi Arabia, and Japan have developed large "buffer" workforces of "have-nots": expatriate, temporary, and contract employees who protect the status of the "haves"—full-time "permanent" employees. Time, however, is running out. The second act has resulted in huge numbers of temporary Chinese workers returning to the countryside, Japanese contract employees losing their jobs, and Saudi expatriates returning to their home countries. As the wave of downsizing begins to affect the permanent employees in these and other collective cultures, organizational leaders will have an even more challenging meaning-making task.

High- Versus Low-Power Distance

Power distance measures the social, emotional, and formal distance between bosses and employees. In low-power-distance cultures, it is easy for both boss and subordinate to have an informal, consultative relationship. In high-power-distance cultures, both parties prefer a more formal, structured, hierarchical connection. There is a similar pattern to that of collectivism versus individualism. Asian, Latin, and Middle Eastern Arab countries rank high on power distance, with Scandinavia, Western Europe (with the exception of France), the United Kingdom, the United States, Canada, Australia, and New Zealand ranking low. It is much easier for managers to form helping relationships with employees in low-power-distance cultures. It is an against-the-grain experience for both boss and employee in high-power-distance cultures. One effect has been an increased use of outsiders such as consultants in organizations experiencing organizational trauma that are located in high-power-distance cultures.

The United States and Japan: Strange Bedfellows on Similar Journeys

Japanese society as a whole has a culture that values conformity, teamwork, fitting in, and subordinating the individual to the system. The United States has a cultural heritage of rugged individualism, of exalting the person over the system. It ranked highest of all the countries studied in "individualism" in Hofstede's original study. In a sense, the old employment contract was a graft of collectivism on an individual-based culture, a mismatch in itself, and one that may account for an undercurrent of individual alienation from, and dissatisfaction with, organizational systems that evolved in the post–World War II era. In Japan, however, the fit between national and organizational cultures is natural. What becomes unhealthy organizational codependency in an individual-centered culture may be the normal order of things in collectivist cultures.

Both the global economic meltdown and social forces are eroding the golden age of overarching Japanese homogeneity. Japan is
just beginning to replicate the U.S. experience of ferment and
seething, deeply felt debate over the implications of plurality, and
such manifestations of diversity as ethnicity, gender, age, disability,
values, and sexual orientation. Young Japanese professionals, particularly those who have worked overseas, are questioning the
spirit-numbing work ethic. Women and ethnic minorities are making inroads into the all-male, all-Japanese business aristocracy. If
diversity is a competitive advantage, Japan is just beginning to pay
its dues. The paradox within the paradox is that although Japan
competes in a diverse, multicultural, global environment virtually
sizzling with change, its own system is fixed, monocultural, and
based on feudal principles of filial obligations.

The United States increasingly operates within a system that
demands instant results. In times of an epidemic of bankruptcies,
mistrust of financial institutions, and massive layoffs, only quarter-
to-quarter (and even sometimes month-to-month) results count.
Strategies that may result in short-term losses in order to develop
long-term markets have fallen victim to the financial meltdown.
Japan is still fighting the good fight to continue to take a long-term
approach, at least with what it considers "real" employees. In Japan,
the acquisition of new professional employees is still seen as one
of the most important activities of a firm. These employees are
long-term assets to be nurtured over time. They are recruited very
young, developed throughout their careers, and retired relatively
early. What in the United States is age discrimination in Japan is
human resource planning.

The new paradigm leadership implications for Japan are staggering. If fully operational, the new employment contract with its
short-term, contractual, individual orientation will tear the heart
out of the collectivist culture. A few years ago, I met with the top
human resource officer of a very large Japanese company. I was
gathering data for a research project on downsizing and asked him
what would happen if his organization experienced a 10 percent
involuntary layoff for all levels of employees. I remember every
word of his answer, and I'll never forget it. He stood, turned,
spread his hands, and gestured to the sprawling complex of buildings that constituted his firm's headquarters and dramatically said,

"The bones of our founder would rattle in his grave if that ever happened!" In our connected world, Japan is but one example of a collective culture entering the new paradigm, and the United States is but one example of an individualistic culture making the same journey. Global leaders will need all the creativity and meaning making they can muster to prevent a worldwide epidemic of "bone rattling" and keep our organizations on track.

Technology: The Global Wild Card

The first act began at a time when the Internet was in its infancy, the United States was the dominant economy, China was just rising from its slumber, and India was still "low tech." The second act is unfolding in a far different environment. We are wired, networked, "flattened," and, as the global financial crisis unfortunately proved, inextricably connected. People are working from their homes, their cars, in airports, and in parks. Virtual organizations, multiple channels of instantaneous communication, and immediate customer feedback are rendering the traditional hierarchical, fixed location, organization if not a knockout punch, a strong, eye-blinking blow.

Layoff survivor sickness is alive and well, but taking place amid the increasing clutter and noise of an accelerating digital and telecommunications revolution. I call this technological explosion a wild card because it isn't clear how it will ultimately affect the forms of organizations, the leadership process, or the shape of a future third act. In an insightful book, futurist Richard Hames (2007) articulates the potential of "appreciative systems" to help leaders link disparate cultures and gain the best of all worlds in terms of productivity and creativity. This is a promising future dimension of global meaning making. Everything is relative in our fast-moving world, and our strategies and perspectives for leading a global workforce in a time of trauma need to take place within the context of a rapidly evolving technology.

Learnings and Implications

In order to be effective in the new reality, leaders must master new or neglected competencies such as transition facilitation, visioning, value congruence, empowerment, self-understanding, and process wisdom. They do not acquire these relevant skills in traditional management development programs or business schools, yet these are the most important capabilities leaders bring to the new paradigm.

No one has yet designed a core curriculum to teach leaders the functional skills necessary to manage a complex business and, in addition, teach them to be authentic, congruent, self-aware, process wise, other centered, and facilitative in the midst of major cultural change. As a precondition to acquiring these needed relevancy skills, leaders must have a strongly developed set of democratic values and possess the courage to understand their own needs and agendas. The arenas in which these skills are cultivated include intrapersonal understanding (self-awareness), interpersonal competence (helping and empathy), and a continuous self-improvement (honing one's own mind and feelings as the primary instruments of leadership).

The complexity of the leadership task is magnified by the fact that it is taking place in a global arena. Relevant leaders must understand the effects of the cultural context of organizational behavior and structure their leadership to accommodate diverse norms of acceptable managerial and employee roles and relationships. This confusing cross-cultural leadership role is taking place in the midst of an explosion of technology that will reshape the nature of work and the concept of a permanent workplace.

The bell tolling for the death of the old paradigm can also be heard as a wake-up call. Leaders, as well as other stakeholders in the organizational system, have a unique opportunity to make a choice. The new employment contract has cleared the air. For the first time in many years, employees can choose to capture their autonomy and self-direction. The final chapter reviews this basic existential challenge.

CHAPTER 14

Life After Downsizing

Revitalizing Ourselves and Our Organizations

"Well, if it goes, I've had a wonderful time. They've paid for my daughter's education, and the food in my mouth, and lots of things over the years. I guess what they're talking about now is they can't promise us life security forever. No company can."

The Top Ten New Reality Managerial and Employee Roles

The old psychological employment contract is experiencing a slow, painful death. It was resuscitated during the economic boom following the new millennium and is now suffering its final decline. In testimony to its seductive and addictive nature, many employees and organizations have forgotten the lessons of the past and once again are paying the toll in terms of lowered productivity and morale. In order to ensure organizational survival and individual relevance, managers and employees must play new roles (Table 14.1). In this concluding chapter, I use the top ten list in the table to summarize some of the concepts and ideas set out in this book. Since managers and other leaders are also employees (something academics and analysts sometimes forget), the roles and behaviors in the "employee" column can also be extrapolated to apply to managers and formal leaders.

Table 14.1. Top Ten New Reality
Managerial and Employee Roles

Manager	Employee
Learn to lead temporary systems.	Adjust your identity to that of a temporary employee.
Learn facilitating, helping skills.	Find ways to externalize your dysfunctional emotions.
Focus on coaching employees to accomplish work and serve customers, not on abstract corporate loyalty.	Define yourself in terms of what you do, not where you do it.
"Know thyself." Constantly work on self-awareness. You *are* the tool!	"Know thyself." Ground your work life in work that is congruent with your unique gifts.
As a manager, your employees are your customers; relentlessly seek to serve them.	Relentlessly seek customers for your work. Without them, you are hedonistic and self-absorbed.
Become a distributor of "realistic optimism."	Become a consumer and codistributor of "realistic optimism."
Don't role-model a mercenary attitude, but keep your options open and maintain marketable skills.	Be cautiously loyal, but cultivate options and keep your skills honed.
Resist the temptation to promise employees a long-term career with employment security.	Don't be seduced by promises of a long-term, secure career with one organization.
Don't weave unrealistic baskets.	Don't put all of your social and emotional eggs in the organizational basket. It will be dropped.
Selfishly guard your uniqueness and cultivate balance and perspective.	Selfishly guard your uniqueness, and cultivate balance and perspective.

The Reality of Temporariness

Leading temporary systems requires a tolerance for ambiguity, a focus on the "here and now," and the ability to celebrate short-term wins. Managing a group of employees who are uncertain that their jobs, or even their organization, will be in existence in twelve months requires a unique blend of optimism, self-confidence, and immediate task focus that unfortunately is in short supply.

In the new reality, we are all temporary employees. As disconcerting as this initially feels, it is also liberating. Employees are free to focus on the task, develop their marketable skills, and pursue work that is congruent with their human spirit without the distracting political gamesmanship that accompanies fitting into an abstract, controlling, bureaucratic organizational culture. Many employees have told me that they have done their best work in the period between either getting or giving notice and their actual departure.

The Need for Empathy

Re-recruiting demoralized employees and leading them through the ambiguity and confusion of the new reality requires managers with helping, not controlling, skills. These were not often the skills that were valued or got managers promoted in the past, but they are the requisite competencies of the future. I have found that most organizational managers have the ability and, with some coaching, the desire to learn basic helping skills. Once learned and applied, they have become an invaluable tool for successful leaders of all levels.

The evidence is overwhelming that employees in most organizations suffer some degree of anger, fear, and anxiety—what I call layoff survivor sickness. Since many organizations have norms that prevent the necessary venting, they are populated with fearful, risk-averse employees at the very time they need creativity and innovation. If the organization won't help, employees need to find ways to externalize these dysfunctional emotions. Their productivity and mental health are at stake.

The Need for Tangibility: Abstractions Are Distractions

In the ambiguous flux of the new reality, leaders need to help their employees focus on their tasks, short-term results, and helping customers. Impression management, fitting in, and abstract concepts such as "loyalty," "commitment," or the "company way," with no behavioral frame or measurement criteria, are artifacts of the old psychological contract. It is not that loyalty and commitment have gone away, but they need to be phrased in clear behavioral language that relates to helping a customer or performing work.

In order to develop immunity to the symptoms of survivor sickness, employees need to ground their self-esteem, purpose, and relevance on their work and their profession, not in the organization where they happen to perform that work or profession. That way, when their job is threatened, their self-esteem stays intact.

The Need for Self-Knowledge

It is not possible to engage in an authentic helping relationship without understanding your own perceptual biases and "hot buttons." You have to know yourself well enough to hold yourself in check so you can truly hear and not judge others. There is always a gap between the way we see ourselves and the way others see us. The manager who wants to make a difference in the new reality needs to find ways to close that gap. The primary tools in helping employees thrive in the new reality are the manager's empathy, authenticity, and interpersonal competence. The way to keep these tools sharp is through an ongoing existential quest for self-awareness.

Good work is nutritious. It occurs in congruence with our unique gifts and human spirit. When employees shift their loyalty from the abstract corporation to good work, they feed their soul. Not all work is "good work," of course, and when we find it, it may not last, but we need to understand ourselves well enough to recognize it when we find it.

The Need for Relentlessly Seeking Customers

Self-centered leaders are not useful generally, and certainly not in the new reality. Leaders who wallow in self-pity or attempt to manipulate the system for their own personal gain are toxic to the chances of organizational survival. Managerial "other-centeredness" has two powerful outcomes: it helps managers open out and escape their own negative internalizations, and it helps others. The primary customers of managers are employees. By helping employees, they help the organization survive. That is not to say that managers don't have outside customers—those who consume their goods or services. They are obviously crucial. However, if managers spend more time with external customers than internal customers—their employees—they are more of an employee than a manager. Managers empower their employees to be at the front line of customer interface.

Employees who cannot clearly identify their value added to a customer—internal or external—are not doing themselves or the organization any good. They too need to open out and be other-centered. That's why it is so crucial for leaders to help them get out of themselves and into focusing on others. Good work always involves doing something for another. Work that is of value only to the employee is not good work; it is narcissism.

The Criticality of Optimism

In difficult times, no one wants a leader who is negative, cynical, or sarcastic. Some leaders think that negative comments are humorous and build camaraderie. In fact, they almost always have the opposite effect. Employees desperately want hope, and competent leaders provide it—not false hope or fraudulent optimism, but a realistic assessment of the upside. The glass is always half full, and even with massive layoffs, there are some positive dimensions of the new paradigm inside or outside the organization. A leader who can't provide this realistic optimism should, voluntarily or involuntarily, step away from the leadership role.

Healthy employees are not only consumers of their leaders' realistic optimism; they pass it on to their colleagues. It is not phony bravado that discounts the seriousness of economic meltdown and employment insecurity. It involves holding up a lantern that illuminates the possibility that with customer focus and good work, the organization can survive—even thrive. It is passing the lantern around so that all can see that losing a job is not the end of the world and can, and often does, lead to a satisfying and balanced life.

The Paradox of Cautious Loyalty

Regardless of the level of organizational fragility, employees look to their leaders for stability and predictability. No one wants to work for a mercenary who will jump ship and leave them in the lurch at the first offer of better compensation. Relevant new paradigm leaders must navigate a precarious path between demonstrating loyalty and commitment to their work and their employees, while concurrently looking out for themselves by keeping their options open and maintaining marketable skills. It is not an easy dance. As in all other things, it is made easier by honesty—sharing the paradox with both employees and peers.

Employees too share the paradox. In order to be congruent and nonmanipulative, they need to be loyal to their work, their colleagues, and their leader. However, the price of this loyalty should not be at the expense of keeping their skills marketable and staying attuned to other options.

The Seduction of Security

Although we are in a new paradigm, we suffer from a cultural lag; the pull of the past is strong. Employees and managers alike yearn for the predictable, long-term security of the old psychological contract. In the heat of battle, when managers are making gut-wrenching decisions and working under enormous pressure, it is tempting to tell employees that after just one more sacrifice and getting through just one more round of layoffs, things will return to "normal." "Normal" will never happen again and, seductive though it may be to promise a return, it won't happen and those who succumb will lose credibility. There is, however, a possibility of long-term employment (not long-term employment security)—in the new paradigm. It takes the form of a series of short-term vow renewals. As organizations gain economic viability, they can offer employment continuity; as individuals discover good work, they can accept the invitation. The relationship is much different from the old paradigm; it is short term, situational, and subject to reciprocal benefits.

Employees must also resist the siren song of long-term security within one organization. When employers tell you the downsizings are over and things will be the way they were, they are making a promise that is undeliverable in the new paradigm. Long-term employment with one organization is possible, but there will be no long-term promises and it will be the result of a number of shorter-term environmental factors.

The Fallacy of Dependency

A managerial tool of the old psychological contract was the creation of mechanisms such as benefits, services, and social systems that tied employees in over a long term. In the new reality, dependent employees are a managerial liability, not an asset. Leading independent, task-oriented, empowered employees requires different skills from those used to lead needy, dependent employees. The payoff in terms of innovation, creativity, and productivity is, however, far greater.

It is not a good proposition, financially or psychologically, for employees to define themselves in terms of their organizational affiliation. Those who allow their self-esteem to be held hostage to the economic viability of any single organizational system are making a fool's bargain. Employees owe their employer good work, not their self-definition.

The Necessary Selfishness of Applied Human Spirit

All levels of employees have unique gifts and a relatively short time—on this planet and in the world of work—to apply these gifts. The new reality has served as a wakeup call to many people who had not been spending their gift—their unique human spirit— wisely. When we work in congruence with our unique gifts and apply our human spirit at work, we are at our best individually and organizationally. When we are working at cross-purposes with our human spirit, we are at our worst, dragging down ourselves and our employers. Applied human spirit is the currency of the realm in the new reality. It is the true competitive edge that will differentiate organizations that thrive from those that flounder. In the old reality, it was often diluted, traded for employment security. In the new reality, we have a fresh opportunity to be intentional in the application of our human spirit. We need to be intentional in where we spend it and selfishly guard against its dilution.

Fragile Choices

The demise of paternalistic organizations and the pain of violated dependency are forcing both individuals and organizations to make difficult choices. People who have taken the risk of breaking

the shackles of organizational codependency require a supportive
environment and organizations seeking to be relevant to the harsh
demands of the new paradigm must move against the grain of
strong past cultures. Here we will look at two adventures into these
uncharted waters, one by an organization and the other by an
employee. We begin with a firm I call Midwest Services.

Midwest Services

Whenever I think of Midwest, I am reminded of the teacher portrayed by Robin Williams in the movie *Dead Poets Society*. Operating
within the constraints of a paternalistic (old paradigm) private
school system, this teacher transformed his students from codependent, information-regurgitating, test-passing robots to empowered, autonomous learners. He gave them a metaphor for paradigm
breaking by having them stand on their desks to see old things in a
new way. In the end, he was fired, replaced by a traditional carrier
of old paradigm values. Paternalistic, control-oriented, codependent values once again ruled the classroom. True learning (good
work) and organizational productivity (turning out adventuresome,
autonomous learners) were sacrificed on the altar of old paradigm
conformity.

Midwest Services was a wholly owned, theoretically independent
subsidiary of a regional financial services organization. A small organization (fewer than fifty people), Midwest offered specialized computer and planning services to financial institutions. For years, it
had operated in a backwater of benign neglect from the parent, but
under the leadership of a new president, it developed a number of
structural innovations. This small organization did a lot of things
right; it now had self-directed teams, a flattened structure, outcome-
related incentive pay, and a near obsession with straight talk and
quality. These new paradigm interventions paid off: profits went up,
and new clients came in. It was a great place to work. You could feel
the spirit when you walked in the door. However, true to the unfor-
tunate but predictable fate of the majority of high-performing sub-
systems, it was not long before the parent organization moved in.
The unit was too different, the systems too unusual, the straight talk
too disrespectful and politically incorrect.

The triggering event was a team incentive plan at Midwest. The parent organization did not have team incentives and would not approve them for the subsidiary. The president implemented one anyway, and he was soon history. His replacement, a longtime parent organization careerist, "regularized," as he said, the organization. It was amazing how quickly the carefully crafted autonomy and good work-oriented culture was replaced by a control-oriented culture and political relationships. In less than a year, the new culture had been driven underground or out the door (some of the employees left or were laid off). After two years, profits had declined to the point that the external business of the subsidiary was dissolved and the few services that the parent was purchasing were brought in-house.

Absurd and wasteful though they may seem, these events are not unusual. The pull of the old culture is strong, and empowered employees and customer service are all too often sacrificed to old values, even though those values are not relevant to the new reality. Organizational response to the wake-up call of the new paradigm is, in all probability, a choice of growth and relevance or of atrophy and eventual death. Reciprocal choices must be made by employees. They can elect organizational codependency, which will almost certainly be violated at some point, plunging them into layoff survivor sickness, or they can choose self-control and empowerment, which will equip them to thrive in the new paradigm.

Ralph's Reevaluation

Ralph was a fast-track design engineer in an organization that developed weapons systems for the federal government. Hired directly out of college, Ralph, through technical competence and labor shortages, floated upward on the rising tide of fat government contracts for the first ten years of his career. At the age of thirty-five, he was a middle manager with two children, whom he didn't see as often as he liked; a large mortgage for a house he was at only to sleep in; and a marital relationship that was becoming frayed. When the contracts stopped coming in and his organization began to "take out" people, Ralph's world began to unravel. Although he struggled to hold on, the layoffs eventually caught up with him, and he became a victim. He was unemployed for nearly six months before being rehired into his former organization in a nonmanagement role at a substantial reduction in pay.

Today, three years after his rehire, Ralph's cash compensation is only slightly less than he made before. His psychic income, however, has increased tremendously. He is doing what he perceives as more interesting and relevant work and putting in fewer hours. He has achieved a balance in his work and his life, seeing his work as a vital part but by no means all of his life. He knows there is a good probability that he will lose his job again, but feels confident that he will be able to make whatever accommodations are necessary to adjust when that time comes.

Paradoxically, by "not playing the game," by approaching his job as an individual entrepreneur, and by "telling the truth," he is getting the best performance reviews of his life, and reports having to "fight" against getting promoted to a managerial role again.

During his forced unemployment, Ralph also clarified his values in these ways:

- S*etting priorities.* The time away from work helped Ralph appreciate his need to spend more time with his family. He decided that the price he was paying in terms of hours and sheer physical fatigue for his managerial role was not worth what he had received from that role.
- *Renewing his vows.* Ralph and his wife had drifted apart. As his job consumed his time and energies, there was not enough of either left to invest in his marriage. He and his wife decided that their personal relationship had priority over any organizational relationship and that they would not allow any new job to get in the way again.
- *Assessing real economic needs.* Ralph and his wife decided they did not need the big house and agreed that there was more to life than servicing a mortgage. Their objective was to get out of a large fixed payment, not to make a huge profit, and they sold the house quickly. They now live in a smaller house in the same school district. They also cut back on some nonessential expenses. Ralph's wife increased her outside work hours during his unemployment and now brings in significant income. Ironically, although Ralph is making less and working shorter hours, he is able to save more in his new situation.

Breaking organizational codependency wasn't easy for Ralph. He went through anger and depression. He and his wife sought financial and career counseling, and Ralph participated in a support group. Although Ralph has achieved a sense of balance in his work life, his future is not without risk. Just like the recovering alcoholic, Ralph must maintain his perspective every day and work hard on maintaining a nondependent work relationship. However, when compared to Charles, the layoff survivor described in Chapter One, Ralph is leading a much more relevant and productive life.

The Existential Act of Choosing Freedom

The new paradigm's gift to us is that it helps us frame our choices. Few of us had the opportunity to wrest our autonomy from our organizational affiliation during the height of the old paradigm; we were too much in the paradigm to assess it. If not fat, dumb, and happy, we were nevertheless woefully ignorant. Certainly many layoff survivors are neither fat nor dumb nor happy. Nor can they claim ignorance. They do, however, have the opportunity to make a real choice, and that may be a once-in-a-lifetime gift. Breaking organizational codependency and taking responsibility for our own work is our ultimate existential challenge. We cannot abstract it, delegate it, or have a task force study it. We must do it and be it. It is a tenet of existential philosophy that as we move away from an artificial dependence, we are moving toward our essential nature, which is freedom. Accepting this natural state of freedom after years of dependence is not easy. To the philosopher Jean-Paul Sartre, we are condemned to be free.

Nevertheless, making the choice to immunize ourselves to layoff survivor sickness by breaking organizational codependency is an affirming act; it is something we do, not something we abstract. We have the opportunity to make a choice. We do not have to be dragged back into old paradigm codependency. Stephen Covey (1989, p. 310) captures the meaning of this opportunity when he celebrates the gap between stimulus and response: "I reflected upon it again and again, and it began to have a powerful effect on my paradigm of life. It was as if I had become an observer of my own participation. I began to stand in that gap and to look outside at the stimuli. I reveled in the inward sense of freedom to choose my response—even to become the stimulus or at least to influence it—even to reverse it."

We hear the death toll of the old paradigm as a wake-up call, and our response defines both our individual sense of relevance and autonomy and our organization's growth and survival. If we claim our independence and shed the manipulation and control of organizational codependency, we embark on an existential voyage of discovery. We will never reach the end of this voyage; another tenet of existential philosophy is that we are always in the process of becoming, and never being. But what a voyage it is, filled with self-esteem, relevance, and pride of contribution fueled by good work and unmarred by manipulation or futile attempts to control the uncontrollable.

Learnings and Implications

I have written about layoff survivor sickness as the symptom and unhealthy dependence as the disease. The phenomena are linked, and we must work on both halves of the equation simultaneously. The depth and toxicity of layoff survivor sickness is not well understood, and it is often denied. Thus, I devoted the first six chapters to deepening our understanding of the pathology and debilitating nature of survivor symptoms.

The next four chapters examined methods of intervention. I described a model with four levels—the first two dealing with symptomatic relief and the last two with root causes. The final four chapters focused on leadership approaches and competencies necessary to ensure organizational sustainability in the new paradigm.

We are living out the ancient Chinese curse of living in interesting times. Despite a global epidemic of layoffs and financial turmoil, we have the opportunity to turn pain into gain. We can use the death toll of the old paradigm as a wake-up call and reclaim our autonomy and self-empowerment. Organizations have the opportunity to form structures and processes that shed the imitations of the old, control-oriented culture. The payoff of empowered employees linked to facilitative organizations by good work is not just elimination of layoff survivor symptoms; it is individual relevance, global competitiveness, and organizational survival.

REFERENCES

Anderlini, J., and Dyer, G. "Downturn Has Sent 20m Rural Chinese Home." *Financial Times,* Feb. 3, 2009, p. A1.

Argyris, C. *Intervention Theory and Method: A Behavioral Science View.* Reading, Mass.: Addison-Wesley, 1970.

Bardwick, J. M. *The Plateauing Trap: How to Avoid It in Your Life.* New York: AMACOM, 1986.

Beattie, M. *Codependent No More: How to Stop Controlling Others and Start Caring for Yourself.* San Francisco: HarperOne, 1987.

Becker, G. *Human Capital: A Theoretical and Empirical Analysis with Special Reference to Education.* Chicago: University of Chicago Press, 1993.

Bennis, W. *On Becoming a Leader.* (2nd ed.) New York: Basic Books, 2003.

Bridges, W. *Transitions: Making Sense of Life's Changes.* Reading, Mass.: Addison-Wesley, 1980.

Brockner, J. "Managing the Effects of Layoffs on Others." *California Management Review,* Winter 1992, pp. 9–27.

Brockner, J., and others. "Layoffs, Self-Esteem and Survivor Guilt: Motivational, Effective, and Attitudinal Consequences." *Organizational Behavior and Human Decision Processes,* 1985, *36,* 229–244.

Brockner, J., and others. "Layoffs, Equity Theory, and Work Performance: Further Evidence of the Impact of Survivor Guilt." *Academy of Management Journal,* 1986, *29,* 373–384.

Business Wire, "Leadership IQ Study: Don't Expect Layoff Survivors to Be Grateful." Dec. 10, 2008. http//findarticles.com/p/articlesmi_m0EINis_2008_Dec_16/ai_n31128154.

Cameron, K. S., Freeman, S. J., and Mishra, A. K. "Best Practices in White-Collar Downsizing: Managing Contradictions." *Executive,* 1991, *5*(3), 57–72.

Cameron, K. S., Kim, M. U., and Whetten, D. A. "Organizational Effects of Decline and Turbulence." *Administrative Science Quarterly,* 1987, *32,* 222–240.

Cascio, W. F. *Responsible Restructuring: Creative and Profitable Alternatives to Layoffs.* San Francisco: Berrett-Koehler, 2002.

Covey, S. R. *The Seven Habits of Highly Effective People: Restoring the Character Ethic.* New York: Simon & Schuster, 1989.

Dorfman, J. R. "Heard on the Street." *Wall Street Journal,* Dec. 10, 1991, pp. C1–C2.

Drath, W. H. *Deep Blue Sea: Understanding the Relational Source of Leadership.* San Francisco: Jossey-Bass, 2001.

Flamholtz, E. *Human Resource Accounting: Advances in Concepts, Methods and Applications.* (3rd ed.) New York: Springer, 1999.

Flint, J. "Who Gets the Parachutes?" *Forbes,* Jan. 12, 1987, pp. 38–40.

Fowler, E. M. "Survivors' Syndrome in Layoffs." *New York Times,* June 3, 1986, p. D23.

Friedman, T. *The World Is Flat: A Brief History of the Twenty-First Century.* (3rd ed.) New York: Picador, 2007.

Goleman, D. *Emotional Intelligence: Why It Can Matter More Than IQ.* (10th ed.) New York: Bantam, 2006.

Gottesfeld, H. *Abnormal Psychology: A Community Mental Health Perspective.* Chicago: Science Research Associates, 1979.

Hallett, J. J. "Worklife Visions." *Personnel Administrator,* 1987, *32*(5), 56–65.

Hames, R. D. *The Five Literacies of Global Leadership: What Authentic Leaders Know and You Need to Find Out.* Hoboken, N.J.: Wiley, 2007.

Hampden-Turner, C., and Trompennars, F. *Building Cross-Cultural Competence: How to Create Wealth from Conflicting Values.* New Haven, Conn.: Yale University Press, 2000.

Harvey, J. B. "Management and Marasmus." Unpublished manuscript, George Washington University, 1981.

Harvey, J. B. *The Abilene Paradox and Other Meditations on Management.* Lanham, Md.: Lexington Books, 1988.

Harvey, J. B. "Eichmann in the Organization: Or You Have to Know Who You Are in Bed With; Otherwise You Can't Tell Whether You Are Making Love or Being Raped." Unpublished manuscript, George Washington University, 1985.

Herzberg, F. "The Motivation-Hygiene Concept and Problems of Manpower." *Personnel Administration,* 1964, *27*(1), 3–7.

Hirsch, P. *Pack Your Own Parachute: How to Survive Mergers, Takeovers, and Other Corporate Disasters.* Reading, Mass.: Addison-Wesley, 1987.

Hoffman, T. "Life After Layoffs: Discarded and Demoralized." *Computerworld,* Aug. 2006. www.computerworld.com/action/article.do?command=viewArticleBasic&articleId=1.

Hofstede, G. "Motivation, Leadership, and Organization: Do American Theories Apply Abroad?" *Organizational Dynamics,* 1980, *9*(1), 42–63.

Hofstede, G. *Cultures and Organizations: Software of the Mind.* New York: McGraw-Hill, 1997.

Kiviat, B. "After Layoffs, There's Survivor's Guilt." *Time,* Feb. 1, 2009. http://www.time.com/time/business/Article/0,8599,187459200.html?imw=Y.

Kübler-Ross, E. *On Death and Dying.* New York: Macmillan, 1969.

Kuhn, T. S. *The Structure of Scientific Revolutions.* (2nd ed.) Chicago: University of Chicago Press, 1970.

Leider, R. *Taking Charge.* Minneapolis, Minn.: Inventure Group, 1992.

Lifton, R. J. *Death in Life: Survivors of Hiroshima.* New York: Random House, 1967.

Lifton, R. J. *The Protean Self: Human Resilience in an Age of Fragmentation.* New York: Basic Books, 1993.

Looney, R. "Saudization and Sound Economic Reforms: Are the Two Compatible?" *Strategic Insights,* 2004, *3*(2). http://www.ccnps.navy.mil/si/2004/feb/looneyFed04.asp.

Marks, M. L. "Regrouping After Downsizing: The O.D. Role." Presentation handout, O.D. Network Conference, Long Beach, Calif., 1991a.

Marks, M. L. "Viewpoints." *Los Angeles Times,* Jan. 6, 1991b, p. D7.

Marks, M. L., and Mirvis, P. "Rebuilding After the Merger: Dealing with Survivor Sickness." *Organizational Dynamics,* 1992, *21*(2), 18–32.

Marrow, A. *The Practical Theorists: The Life and Work of Kurt Lewin.* New York: Basic Books, 1969.

Marshak, R. J., and Katz, J. H. "The Symbolic Side of OD." *OD Practitioner,* 1992, *24*(2), 1–5.

Merry, U., and Brown, G. *The Neurotic Behavior of Organizations.* Cleveland, Ohio: Gestalt Institute Press, 1987.

Moses, J. L. "A Psychologist Assesses Today's AT&T Managers." *Teleconnect,* Mar. 1987, pp. 32–36.

Poornima, M. "Motorola Confirms Layoffs in India." *Wall Street Journal,* Feb. 2, 2009. http://www.livemint.com/2008/11/04230233/Motorola-confirms-layoffs-in-I.html

Porter, L. "Some Extrapolations, Metaphors, and Inferential Leaps." *OD Practitioner,* 1978, *10*(3), 3.

Prokesch, S. "Remaking the American CEO." *New York Times,* Jan. 25, 1987, p. F1.

Right Associates. *Lessons Learned: Dispelling the Myths of Downsizing.* (2nd ed.) Philadelphia: Right Associates, 1992.

Rosinski, P. *Coaching Across Cultures: New Tools for Leveraging National, Corporate and Professional Differences.* London: Nicholas Brealcy, 2003.

Schaef, A. W. *Co-Dependence: Misunderstood—Mistreated.* San Francisco: HarperOne, 1986.

Schwadel, F., Moffett, M., Harris, R., and Lowenstein, R. "Thousands Who Work on Shuttle Now Feel Guilt, Anxiety, and Fear." *Wall Street Journal,* Feb. 6, 1986, p. 27.

Solzhenitsyn, A. I. *One Day in the Life of Ivan Denisovich.* Westport, Conn.: Praeger, 1963.

Solzhenitsyn, A. I. *The Gulag Archipelago, 1918–1956: An Experiment in Literary Investigation.* New York: HarperCollins, 1974.

Tichy, N. M., and Devanna, M. A. *The Transformational Leader.* Hoboken, N.J.: Wiley, 1986.

Vaill, P. B. "Process Wisdom for a New Age." In J. D. Adams (ed.), *Transforming Work: A Collection of Organizational Transformation Readings.* Alexandria, Va.: Miles River Press, 1984.

Vaill, P. B. *Management as a Performing Art.* San Francisco: Jossey-Bass, 1989.

Whyte, W. H. *The Organization Man.* New York: Simon & Schuster, 1956.

Wilson, S. *The Man in the Gray Flannel Suit.* New York: Simon & Schuster, 1955.

Wudunn, S. "Wuhan Journal; Layoffs in China: A Dirty Word, But All Too Real. *New York Times,* May 11, 1993. http://query.nytimes.com/gst/fullpage.html?res=9F0CE3DC1F38F932A25756C0A965958260&sec=&spon=&pagewanted=2.

Wyatt Company. "Restructuring—Cure or Cosmetic Surgery: Results of Corporate Change in the '80s with RXs for the '90s." Washington, D.C.: Wyatt Company, 1991.

ACKNOWLEDGMENTS

Most of all, I thank my wife, Diana, for her love, support, and encouragement. Without these gifts, not only would this book not have been possible, my life would be dreary and my spirit diminished.

I also need to thank my amazing clients, many of whom have become friends and moved beyond a consultant-client relationship to partner with me to explore new and untested intervention strategies. For the most part, the pain was worth the gain, and we grew together.

I acknowledge the care, professionalism, and responsiveness of the Jossey-Bass team. You are the best.

A special thanks to Tim Rickard, whose talent and creativity resulted in illustrations that were worth very much more than the fabled thousand words.

Finally, my profound appreciation goes to Nicholas for his unconditional positive regard. Nicholas is my wife's black cocker spaniel who sleeps outside my office door and is always there for me with a wag of his tail and a roll on his back regardless of the muse's generosity or parsimony.

THE AUTHOR

David Noer is an author, consultant, speaker, and executive coach. His career has spanned corporate management, global consulting, and higher education. He has been named a senior fellow at the Center for Creative Leadership and professor emeritus at Elon University. His professional practice involves executive coaching, speaking, building high-performance teams, and helping individuals and organizations recover from the trauma of downsizing.

Concurrently with his global consulting, he served as the Frank S. Holt Jr. Professor of Leadership at Elon University for seven years. He previously was senior vice president of the Center for Creative Leadership and was responsible for that organization's worldwide training and education activity. He also served as a consultant to top organizational leaders and executive teams.

He has held positions as dean of the Control Data Academy of Management and its vice president of human resource development. He has served as president and CEO of Business Advisors, a firm specializing in technology-based management consulting, with offices in the United States, England, and Australia In addition to managing the firm, Noer provided diagnostic and developmental consulting to executives in many client systems, particularly those dealing with the human dimensions of restructuring, mergers, and layoffs. His previous position was senior vice president of administration and human resources for Commercial Credit Company, a holding company with operations in insurance, finance, consumer lending, banking, and real estate.

For much of his business career Noer resided and worked outside the United States, holding line and staff positions in Europe and Australia. He is the author of numerous book chapters and both academic- and practitioner-oriented articles on consulting skills, cross-cultural leadership, downsizing, and executive development. In addition to *Healing the Wounds,* he has written four other books: *Multinational People Management, How to Beat the Employment Game, Jobkeeping,* and *Breaking Free.* He also writes a monthly column for the *Greensboro News and Record.*

He received a B.A. degree from Gustavus Adolphus College, an M.S. degree in organization development from Pepperdine University, and a doctorate in business administration, with a concentration in organizational behavior and a supporting field of executive mental health, from George Washington University.

INDEX